REAL FOOD
by MIKE

REAL

Seasonal wholefood recipes for wellbeing

FOOD
by MIKE

MIKE McENEARNEY

BEET·KVAS

MAPLE-TOASTED
BUCKWHEAT

hardie grant books

My food philosophy _____ 7

About this book _____ 10

1 SUMMER
12–71

BREAKFAST _____ 16
SOUPS _____ 22
SALADS _____ 26
VEGETABLES _____ 34
MEAT _____ 42
FISH _____ 51
AFTERS _____ 58
DRINKS _____ 68

2 AUTUMN/ FALL
72–119

BREAKFAST _____ 76
SOUPS _____ 83
SALADS _____ 86
VEGETABLES ____ 94
MEAT _____ 102
FISH _____ 107
AFTERS _____ 112
DRINKS _____ 118

3 WINTER
120–175

BREAKFAST _____ 124
SOUPS _____ 130
SALADS _____ 134
VEGETABLES ____ 142
MEAT _____ 152
FISH _____ 157
AFTERS _____ 164
DRINKS _____ 172

4 SPRING
176–229

BREAKFAST _____ 180
SOUPS _____ 186
SALADS _____ 190
VEGETABLES _____ 198
MEAT _____ 206
FISH _____ 215
AFTERS _____ 220
DRINKS _____ 228

5 LARDER
230–245

Index _____ 246

Acknowledgements _____ 252

About the author _____ 254

My food philosophy

Some people are slow learners. I unashamedly put my hand up to being such a person. It took 20 years of cooking before I had my epiphany, and since that moment it has influenced every day of my life.

The year 2009 was very big on all fronts in my household. My wife, Joss, and I had been back in Australia for three years and were desperately missing Europe. Joss was also pregnant with our third child, who was due in autumn, and she wanted to be near her family in England. And I – well, I knew it was time for me to make a change and think about opening my own restaurant, instead of working in someone else's.

So when William was born we made the pivotal decision to pack up our life in Australia and fly back to the UK in search of utopia.

One week before our flight, we had a catastrophe. William got very sick. He was only 6 weeks old and was diagnosed with meningitis. During his time in hospital, it really hit home that there was a lack of fresh nutritional food available to patients. The food consisted of things like dehydrated mashed potato, heavily processed bread, preservative-laden juices and sugared cereals. There was simply no fresh food to heal and nourish – just processed food to poison.

We landed in the UK in July of 2009 to the most glorious summer. The hedgerows were bursting with berries, the sun was shining and life was good. Our aim was to base ourselves at my mother-in-law's small-holding farm in Wales and travel through the UK in short spurts, looking for our new place to call home. The best way to achieve this was to send our two eldest boys, George and Alfie, to the local village school and take William with us.

On our travels we saw some beautiful countryside, but what interested us most was life on the farm. Joss's family farm is a truly beautiful property. Some 12 hectares (30 acres) of organic farming land are used to raise speckle-faced lambs, Hereford and longhorn cattle and saddleback pigs, and there is one of the oldest apple orchards in Wales as well as a fertile kitchen garden. Joss's family was self-sufficient and a picture of health and happiness. They cut their own wood for the fires, had photovoltaic cells and wind turbines to generate power, and grew nearly all of their food. I was hooked and I loved it.

WE LANDED IN THE UK IN JULY OF 2009 TO THE MOST GLORIOUS SUMMER. THE HEDGEROWS WERE BURSTING WITH BERRIES, THE SUN WAS SHINING AND LIFE WAS GOOD.

8

To complete the idyll, I built a brick oven next to the wood shed, using a set of Alan Scott plans, and started baking sourdough. I kneaded 30 kg (66 lb) of dough by hand twice a week. I fired up the oven at 2 in the morning and baked 1.5 kg (3 lb 5 oz) loaves to sell to the locals at school drop-off.

We were living the dream, picking blackberries, gooseberries, raspberries and currants in summer; damsons and early pears and apples in autumn, eating what we could and turning the rest into jam. The garden was a true revelation. I had lived in Europe previously and understood the seasons very well, but growing the produce and eating it straight from the tree was another level. This was my 'road to Damascus' moment, a cartoon light bulb going 'ping' over my head.

WE WERE LIVING THE DREAM, PICKING BLACKBERRIES, GOOSEBERRIES, RASPBERRIES AND CURRANTS IN SUMMER; DAMSONS AND EARLY PEARS AND APPLES IN AUTUMN.

At the time we were at the farm, a local 'apothecary' naturopath had also begun to section off four beds in the kitchen garden to create a Hippocratic garden, using the four humours of the body as her guide. Not only were these beds beautiful to look at, they were also stuffed full of medicinal plants and herbs to help relieve medical symptoms. The beds were divided into the humours, or temperaments: sanguine, choleric, melancholic and phlegmatic. It was fascinating to me that she looked at these herbs as medicinal, while I saw them as culinary. From that moment, the phrase 'you are what you eat' became truly profound to me.

For the past decade I have noticed the rise in people's interest in good health, and so many fads and diets have been and gone. At Kitchen by Mike, and No. 1 Bent Street by Mike, I have always focused on fresh, seasonal food and, in doing so, have unconsciously endorsed and promoted healthy eating and wellbeing. It has shaped what my restaurants have become. My interest in health is neither Western nor Eastern. I simply believe in a balanced diet, eating whole foods and all things in moderation. I also believe in using natural medicines to stimulate and assist the body when it's not 100 per cent healthy. I believe that food – and by food I mean all edible flora and fauna in its purest form – is nature's medicine.

This book is intended to inspire and empower those who read it by providing simple recipes with notes on the health benefits of the ingredients. I hope it has the potential to tie together the idea of 'food' and 'medicine', and will inevitably help guide you towards a more natural and sustainable way of nourishing and healing yourselves.

10 About this book

Let's get this out in the open first. I am not a doctor, naturopath or nutritionist. I am an inquisitive chef who loves all things food. I am not claiming to cure cancer or add 50 years to your life, but merely providing notes for each recipe, which list the benefits of quality wholefoods and demonstrate how a small amount of education about the medicinal benefits of ingredients can truly have a positive effect on your overall wellbeing.

Since time began, people have been living in accordance with the seasons and with nature. Right now, with the economic and geographical climates in peril, we have begun to realise the importance of respecting the seasons – and in the process are discovering a simpler, ultimately richer way of life. Waiting for the arrival of each season is like waiting for a birthday – it only comes once a year, so you really look forward to it and enjoy every moment when it's here.

Cooking food that's in season is better for you, both nutritionally and ethically. I don't want to eat (and I certainly don't want my kids to eat) food that's pumped full of chemicals to force it to grow, or that has been flown halfway around the world at all times of the year. The bottom line for me is that it's all about flavour. Food in season just tastes better – the food and its flavour both in their prime.

The recipes in this book are arranged by season, ranging from breakfast ideas to salads, more substantial dishes, sweet things and even drinks. Many of them are simple and take only minutes to prepare; others are broken up into stages to fit in with our busy lives.

At the back of the book is the Larder section, to inspire you to make the most of what's plentiful each season – and give you a head start in the kitchen. Having a well-stocked larder is a saviour in so many ways. Not only can it halve your cooking time, but it will also save you a fortune as you'll have preserved the ingredients when they were at their best and their cheapest.

If stored correctly, many of these preparations have a long shelf-life and are invaluable for adding flair to your daily cooking. A good example is to try freezing the Ponzu (page 234) into a granita to serve on top of freshly shucked oysters. Or add an equal amount of olive oil to it and turn it into a dressing to spoon over steamed fish or grilled vegetables. My favourite use for ponzu is as a dipping sauce for sashimi.

You'll notice that a lot of the recipes cross-reference each other, and I hope this will encourage you to try various combinations.

I know every day what my body is craving and what I need to eat if I am not feeling 100 per cent. The ultimate aim of this cookbook is to assist you in maintaining good health while enjoying real food that will enhance your life.

COOKING
MEASUREMENTS
· NOTES ·

Australian 20 ml (3/4 fl oz) tablespoon measures are used in the recipes, so cooks with 15 ml (1/2 fl oz) tablespoons should be generous with their tablespoon measurements.

Metric cup measurements are used, i.e. 250 ml (8 1/2 fl oz) for 1 cup. In the US a cup is 237 ml (8 fl oz), so American cooks should be generous with their cup measurements. In the UK a cup is 284 ml (9 1/2 fl oz), so British cooks should be scant with their cup measurements.

FIGS, ROAST ONIONS, WALNUTS

French toast with nectarines and cinnamon sugar
Sheep's kefir with gooseberries and lemon verbena
SMASHED AVOCADO, TOMATO AND PERSIAN FETA ON TOAST
Coconut bread with blackberry butter
MALAYSIAN SPICED PUMPKIN AND COCONUT SOUP
— WHITE GAZPACHO —
Melon salad with fregola, gorgonzola, olives and brazil nuts
Figs, roast onions, walnuts and radicchio
Grilled haloumi, grapes and red rice
MANGO, AVOCADO, LIME AND LENTIL SALAD
Baked okra with tomato, ginger and mustard seeds
LEEKS À LA GRECQUE
ROAST BABY SQUASH WITH OREGANO AND LIME
— TOMATOES PROVENÇAL —

SUMMER
12-71

Grilled marinated lamb skirt with bread and butter cucumbers
Glazed ham with prickly pear chutney
ROAST CHICKEN WITH VERJUICE, WHITE GRAPES AND TARRAGON
Picnic ocean trout, wild black pepper and verjuice mayonnaise
Baked scallops with watermelon and hazelnut curry
PAELLA ON THE BARBECUE
Poached apricots with lemon thyme junket
PAVLOVA WITH RASPBERRIES IN VINEGAR
Gluten-free plum, rosemary and hazelnut cake
— PEACH MELBA —
Pineapple, mint and kombucha iceblocks
— KOMBUCHA —
LILLY PILLY CHAMPAGNE COCKTAIL

MEDICINAL
BRAIN, SKIN,
HEART
·BENEFIT·

BLUEBERRIES

The sun shines, berries ripen, stone fruits burst with fragrant juice, and crisp, leafy greens are at their best. Summer cooking demands simplicity, tons of salads, bright flavours and a generally lighter touch in the kitchen. I find myself hankering for foods rich in skin-protecting antioxidants and prefer cooking dishes that are fresh, colourful and energising.

STRAWBERRIES

MEDICINAL
EAR, NOSE &
THROAT
· BENEFIT ·

RASPBERRIES

MEDICINAL
MUSCLES,
BONES & JOINTS
· BENEFIT ·

MULBERRIES

MEDICINAL
BRAIN, HEART,
SKIN
· BENEFIT ·

16

French toast with nectarines and cinnamon sugar

SERVES 4 GENEROUSLY

6–8 nectarines, cut into sixths,
  skin left on

50 g (1¾ oz) caster (superfine)
  sugar, plus 1 tablespoon extra

20 g (¾ oz) butter

1 cinnamon stick

2 teaspoons verjuice, or
  1 teaspoon apple-cider vinegar
  mixed with 1 teaspoon water

250 ml (8½ fl oz/1 cup) milk

1 vanilla bean, split lengthways
  and seeds scraped

50 ml (1¾ fl oz) sherry

5 eggs

4 thick slices brioche or
  good-quality white bread

125 g (4½ oz) Clarified butter
  (page 234)

CINNAMON SUGAR

2 tablespoons panela sugar
  (see Note)

1 teaspoon ground cinnamon

Making French toast, otherwise known as *pain perdu* (lost bread), is one of my favourite things to do with stale bread. There are many different ways to cook French toast but my method is to not cook it too long in the pan as I want it crispy on the outside but to have a gooey, custardy centre. However, you can cook it a little longer and the interior will firm up. This is delicious with any fruit or just with maple syrup.

Preheat the oven to 200°C (400°F).

In a bowl, toss the nectarines with the extra 1 tablespoon caster sugar.

In a heavy-based, ovenproof frying pan over medium heat, melt the butter. Add the nectarines, cinnamon stick and verjuice. Give the pan a shake to combine the ingredients, then pop the pan in the oven to cook for 10 minutes, turning the nectarines occasionally until a caramel forms. Remove from the oven and set aside.

For the cinnamon sugar, mix the panela sugar with the cinnamon. Set aside.

In a small saucepan over medium–low heat, simmer the milk with the vanilla bean and seeds and half the caster sugar. Stir in the sherry and remove the pan from the heat. Set aside to cool, then strain into a container.

Whisk the eggs with the remaining sugar until pale and fluffy. While whisking, add the milk mixture to combine. Soak the brioche or bread slices, fully submerged, in the milk mixture for 5 minutes.

Warm a little of the clarified butter in a large frying pan over medium heat and fry the soaked bread until brown on both sides. Remove from the pan. The bread should be crispy on both sides but still a little gooey in the middle. Sprinkle with the cinnamon sugar and serve with the nectarines.

Note: *Panela or rapadura sugar is a raw, unprocessed sugar that retains all the natural benefits of sugarcane. Other sugars to use in place of panela would be dark brown sugar, coconut sugar or any other raw, unprocessed sugars you may find.*

The vitamin C in nectarines boosts your immune system. It also helps make collagen that in turn helps heal wounds and give support to blood vessels. Nectarines contain vitamin A, essential for good vision and bone growth, and vitamin E, which does wonders for overall immunity. It's also great for skin and hair.

18

Sheep's kefir with gooseberries and lemon verbena

SERVES 4

SHEEP'S MILK KEFIR

500 ml (17 fl oz/2 cups) sheep's milk

1 teaspoon milk kefir grains (see recipe introduction)

GOOSEBERRIES IN LEMON VERBENA

100 ml (3½ fl oz) boiling water

1½ tablepoons lemon verbena leaves, chopped

100 g (3½ oz) caster (superfine) sugar

375 g (13 oz) gooseberries

½ lemon, juiced

This is my ideal start to the day – fruit and a probiotic. You can buy ready-to-drink milk kefir from health food stores. However, if you want to follow the recipe and make your own sheep's milk kefir, you can buy milk kefir grains at a health food store or online. These grains are the bacteria that ferment the milk into a probiotic drink. When you strain your kefir milk you will be left with the grains. You do not eat these milk kefir grains – these are used as a starter for making the drinking kefir in the recipe. Remember that the milk kefir grains after every batch will grow and, after a handful of times, you will have enough milk kefir grains to give some to your friends. When you are not making kefir, store the milk kefir grains in a puddle of milk in the refrigerator to keep them hydrated. Please note that milk kefir grains are different from water kefir grains, and you cannot interchange them.

Mix the sheep's milk and milk kefir grains in a 750 ml (25½ fl oz/3 cup) glass jar. Cover the jar with a piece of muslin (cheesecloth), secured with an elastic band, to allow the carbon dioxide to escape during fermentation. Keep in a dark place at room temperature for 24–48 hours. The timing depends on the ambient temperature – the cooler the temperature, the longer it will take. The texture should be similar to pouring cream. Once you have this consistency, strain the mixture through a sieve to catch the milk kefir grains. Store the strained drinking kefir in the refrigerator. It will last for about 1 week.

For the gooseberries in lemon verbena, pour the boiling water over the lemon verbena leaves and allow to steep for 5 minutes until cool (if you can only find dried lemon verbena, use 1 teaspoon as it will be stronger than fresh). Strain the tea and pour it into a saucepan over medium heat with the sugar and bring to the boil. Add the gooseberries and simmer until they are soft and a syrup has formed – the temperature should have reached 100°C (212°F) on a thermometer. Add the lemon juice to taste to add a tart flavour. Allow to cool to let the syrup set.

Serve the gooseberries in a small bowl and serve the drinking kefir in a glass to sip with it, or pour it over the top.

Gooseberries contain a strong antioxidant called anthocyanin, which is anti-inflammatory, helps regulate blood sugar metabolism and also helps in reducing cholesterol. Lemon verbena contains essential oils that have a calmative effect on the nerves, are antiseptic, antibacterial and also help with digestion.

Smashed avocado, tomato and Persian feta on toast

SERVES 4

4 slices good-quality sourdough
   bread
2 avocados
24 cherry tomatoes
1 generous handful basil leaves,
   torn
4 tablespoons dill sprigs
1 lemon, juiced
60 ml (2 fl oz/¼ cup) Basil oil
   (page 233)
100 g (3½ oz) Persian feta

This became a quick staple at my restauraunt Kitchen by Mike. The reason for this was that you could replace the Persian feta with smoked salmon or have it with a poached egg. It gave diners the sense that they were creating their own bespoke breakfast. Always choose ripe avocados as waxy ones won't squash onto your toast and form what I like to think of as a butter-like substance. If you don't have time to make the basil oil, try using lemon oil or quality extra-virgin olive oil.

Toast the bread and squash half an avocado onto each slice.

Roughly chop the tomatoes and toss them with the torn basil leaves, dill sprigs, some salt and freshly ground black pepper, the lemon juice and basil oil. Spoon the mixture onto the avocado, then crumble over the feta. Drizzle over any juices left in the bowl, add another grinding of pepper and serve.

MEDICINAL
GUT, HEART
BENEFIT

We discuss avocado on page 189, so let's look at the health benefits of feta. As a quality, non-meat protein, feta is great for vegetarians. It contains chloride, which helps balance body fluids, and also helps produce the stomach acid required to break down and digest food. It has plenty of phosphorus, which is important for converting food to energy and, in conjunction with calcium, for building and protecting bones. It's also a source of vitamin B12, essential for preventing plaque build-up in the arteries, thus reducing the risk of heart disease.

Coconut bread with blackberry butter

SERVES 8

100 g (3½ oz/1 cup) coconut flour

½ teaspoon bicarbonate of soda (baking soda)

1 teaspoon baking powder

2 eggs

6 egg whites

125 ml (4 fl oz/½ cup) extra-virgin olive oil

120 ml (4 fl oz) maple syrup

2 tablespoons fresh coconut, grated (see recipe introduction)

1 quantity Blackberry butter (page 236)

Although you can use desiccated coconut for the coconut bread, I use grated fresh coconut as it gives a chunkier finish. If you don't have any baking powder, try combining the same amount of bicarbonate of soda (baking soda) with vinegar to get a fizz. The carbon dioxide reaction will be your raising agent. If you're using this method, don't add this at the beginning with the flour. Instead you'll need to add it to the batter at the very last stage before it goes into your cake tin and then bake it immediately. Every second this reactive agent is in your batter it is fizzing and slowly decreasing in power, so you need to act fast or your bread will be flat.

Preheat the oven to 175°C (350°F). Grease and line the bottom and sides of a 21 x 11 cm (8¼ x 4¼ in) loaf (bar) tin with baking paper.

Sift the flour, bicarbonate of soda, baking powder and ½ teaspoon salt into a mixing bowl.

In a separate bowl, using an electric mixer, beat the whole eggs and egg whites with the oil and maple syrup at low speed (or swiftly by hand) to combine, before raising the speed to whip the mixture to a fluffy texture. Add the flour mixture and beat at low speed until just combined, then fold through the grated coconut.

Pour the batter into the prepared tin and smooth the surface. Bake for 1 hour or until a skewer inserted in the centre comes out clean. Leave to cool for 20 minutes in the tin, then turn the cake out and cool on a wire rack.

Serve the bread fresh with lashings of blackberry butter, or toast the bread to give it a nice crisp texture – this will also enable the butter to melt.

This coconut bread is sugar- and gluten-free, helpful to those with intolerances and dietary preferences. Coconut contains a substance called lauric acid, which increases the 'good' cholesterol levels in the blood, beneficial in preventing plaque build-up in the arteries. Blackberries contain anthocyanidins, a specific set of compounds that give pigmentation to various fruits and vegetables. As antioxidants, they're anti-inflammatory and anticarcinogenic. Blackberries also contain immune-boosting vitamin C, vitamin A for good vision, vitamin E and vitamin K, the last of which helps with blood clotting.

22

Malaysian spiced pumpkin and coconut soup

SERVES 4

400 ml (13½ fl oz) coconut milk

1 scud chilli, chopped

1 long red chilli, halved (seeded if you want it milder)

1 lemongrass stem, pale part only, bruised

1 kaffir lime leaf, thinly sliced

12 g (¼ oz) galangal, peeled and sliced

1 tablespoon palm sugar (jaggery)

50 ml (1¾ fl oz) fish sauce

40 g (1½ oz) chilli paste

800 g (1 lb 12 oz) pumpkin (squash), diced into large chunks

1 lime, juiced

½ bunch coriander (cilantro), leaves picked

This soup is good for using up any left-over roast pumpkin. If using cooked pumpkin, add it to the pan at the end, simmer for a moment to combine the flavours, then serve. Another serving suggestion is to add a dollop of coconut yoghurt to cool your palate. All the ingredients are readily available in most supermarkets.

In a large heavy-based saucepan over medium heat, warm the coconut milk. Add the chillies, lemongrass, kaffir lime leaf and galangal and simmer for 2 minutes until very aromatic.

Add the palm sugar, fish sauce and chilli paste and simmer until the palm sugar has dissolved. Add the pumpkin and simmer for about 30 minutes or until tender. Remove from the heat and add the lime juice to taste (it will balance the flavours). The soup should first taste hot, then sour and then sweet from the pumpkin and coconut.

Finish with a healthy scattering of coriander and serve.

Pumpkin is rich in vitamin A and beta-carotene, both essential for good vision. Coconut milk is not only high in a saturated fatty acid called lauric acid, which increases the levels of 'good' cholesterol in the blood, but it also contains B complex vitamins and potassium. Chilli is loaded with vitamins C and A, the latter useful for protecting from the free radicals that are generated when you're stressed or sick. Chilli also has decent amounts of vitamin B6, which can prevent plaque build-up in the arteries. Coriander contains antioxidant and anti-inflammatory compounds and is rich in vitamins A, C and K.

White gazpacho

SERVES 4

350 g (12½ oz) activated
  almonds (see page 237),
  flaked

450 g (1 lb) sourdough bread,
  torn into pieces

5 garlic cloves, peeled

1 pinch sea salt

350 ml (12 fl oz) extra-virgin
  olive oil

150 ml (5 fl oz) verjuice

375 g (13 oz) Lebanese (short)
  cucumbers, peeled

625 g (1 lb 6 oz) white grapes,
  halved

almond oil for drizzling

This is one of my favourite light lunches. It has substance from the almonds and bread, a fresh zing from the garlic and cucumbers. If you can't find verjuice, you could use half the amount of apple-cider vinegar or white-wine vinegar. I always find the short (Lebanese) cucumbers the sweetest and juiciest for this recipe, but long (telegraph) cucumbers will also work nicely. If you don't have almond oil, a drizzle of olive oil is a great alternative.

Blitz the almonds to a fine texture in a food processor or blender. Add the remaining ingredients, except the grapes and almond oil, and blend to a smooth paste. Transfer the gazpacho to the refrigerator.

Serve chilled with a garnish of grape halves and a drizzle of almond oil.

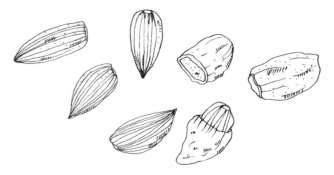

MEDICINAL
MUSCLES,
BONES & JOINTS
BENEFIT

Almonds are full of cholesterol-friendly monounsaturated fatty acids, plus vitamin E for healthy skin, and B complex vitamins for muscle growth. Cucumbers are high in antioxidants and vitamins A, C and K; vitamins A and K are fat-soluble and can be stored in the body for long periods. As well as vitamin K's role in blood clotting, it also plays a part in preventing tooth decay and osteoporosis.

26

Melon salad with fregola, gorgonzola, olives and brazil nuts

SERVES 4

125 g (4½ oz/1 cup) fregola

125 ml (4 fl oz/½ cup) extra-virgin olive oil, plus extra for folding through the fregola when cooked, and for drizzling

½ honeydew melon, seeds removed

½ rockmelon (cantaloupe), seeds removed

½ cup (95 g/3¼ oz) activated brazil nuts (see page 237)

1 lemon, juiced

1 teaspoon verjuice

½ bunch basil, leaves picked, large ones torn, small ones left whole

½ cup (80 g/2¾ oz) kalamata olives, squashed on a board to remove the pit, then left in a nice squashed shape

150 g (5½ oz) gorgonzola

Fregola is a type of pasta from Sardinia. It comes in varying sizes, but typically consists of semolina dough that has been rolled into tiny 2–3 mm (¹⁄₁₆–⅛ in) balls, then toasted in the oven. Any type of melon can be used for this recipe as long as it's sweet and juicy. The choice of cutting it into wedges or cubes is entirely up to you. I find that larger pieces are nicer if you need to add other ingredients, so the melon doesn't get lost. The cheese adds a lovely salty flavour to the salad but, if you have dairy issues, you can add some sliced Serrano ham instead.

Simmer the fregola in salted boiling water until al dente, then drain and rinse in cold water. Fold through a little olive oil.

Remove the skin from the honeydew melon and rockmelon. Cut the melons into large wedges or cubes.

Break up the brazil nuts a little by putting them on a board and hitting them with a rolling pin.

To make a melon dressing, put ½ cup of the melon flesh, a large squeeze of lemon juice, the verjuice, some salt and freshly ground black pepper, the olive oil and a few of the basil leaves in a jug or tall container and blitz using a hand-held blender until smooth. The dressing should first taste of melon, then have some acidity from the lemon and spiciness from the olive oil.

To serve, scatter the fregola on a platter. In a bowl, toss the remaining melon, the remaining basil leaves, the olives and brazil nuts in the dressing and spoon it over the fregola. Crumble over the gorgonzola or serve it on the side for your friends to add as much as they like. Finish with a good grinding of black pepper and a hit of extra-virgin olive oil.

Melons contain vitamin A, a powerful antioxidant that's essential for keeping teeth, skin, bone and mucous tissue healthy. They're also high in vitamin C and in potassium, which is so essential for heart health and keeping blood pressure in check. Brazil nuts are packed with vitamins (including E), antioxidants and a whole slew of minerals including selenium (vital for a healthy immune system), for which they're the highest naturally occurring source.

28

Figs, roast onions, walnuts and radicchio

SERVES 4

1 large head radicchio
sea salt or Himalayan rock salt
2 small red onions
8 figs, sliced or quartered
extra-virgin olive oil, if needed
balsamic vinegar, if needed
Maple vinaigrette (page 234)
250 g (9 oz) activated walnuts
   (see page 237)
¼ bunch mint, leaves picked

This salad is all about the sweet flavours of the figs and onions being balanced by the bitter flavours of the radicchio leaves. Other bitter leaves, such as chicory (endive), trevisiano or dandelion are a good substitute for the radicchio. The salad can be served warm, or made in advance and served at room temperature.

Preheat the oven to 150°C (300°F).

Cut the radicchio into large wedges and toss it with some salt in a bowl. Allow the radicchio to bleed for 30 minutes – this will bring out its colour and make it slightly tender, but keep it crisp for the salad without cooking.

In a roasting tin, on a little bed of sea salt, roast the onions in their skins for 2 hours. When they are cooked, cut off the onion tops and squeeze out the slow-baked onion flesh.

If the figs are at the height of their season and absolutely perfect, I wouldn't want to do anything but leave them as they are. If they are a little dry, I suggest you halve them, drizzle over a tiny dash of olive oil, balsamic vinegar and salt and warm them in a 150°C (300°F) oven until they go soft. This will in some way bring their flavour back to life.

To construct the salad, you can serve everything straight from the roasting tin. Or, to compose a more delicately styled salad, toss the radicchio with a very small amount of the maple vinaigrette and scatter it on a serving plate. Toss the onions in more vinaigrette and strew them over the radicchio. Scatter the figs and walnuts on top, and spoon over more vinaigrette. A final scattering of mint leaves adds a fresh zing.

Figs are particularly rich in polyphenols, chemicals that have antioxidant, anti-inflammatory and anticarcinogenic properties. They contain vitamins A, E and K, plus something called chlorogenic acid. This helps slow down the body's absorption of fat from a regular food intake, and can help balance blood sugar levels. Radicchio contains a unique compound called lactucopicrin, which gives it its characteristic bitter flavour. This compound is said to have a potent sedative and painkiller effect.

30

Grilled haloumi, grapes and red rice

SERVES 4

200 g (7 oz) haloumi

½ red onion, very thinly sliced
into rings

sea salt

1 tablespoon sherry vinegar

60 ml (2 fl oz/¼ cup) extra-
virgin olive oil, plus extra
for drizzling

125 g (4½ oz/1 cup) red rice

1 red capsicum (bell pepper)

2 preserved vine leaves

180 g (6½ oz/1 cup) red or
white grapes

½ trevisiano or radicchio, leaves
broken off and torn
lengthways (you want nice
long pieces of leaf)

¼ bunch flat-leaf (Italian)
parsley, sprigs picked

**This dish is best served hot while the cheese is still slightly soft and
stretchy – when it's cold it becomes like rubber. You can use a barbecue
or a chargrill pan to cook the haloumi and capsicum. When grilling I
always prefer to use wood and charcoal, as these flavours can't be
replicated and give a distinct character to the dish. The grapes you want
to use are those picked during harvest time, from the very end of
summer into the first couple of weeks of autumn. Look for sweet muscat
grapes or concord grapes for a sweet punch.**

Soak the haloumi in cold water in the refrigerator overnight. (This takes away
the intense saltiness, which increases when you cook it.)

Put the onion slices in a small bowl, sprinkle them with with sea salt and leave
for 10 minutes. Pat dry and add the sherry vinegar to cure the onion. Add the
olive oil and combine to make the dressing.

Cook the red rice by boiling it in water until tender (about 25 minutes).
(Red rice cooks best if you boil it, rather than using the absorption method, as
it has a husk much like brown rice and benefits from being boiled and rinsed.)

Grill the capsicum to blacken the skin. Remove it from the grill, put it in
a plastic bag, allow to cool, then rub off the black skin. Cut the capsicum
into strips.

Wrap the drained haloumi in the vine leaves and secure with toothpicks.
On a hot grill, cook the haloumi for 3 minutes on each side – the vine leaves
will turn a lovely ash colour and have a smoky flavour. Remove from the grill,
set aside and keep warm.

Dress the red rice in the onion vinaigrette. Halve the grapes to expose the
lovely insides and add them to the rice, along with the capsicum strips. Lay
the trevisiano leaves on a platter and spoon over the rice mix. Cut the hot
haloumi into wedges and place on the rice and trevisiano. Finish with a drizzle
of olive oil and the parsley leaves.

Grapes contain a substance called resveratrol, which helps protect the arterial lining, reducing the
risk of heart disease. They also contain a certain type of tannin that binds to cancer-causing toxins
in the colon, thereby offering some protection from inflammatory bowel disease, certain cancers
and diverticulitis. As well as all this, they have a particularly high concentration of antioxidants.

Mango, avocado, lime and lentil salad

SERVES 4

1 handful wild rocket (arugula), washed

100 g (3½ oz) black or green lentils, soaked and steamed (see page 141 for cooking instructions)

2 mangoes

1 avocado

100 g (3½ oz/½ cup) activated walnuts (see page 237)

45 g (1½ oz) taggiasca olives (see Note)

45 g (1½ oz) green olives

½ lime, juiced

1 tablespoon walnut oil

1 tablespoon salted capers, rinsed

If you're taking this salad to a picnic, make the dressing at home, place it in a jar, then all you need to do is give it a shake to emulsify it before pouring it over the salad. I like to leave my olives whole with the pit in. However, if you are outdoors on a picnic you will be eating while holding the plate with one hand and a fork in the other, so I suggest you remove the pits for ease.

Place the wild rocket in a large bowl or on a board, and spoon over the cooked lentils.

Remove the skin from the mangoes and avocado, cut the flesh into wedges and place it on top of the salad. Scatter over the walnuts and olives.

For a light dressing, combine the lime juice, walnut oil and capers and pour over the salad. Serve.

Note: *Italian taggiasca, or cailletier, olives are very small and purplish green. They have an intense flavour and a lovely crisp texture. If you can't find taggiasca olives, lovely riviera olives from southern France are also delicious, or kalamata will work too. It's all about the crisp texture, as the mango and avocado are soft.*

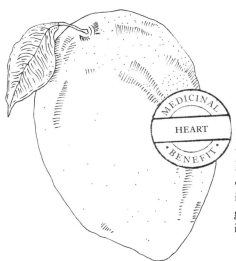

MEDICINAL
HEART
BENEFIT

Mangoes are an excellent source of beta-carotene, which is converted to vitamin A inside the body. Vitamin A is essential for good vision and for keeping organs like the heart, lungs and kidneys working well. They also contain vitamin B6, which helps reduce the risk of heart disease, boosts immune function and helps make red blood cells. Mangoes are also a good source of vitamin C and potassium, and of copper, which plays an important role in iron metabolism and the production of red blood cells.

34

Baked okra with tomato, ginger and mustard seeds

SERVES 4

1 teaspoon brown mustard seeds

30 g (1 oz) fresh ginger, finely
chopped

75 ml (2½ fl oz) extra-virgin
olive oil

500 g (1 lb 2 oz) okra, washed

1 garlic clove, crushed

1 pinch chilli flakes

1 handful baby English spinach
leaves, washed

75 g (2¾ oz) labne (see page
181)

1 bunch coriander (cilantro),
leaves picked in sprigs

TOMATO JAM
(MAKES 1 KG/2 LB 3 OZ)

2.5 kg (5½ lb) truss tomatoes

50 ml (1¾ fl oz) extra-virgin
olive oil, plus extra for the jar

1 pinch freshly ground white
pepper

1 small brown onion, diced

1½ tablespoons red-wine vinegar

1½ tablespoons caster
(superfine) sugar

5 garlic cloves, peeled and
chopped

Okra is super seasonal and can always be replaced with green beans. When I cook okra I always roast it first before folding it into a sauce, in order to keep it crisp. If you cook it for too long in the sauce the okra will become gooey and lose its shape. The labne adds a cooling element to the spicy sauce and the dish is lovely served hot or at room temperature. Try using young sorrel leaves instead of the spinach leaves for a nice tart flavour.

For the tomato jam, preheat the oven to 200°C (400°F).

Put the whole tomatoes on a baking tray, drizzle them with half the oil, a couple of pinches of salt and the white pepper and roast them for 10 minutes until soft and lightly caramelised.

In a frying pan over medium heat, sweat the onion in the remaining oil for a couple of minutes until translucent. Add the roasted tomatoes to the pan and squash them with a wooden spoon to break them down. Add the remaining ingredients and simmer for 20–30 minutes until thick and jammy.

Pass the mixture through a sieve, then store in the refrigerator with a film of oil on top until ready to use. This will keep for 1 month in the refrigerator.

Preheat the oven to 180°C (350°F).

In a small frying pan over medium heat, toast the mustard seeds and ginger in a little of the olive oil for 1 minute until fragrant, then remove from the heat.

In a large baking tin, toss the okra with half the remaining olive oil. Add the ginger and mustard seed mix, the garlic and chilli flakes. Bake for 20 minutes until tender.

While still hot, fold 250 g (9 oz) of the tomato jam through the okra with the baby spinach, then dollop with labne. Garnish with coriander, then drizzle over the remaining olive oil and serve.

Okra contains plenty of mucilage, a thick, gooey substance full of soluble fibre that helps move food through the gut. It also contains good levels of folates, vital for cell production, as well as vitamins A, C, K and B6, and appreciable amounts of magnesium (for bone health and energy metabolism) and manganese (for regulating blood sugar and supporting the nervous system).

37

Leeks à la grecque

SERVES 4

1 pinch saffron

2 tablespoons white wine

2 teaspoons extra-virgin olive oil

½ teaspoon coriander seeds

½ teaspoon whole white
peppercorns

1 bay leaf

¼ bunch thyme, chopped, or left
in sprigs if young and tender

2 garlic cloves, peeled and thinly
sliced

4 leeks as thick as your thumb,
the top third of the green
discarded

2 tablespoons white-wine
vinegar

You can use any size leeks you can find, but you will need to adjust the cooking time accordingly – pencil leeks will cook very quickly and large leeks will take longer. A good way to test if they are ready is to insert the point of a knife into the leek. If it enters with very little pressure it is ready. If you feel there are still crisp layers of leek then it will need further cooking. This recipe can stand on its own if served with a grated hard-boiled egg and maybe a cheeky anchovy to top it off.

Steep the saffron in the white wine overnight in the refrigerator.

Preheat the oven to 135°C (280°F).

Gently warm the olive oil in a large ovenproof frying pan over medium–low heat. Add the coriander seeds, peppercorns, bay leaf, thyme, garlic and leeks and toss for 2 minutes until the coriander is aromatic. Add a pinch of salt, the saffron-infused wine and vinegar, bring to the boil and cover with baking paper. Transfer the pan to the oven and bake for 1 hour or until the leeks are tender.

Remove the leeks from the oven and allow to cool slightly, but make sure to eat them when they're still a little warm.

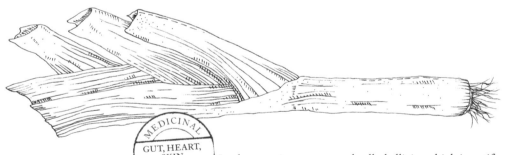

MEDICINAL · BENEFIT ·
GUT, HEART, SKIN

Leeks contain a compound called allicin, which is antifungal, antiviral, antibacterial and an immunity booster. You'll recognise the pungent smell as it's shared with other members of the allium family (chives, garlic and onions, for example). Leeks are a great source of folic acid (essential for DNA synthesis and cell division), and of B vitamins (which help convert food into energy and also help prevent the build-up of plaque in arteries). Leeks contain vitamin A (good for eyes and immunity), vitamin C (also for immunity), vitamin K (for blood clotting) and vitamin E (for the skin and to help protect cells).

38

Roast baby squash with oregano and lime

SERVES 4

12 baby (pattypan) squash
1 tablespoon extra-virgin olive oil
½ quantity Oregano lime butter (page 236)

There is always a ton of baby squash at the market. I don't know if it's because nobody likes it, or because it's easy to grow yourself. I love it as it's small and very versatile. Its flavour is reasonably neutral, which means it works well when you play with tasty seasonings. With its great skin texture, as well as roasting, it also boils very well.

Preheat the oven to 220°C (430°F).

Put the squash in a roasting tin and drizzle with the olive oil, tossing to coat. Roast the squash in the oven for 20 minutes or until tender – insert a skewer or knife to check.

Remove the squash from the oven and allow it to cool for a moment then, using a small sharp knife, cut a cross on the top, cutting halfway through the squash. Spoon the oregano lime butter into the cavities and serve with plenty of freshly ground black pepper and some salt.

MEDICINAL
EAR, NOSE & THROAT
·BENEFIT·

Squash are a good source of folates, which are absolutely vital for new cell production. They also contain vitamin C, vitamin A and other powerful compounds that have antioxidant, anti-inflammatory, anticarcinogenic and other protective abilities. Oregano is full of essential oils with a range of benefits, from antiseptic to carminative (eliminating gas) properties to helping with gall bladder function. Use the herb in a warming tea for the treatment of colds, flu, mild fevers, indigestion, stomach upsets and period pain.

Tomatoes provençal

SERVES 4

3 oxheart tomatoes (or any other large plump variety)

80 ml (2½ fl oz/⅓ cup) extra-virgin olive oil

1 pinch sea salt

120 ml (4 fl oz) white wine

80 g (2¾ oz/1 cup) fresh breadcrumbs

4 garlic cloves, peeled and thinly sliced

¼ bunch thyme, roughly chopped

¼ bunch flat-leaf (Italian) parsley, roughly chopped

¼ bunch marjoram, roughly chopped

If I were to think of something that reminds me of being in southern France it would be this dish. A couple of these tomatoes and a glass of rosé and I am in heaven. I love oxheart tomatoes for this recipe as they are very flavoursome and hold a lot of pulp, so they don't go too mushy when cooked. It's nice to mix a couple of heirloom tomatoes in to add colour. Fresh breadcrumbs are best for this dish, as you get two different textures – crispy on top, and soft underneath to soak up the beautiful tomato juices. I prefer this dish at room temperature, as the tomatoes are very steamy when hot and a little harder to eat.

Preheat the oven to 220°C (430°F).

Cut the tomatoes in half crossways and season them with some salt. Heat half the olive oil in a large, flameproof casserole dish over medium heat. Place the tomatoes in the pan, cut side down, and cook for 1–2 minutes until lightly browned.

Remove from the heat and turn the tomatoes cut side up. Put the casserole dish back on the stove top, sprinkle the tomatoes with the sea salt, drizzle with the wine and cook until the liquid is reduced to a glaze.

Put the breadcrumbs, garlic, herbs, the remaining olive oil and any pan juices in a bowl and rub them together with your hands with a pinch of salt and some freshly ground black pepper. It's important to keep the crumbs loose, and handle the mixture very gently so as not to create a dough.

Scatter the loose, oily crumbs over the tomatoes, transfer the casserole dish to the oven and bake the tomatoes for 15–20 minutes until the breadcrumbs are golden on top and the tomatoes are soft and tender. Spoon over any juices before serving.

Tomatoes are high in lycopene, which helps protect cells from harmful oxygen free radicals. Lycopene gives the red colour to tomatoes (and other red and pink fruit) and is said to help protect the skin from UV rays. Tomatoes also contain flavonoids, which help protect the eyes from macular disease by filtering out harmful ultraviolet rays. They also contain potassium, an important component of cell and body fluids that helps control the heart rate and blood pressure.

Grilled marinated lamb skirt with bread and butter cucumbers

SERVES 4

1 kg (2 lb 3 oz) lamb skirt

125 ml (4 fl oz/½ cup) balsamic vinegar

1 teaspoon salt

1 fresh bay leaf

¼ bunch rosemary, leaves picked

3 garlic cloves, squashed with the heel of your hand

125 ml (4 fl oz/½ cup) extra-virgin olive oil

plain yoghurt, to serve

¼ quantity Bread and butter cucumbers (page 241)

This lamb is delicious on flatbread with a dollop of yoghurt, or just as it is for finger food. Ask your butcher for the skirt of the lamb, otherwise known as the breast. You can get it with the rib bones attached or none at all, but it's basically the large bit of flesh that holds the belly in. The pickled cucumbers balance the sweetness of the balsamic and the lovely rich-flavoured lamb. Instead of pickling your own cucumbers, you could buy a quality brand from a reputable store.

If the skirt is too fatty, trim a layer off so the fat is evenly dispersed across the belly. Place the lamb in a non-reactive tray – such as stainless steel, earthenware or plastic – and pour all the ingredients over it, except the yoghurt and cucumbers, massaging them into the meat well. Leave to marinate in the refrigerator for a few hours, or preferably overnight.

When you're ready to cook the lamb, fire up the barbecue or chargrill pan to super hot.

Lift the lamb out of the marinade and sit it on a wire rack set over a bowl, to allow the liquid to drain so it doesn't spit and steam everywhere when it hits the pan.

Depending on the size of your grill, you may need to cut your meat to fit. Cut it in half or thirds but don't cut it into smaller pieces – you want the pieces as large as possible.

Place the meat on the grill and allow it to sizzle and smoke hard for a good 10 minutes. Then turn it over and give it another 10 minutes. Don't be worried by its very dark colour, as this is simply the balsamic vinegar caramelising – the flavour of the balsamic is robust and helps cut through the fattiness of the lamb.

Remove the meat from the grill and rest for a minimum of 5 minutes, although 10 is preferable. Slice the lamb into strips and serve with a dollop of yoghurt and the bread and butter cucumbers.

Lamb is rich in vitamins B3 and B12, essential for a variety of functions including the maintenance of the nervous and digestive systems. It also contains zinc, which plays an important role in immune function as well as in the synthesis of proteins and DNA. Phosphorus is in the mix (good for bones and teeth), as is iron (vital for the healthy production of red blood cells).

Glazed ham with prickly pear chutney

SERVES 10, WITH EXTRA FOR SANDWICHES THE NEXT DAY

1 leg of ham (about 4 kg/
8 lb 13 oz) bone in, or buy an
'easy-carve' ham, which has
the femur and hip bone
removed

30–40 cloves

60 g (2 oz/¼ cup) English
mustard, or 1 tablespoon
English mustard powder

55 g (20 oz/¼ cup) soft
brown sugar

a water sprayer

PRICKLY PEAR CHUTNEY (MAKES 1 KG/2LB 3 OZ)

125 g (4½ oz/1 cup) sultanas
(golden raisins)

5 g (¼ oz) salt

150 g (5½ oz) caster (superfine)
sugar

1 brown onion, finely chopped

1 orange, zested and juiced

1 teaspoon ground cinnamon

½ teaspoon freshly grated
nutmeg

4 cm (1½ in) piece fresh ginger,
finely diced

250 ml (8½ fl oz/1 cup) white-
wine vinegar

1 pinch saffron

1 kg (2 lb 3 oz) prickly pears,
cut into 1 cm (½ in) dice (see
Note, page 46)

There is no such thing as a boneless leg of ham, as that would be gammon. However, you are welcome to make this recipe with a piece of gammon if you choose. Although if it's Christmas, you really should bring out the big guns and do the whole leg of ham. (Note that when you order a leg of ham, it comes already cured and cooked. If it was raw it would be a leg of pork.)

For the prickly pear chutney, heat a large heavy-based saucepan over medium–low heat. Add all the ingredients, except the prickly pear, and simmer for 5 minutes. Add the prickly pear and boil for 5–10 minutes until the mixture becomes glossy and starts to bubble like a volcano.

Remove the pan from the heat and immediately transfer the contents to a 1 litre (34 fl oz/4 cup) sterilised jar (or several smaller jars). The chutney will need to be above 85°C (185°F) when the lid is put on, in order to form a vacuum to preserve the chutney. Use a thermometer to check the temperature.

Place the ham on a board, skin side up. Using your fingertips or a small knife, prise the skin away from the fat, to separate it from the flesh, then fully peel the skin back.

Take an educated look at the ham, searching for the very fatty pieces and trim it so there is about a centimetre (half an inch) of fat covering the leg. Then score the fat into a lattice or diamond pattern just down to the meat, making sure not to penetrate into the flesh. Place a clove at the intersection of every diamond, pushing the cloves in firmly so they're secure. (These will perfume the flesh as they warm in the oven.)

Preheat the oven to 220°C (430°F) – remember that the ham is already cured and cooked and all you are doing is glazing it to serve.

Place the leg of ham on a wire rack set in a large, heavy-based baking tin, with a little water in the bottom of the tin so the ham doesn't burn and smoke out your oven.

In England, you will find that the best mustard comes in powdered form. If you can find a good-quality powder, lightly dust it over the leg. However, quality prepared English mustard is almost as good. If using mustard from a jar, smother a thin layer all over the fat so the ham is covered. Scatter brown sugar all over your ham so it sticks to the mustard and forms a beautiful layer on top. ➤

46

<

Put the ham in the oven and watch it carefully – you don't want the sugar to clump and go hard. If you notice any pockets of sugar, they will set like toffee. Get the water sprayer and give the ham a little spritz to hydrate the sugar and help to melt it and glaze the ham.

Your ham will be beautifully glazed in about 30 minutes. If you think it's getting too dark too soon, reduce the oven temperature and continue to cook until you have a lovely caramel sheen over the layer of fat.

It's best to warm the ham in the oven just before you're ready to serve. If you do it too early, the ham fat will solidify and not be as pleasant to eat.

Remove the ham from the oven and allow it to rest for 20 minutes while you call your friends to the table and prepare the accompaniments. Slice the ham thinly across the grain for the tenderest pieces. Serve with chutney on the side.

Note: *Be very careful peeling the prickly pears – if you get those needles in your fingers, chances are you won't get them out till the next day. I find the best thing to do is handle the pears with gardening gloves. Using a sharp knife, take the top and bottom off, then run a knife down the length of the fruit to remove the skin.*

Pork is rich in B complex vitamins. These help convert food into energy, lower plaque build-up in arteries and help make serotonin, which plays a key role in regulating sleep, moods and appetite. B vitamins also help make red blood cells and boost the function of the immune system. Pork is a good source of selenium, which helps with healthy thyroid activity, and zinc, which is essential for a sharp sense of taste and smell and the healing of wounds. Prickly pears are a rich source of dietary fibre, helpful for digestion but also for reducing cholesterol and blood sugar levels. They contain vitamin A (good for the eyes), B complex vitamins, vitamin C and flavonoids (which help protect the skin).

Roast chicken with verjuice, white grapes and tarragon

SERVES 4

4 garlic cloves, peeled

1 × 1.5 kg (3 lb 5 oz) free-range
   chicken

200 ml (7 fl oz) verjuice

1 handful thyme sprigs

extra-virgin olive oil

sea salt

360 g (12½ oz/2 cups) picked
   white grapes

1 handful activated walnuts
   (see page 237)

1 bunch tarragon, leaves picked

6 radicchio leaves

There is a famous French fish dish called *sole veronique*. I was inspired by the ingredients to make it with chicken, another white-fleshed meat. I have also eaten a very similar dish in France served with quail. I really love the sweet flavour from the grapes juxtaposed with the bitter flavour of the radicchio. Adding radicchio to the warm juices will make it wilt slightly and lose some of its bitterness, and it's delicious for soaking up the juice. The walnuts give the dish a nice crunch and tarragon just happens to be my favourite herb.

Place the garlic cloves inside the chicken, then place the chicken in a large zip-lock plastic bag. Pour in half the verjuice and add the thyme sprigs. Fasten the bag and shake well. Leave to marinate for 1 hour in the refrigerator, shaking every so often as you walk past.

Preheat the oven to 220°C (430°F).

Tip the chicken into a terracotta or non-reactive baking dish (you might like to serve it in the same dish you cook it in) with a healthy splash of olive oil and a sprinkling of sea salt. Put the dish in the oven and cook the chicken for 15 minutes, then reduce the heat to 200°C (400°F) for 20 minutes – until the drumstick easily twists out of the socket of the thigh when tested. The chicken will colour fast because the verjuice is high in residual sugar. If you find that it's colouring too fast, reduce the heat by 10°C (50°F) and cover the chicken with aluminium foil. ❯

⟨

When you think it's about 10 minutes until the chicken is cooked, add the remaining verjuice and the grapes. Scatter over the walnuts. Allow to sizzle and roast for a final 10 minutes. The grapes will swell and burst. (A purist would say you need to peel them, but I say this is too much work.) The time to add the grapes is really up to you – you can cook them longer so they blister, or just enough so they go soft.

Remove the pan from the oven and scatter over the tarragon leaves. Leave to rest for 15 minutes to allow all the flavours to mingle.

The best way to cut the chook is with poultry shears if you have them. Cut up the breast plate to divide the chicken. Remove the leg and thigh and use your shears to cut up the breast – don't be precious.

Finish with a few torn radicchio leaves thrown into the warm juices and a fresh grinding of black pepper.

MEDICINAL

MUSCLES,
BONES & JOINTS

BENEFIT

Chicken is a quality source of lean protein, needed to build muscle. It contains selenium, which helps regulate thyroid hormone activity, and is high in vitamin B (which helps convert food into energy). It's also rich in phosphorus and calcium, two minerals that help build and protect bones. Tarragon has one of the highest antioxidant levels of all the common herbs. It also contains compounds that help restrict blood clotting inside the tiny blood vessels of organs, such as the heart and brain, and this protects from heart attack and stroke.

Picnic ocean trout, wild black pepper and verjuice mayonnaise

SERVES 5–6

1 copy of your least favourite newspaper, which you're happy to burn

2 kg (4 lb 6 oz) ocean trout, scaled, gutted and gills removed (ask your fishmonger to do this for you, as it can be messy)

1 lemon, sliced

1 tablespoon extra-virgin olive oil

1 packet dried dulse seaweed, rehydrated in cold water for 30 minutes, then drained

WILD BLACK PEPPER AND VERJUICE MAYONNAISE

2 teaspoons voatsiperifery peppercorns (see Note, page 52)

1 egg yolk

1 tablespoon verjuice

1 teaspoon dijon mustard

200 ml (7 fl oz) grapeseed oil

Christmas lunch in Australia is always a fun affair for us. I love the freedom to be either at home with family, or to wander down to the beach to eat. This flexible way of cooking fish works for both options, as the fish will keep warm for 45 minutes after cooking. The seaweed is used to wrap around the fish, to help give it a natural salty seasoning from the sea. If you can't find dulse, try using other seaweeds such as wakame, kombu or any other leaf seaweed. Mayonnaise is always on my radar with trout or salmon, and the wild pepper and verjuice mayonnaise here uses the softer tones of verjuice rather than vinegar, which allows the wild peppercorns to sing. Take the jar of mayonnaise with you to the picnic to have on the side with the trout. Serve with Mango, avocado, lime and lentil salad (page 33) – the fruity mango salad with the zing of lime and the saltiness of capers and olives is a perfect match for the rich ocean trout flavours.

For the wild pepper and verjuice mayonnaise, lightly toast the peppercorns in a frying pan over low heat for 2 minutes, just to refresh them. Allow to cool, then crush half of them roughly in a mortar and pestle.

In a bowl, whisk together the egg yolk, verjuice and mustard. While whisking, gradually pour in the grapeseed oil to create the mayonnaise. Add the ground peppercorns and adjust the seasoning with some salt and a little more verjuice to suit your palate – it should taste aromatic and spicy. Transfer the mayonnaise to a sterilised jar and scatter with the remaining peppercorns.

To cook the fish, preheat the oven to 220°C (430°F).

Open your newspaper out to the centre page. Pour 1 litre (34 fl oz/4 cups) water over the newspaper to drench it and place a large piece of baking paper in the middle – as we don't want the ink to come in contact with the fish. Place the sliced lemon in the fish's belly. Rub the fish with the olive oil and a pinch of salt and wrap the dulse seaweed around the fish. Wrap up the fish tightly in the newspaper, making sure the baking paper is between the fish and the newspaper, and secure it with string. Now soak the entire package in water until the paper is sopping wet. ➤

<

Place the package on a wire rack set in a baking tin and bake for 25 minutes. It's now ready to eat. However, the beauty of this dish is that it will stay warm in its little cocoon for another 45 minutes, which gives you ample time to get to your picnic destination. If serving the fish immediately, allow it to rest for 10–15 minutes before cutting open the package, to allow the flesh to relax and the fish to finish cooking a little more inside the paper.

If you take the package to a picnic, take a pair of scissors with you to snip the string and prise the package open from the top.

Use a spoon to pull some fish from the bone and place it on a serving plate – it will flake off the bone very easily, as the fish has been steamed in the wet newspaper and will hold together beautifully before portioning. Serve with a dollop of the mayonnaise.

Note: *A mix of sichuan and black peppercorns is a good option if you can't find voatsiperifery peppercorns, which come from Madagascar.*

Salmon is rich in a particular omega-3 fatty acid that helps control blood sugar and can therefore help with diabetes. It can also prevent heart disease by lowering 'bad' cholesterol. It's high in selenium (for thyroid regulation) and potassium, to balance bodily fluids, maintain a steady heartbeat and help lower blood pressure. Salmon also contains an antioxidant called astaxanthin, which gives the flesh its orange colour. The benefits of this antioxidant mainly involve the skin as it has powerful UV-blocking properties. It helps protect fish eggs from sun damage; in humans, it's been shown to reduce wrinkles.

Baked scallops with watermelon and hazelnut curry

SERVES 4

12 scallops
olive oil
sea salt
lime wedges, to serve

WATERMELON CURRY

350 g (12½ oz) watermelon,
   diced
½ bunch coriander (cilantro),
   with roots
1 garlic clove, peeled and
   crushed
1 teaspoon chilli powder
¼ teaspoon ground coriander
1 pinch ground turmeric
50 ml (1¾ fl oz) extra-virgin
   olive oil
¼ teaspoon cumin seeds, toasted
   and lightly crushed
50 g (1¾ oz) hazelnuts
½ lime, juiced
½ teaspoon caster (superfine)
   sugar

You can buy scallops in many different forms. Alive is of course best, but you can also buy them on the half shell (these usually come frozen), or as just scallop meat. If you buy a large live scallop in its shell, hold it firmly and place a blunt palette knife between the top and bottom of the shell. Scrape the flat shell to separate it – the flat part is the top of the shell, and the round part is the bottom. Discard the top. The scallop flesh is connected to the bottom shell by a muscle. Remove the muscle and also the frill, but leave the roe. You can ask your fishmonger to do this if you prefer.

For the watermelon curry, purée 150 g (5½ oz/1 cup) of the diced watermelon with the coriander roots in a blender until a smooth juice is formed.

Using a mortar and pestle or a food processor, make a paste from the garlic and ground spices with a pinch of salt.

Heat the olive oil in a frying pan over medium heat and fry the paste for 30 seconds or until the garlic is aromatic. Add the toasted cumin seeds and watermelon purée and reduce for 5 minutes to form a thick curry sauce. Remove from the heat and add the remaining diced watermelon and the hazelnuts. Adjust the flavour to taste with the lime juice, sugar and salt. Garnish with half the coriander leaves.

Preheat the oven to 220°C (430°F).

Place the cleaned scallops back in the bottom halves of the shells, drizzle with olive oil and sprinkle with sea salt. Place the scallops on the tray and bake for 3 minutes. The scallops are ready when you press the flesh and it feels springy and bounces back. If it still feels dull to the touch, it's still raw in the centre.

Remove the scallops from the oven and transfer to serving plates. Spoon the watermelon curry over the scallops, garnish with the remaining coriander leaves and serve with the lime wedges.

Scallops are rich in the omega-3 fatty acids that can help blood sugar levels (thus helping control diabetes) and prevent heart disease by lowering 'bad' cholesterol. Scallops contain iron, potassium and magnesium, known to reduce muscle cramps and help regulate blood pressure.

56

Paella on the barbecue

SERVES 8

1 kg (2 lb 3 oz) green (raw) king prawns (jumbo shrimp), peeled with the shell left on the tip of the tail (reserve the heads and shells)

2 pinches saffron threads

50 ml (1¾ fl oz) extra-virgin olive oil

50 g (1¾ oz) French shallots, peeled and thinly sliced

20 g (¾ oz) garlic, crushed

½ bunch thyme, leaves picked

¼ bunch rosemary, leaves picked and chopped

2 boneless, skinless chicken breasts (about 180 g/6½ oz each)

1 pinch sea salt

400 g (14 oz) calasparra rice (see Note)

125 ml (4 fl oz/½ cup) white wine

250 g (9 oz) tomato passata (puréed tomatoes)

500 g (1 lb 2 oz) mussels

500 g (1 lb 2 oz) broad (fava) beans, shelled

2 lemons, cut into wedges

Before we start, let's note that you can of course cook paella on a conventional stove top. I choose to use the barbecue because, traditionally, a paella is cooked over coals. A round kettle barbecue also has two flaps on either side of the grill to lift the pan higher, away from the heat, if you need to slow the cooking down. You can prop the pan up with a brick or similar, if you don't have a kettle barbecue.

Fire up a round kettle barbecue with a full basket of coals.

Put the prawn heads and shells in a saucepan of water over medium heat and simmer for 15 minutes to obtain a red stock. Strain the stock into a bowl through a sieve, add the saffron and top up with a little water to give you 1.25 litres (42 fl oz/5 cups). Set the stock aside but keep it hot.

When the coals are glowing, put a paella pan (with a 32 cm/12¾ in base) on the grill over the coals and add the olive oil – the oil will get hot quickly as a paella pan is quite thin. Add the shallots, garlic, herbs and chicken and season with the sea salt. Stir to soften the shallots and lightly cook the chicken for about 5 minutes.

Before you add the rice, rinse it until the water runs clear. Add the rice to the paella pan and stir for 30 seconds to coat the rice in oil, then add the wine and continue to stir for 2 minutes until the rice has absorbed the wine. Add the tomato passata and stir to coat the rice, then add the reserved hot prawn head stock. Bring to the boil and simmer slowly, stirring occasionally, for 5 minutes. Add the mussels and broad beans and stir one last time.

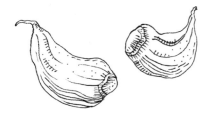

Lift the grill flaps up on the barbecue (if it has them) and suspend the paella high off the coals to maintain a slow simmer (or use a brick to prop up the pan). Don't stir anymore as a light caramelised crust will begin to form under the rice when cooked, called a socarrat, and this is a highly prized element of the dish.

After 5 minutes place the prawns on top to steam gently from the heat of the rice. Make sure to turn them after 5 minutes.

Soon the rice will have absorbed most of the stock and little steam vents will form. Taste the rice on top to see if it is cooked. Like risotto, it should be al dente, but it won't be creamy in texture as it isn't stirred. When you are satisfied, lift the pan off the barbecue and place it on the table with a tea towel (dish towel) over it and rest it for 15 minutes. (This is the perfect time to have a sherry!)

Remove the tea towel and divide the paella among serving plates, scraping some of the trophy socarrat crust into each portion. Serve with the lemon wedges for squeezing.

Note: *Calasparra is an ancient rice strain from the region of Murcia in southeastern Spain. Calasparra has a short, round grain that can absorb 30 per cent more liquid than ordinary rice. Also look for bomba, another Spanish rice variety perfect for paella.*

There are many healthy ingredients in this paella, but let's focus on the rice. There's no question that brown rice is healthier for you, but using carefully sourced organic white rice, such as calasparra or bomba, has benefits. Because rice is low in sodium, it's a fantastic food for those suffering from high blood pressure. Rice is also rich in carbohydrates, which are the body's main source of energy. And, it's a good source of vitamin B3 (also called niacin and helpful for regulating cholesterol), vitamin D (important for maintaining normal blood levels of calcium and phosphorus, which strengthen and build bone) and vitamins B1 and B2 (to convert food to energy as well as help maintain healthy hair, skin, muscles and brain).

58

Poached apricots with lemon thyme junket

SERVES 4

200 ml (7 fl oz) water

200 ml (7 fl oz) white wine

200 g (7 oz) caster (superfine) sugar

1 vanilla bean, split and seeds scraped

10 apricots, stoned and halved

60 ml (2 fl oz/¼ cup) brandy

LEMON THYME JUNKET

1½ junket (rennet) tablets

1 tablespoon cold water

430 ml (14½ fl oz) full-cream (whole) milk

40 g (1½ oz) caster (superfine) sugar

10 g (¼ oz) lemon thyme leaves, chopped

Junket is something my grandmother made for me. It was one of those dishes from wartime that have few ingredients but taste absolutely delicious. The texture of junket is very delicate, and this is what I love. It's like the softest jelly you could imagine, so set it in your jars and try not to move it too much or it will crack. Junket is also good with other infusions – try bay leaf or lavender. The apricots here are very simply poached. However, if you happen to find a whole box at the market, make the syrup from the water, wine, vanilla bean and brandy with double the amount of sugar, placing all the ingredients in jars, and cook it like the Bottled pears on page 166. These will stay in your larder, at ambient temperature, for a year or until you decide to eat them.

For the lemon thyme junket, dissolve the junket tablets in the cold water.

In a saucepan over low heat, warm the milk, sugar and lemon thyme until tepid (36–40°C/97–104°F), using a cooking thermometer to check the temperature.

Remove the pan from the heat and add the dissolved junket, stirring well. Strain the mixture into sterilised jars and refrigerate until set (2–3 hours).

For the apricots, combine all the ingredients, except the apricots and brandy, in a large saucepan over medium–high heat. Simmer for 2 minutes before adding the apricots. Remove the pan from the heat and let the apricots steep for 10 minutes. When tender, remove the apricots and set them aside.

Simmer the syrup left in the pan for 5 minutes or until it reduces to a glossy consistency. Take the pan off the heat, stir in the brandy and set aside to cool. Return the apricots to the syrup and they are now ready to serve or store in jars in the pantry.

Apricots are an excellent source of dietary fibre, antioxidants, vitamins and minerals. They're particularly rich in vitamin A and carotenoids, which are vital for healthy eyes. Lemon thyme, and regular thyme for that matter, contain thymol. This essential oil is antiseptic and antifungal and is useful for respiratory ailments, indigestion and easing menstrual cramps. Thyme can also be used to treat depression, insomnia and headaches.

Pavlova with raspberries in vinegar

SERVES 4

100 g (3½ oz) mascarpone
½ quantity Chantilly cream
   (page 245)
left-over raspberries from
   Raspberry vinegar (page 233)
mint leaves, to finish (optional)

MERINGUE

50 g (1¾ z) panela sugar (see
   Note, page 16)
4 egg whites
200 g (9 oz) caster (superfine)
   sugar
1 teaspoon vanilla bean paste
¼ teaspoon cream of tartar

Of course, you can use fresh raspberries for this recipe; however, I like to get as much use out of an ingredient as possible. I love making raspberry vinegar, which can be used to make salad dressings instead of standard vinegars. The sharp flavour of the raspberries from the vinegar counterbalances the sweet, sugary meringue in this recipe. When you make the vinegar, reserve the berries in the colander for the pavlova. The meringues will last for days in a sealed container.

Preheat the oven to 130°C (270°F). Line a baking tray with baking paper.

To make the meringue, using a spice grinder, grind the panela sugar until it is very fine.

In a very clean bowl, whisk the egg whites on either the second-highest speed of your electric mixer, or by hand. When they reach soft peaks, begin to add the caster sugar, 1 tablespoon at a time, making sure the sugar is dissolved between each addition. Continue to whip until you have stiff peaks, the sugar is completely dissolved into the egg whites and the appearance is very shiny. Add the panela sugar last and whisk to dissolve it. To test this, rub a little mix between your fingers. If you can't feel any sugar granules between your fingertips you're good to go. If not, keep whisking. Gently fold in the vanilla and sifted cream of tartar.

Using a spoon, place heaped dollops of the meringue mixture to form nests on the baking tray. You can make the meringue nests as large or small as you wish, but I think 10 cm (4 in) diameter is nice. If you want to refine the shape any more, you can quenelle the meringue using two large spoons. Bake for 1 hour. Leave to cool in the oven with the door ajar.

Gently fold the mascarpone through the chantilly cream to thicken it and cut through the sweetness.

When the pavlovas have cooled, spread over the chantilly cream mixture and spoon the raspberries over the top. Finish with mint leaves if desired.

MEDICINAL
BRAIN, GUT,
HEART
·BENEFIT·

High-quality unfiltered apple-cider vinegar has many health benefits. It contains pectin, which helps stabilise blood glucose levels and can lower 'bad' cholesterol. There's also vitamin B, folic acid (to help create new cells) and potassium (for balancing fluids and helping maintain a steady heartbeat). Malic acid supports energy production, increases muscle performance and mental focus, and reduces fatigue after exercise.

62

Gluten-free plum, rosemary and hazelnut cake

SERVES 9

5 eggs

75 g (2¾ oz/⅓ cup) raw (demerara) sugar

125 ml (4 fl oz/½ cup) honey

125 g (4½ oz) butter, softened

1 tablespoon chopped rosemary leaves

1 orange, zested

220 g (8 oz/2 cups) ground hazelnuts

15 plums, stoned and halved

1 tablespoon icing (confectioners') sugar

5 grindings of black pepper

vanilla ice cream or cream, to serve

I really enjoy a piece of cake for afternoon tea, but sometimes my body tells me I have had too much gluten. This recipe uses ground nuts to thicken the batter and whole eggs for aeration. If you can't find plums, try stoned apricots or small peaches. The black pepper is the perfect friend for the rosemary, and the lovely orange tang further helps bring the ingredients together.

Preheat the oven to 180°C (350°F). Line a 20 x 28 cm (8 x 11 in) cake tin with baking paper (a round tin will also work fine, but the batter is dense and it can't be too deep or it won't cook through).

Break the eggs into a large bowl. Add a pinch of salt and the raw sugar and whisk with an electric mixer, or by hand, until the mixture becomes pale and thick. Whisk in the honey, butter, rosemary and orange zest. Stir in the ground hazelnuts.

Scrape the batter into the prepared cake tin and arrange the plum halves, cut side up, on top of the mixture. Dust with half the icing sugar. Bake for about 1 hour, until golden brown and cooked through.

Let the cake cool in the tin before serving, as it is a very soft mix and will firm up as it cools. Dust with icing sugar and finish with a grinding of black pepper. Serve with ice cream or cream.

Plums are full of dietary fibre, for healthy digestion. They also have ample vitamin A, for the health of the eyes, B complex vitamins, to help convert food into energy, and vitamin C, to bolster the immune system. Rosemary is also a good source of vitamins A and C, plus it contains rosmarinic acid. Rosmarinic acid has anti-inflammatory and antimicrobial properties, and its antioxidant potency is stronger than that of even vitamin E when it comes to preventing cell damage. It's also good for sharpening the memory.

64 Peach Melba

SERVES 10

2 vanilla beans, split lengthways
    and seeds scraped
350 g (12½ oz) caster
    (superfine) sugar
1 litre (34 fl oz/4 cups) sparkling
    white wine
1 litre (34 fl oz/4 cups) water
10 peaches
vanilla ice cream, to serve

RASPBERRY COULIS

500 g (1 lb 2 oz) fresh
    raspberries (not frozen)
250 g (9 oz/2 cups) icing
    (confectioners') sugar, sifted

Peach Melba is my favourite summer dessert. It's all about things on a plate that complement each other perfectly. The peaches really need to be ripe and ready to eat before you poach them, or else you'll find that they will take too long to poach and become soft and bloated. A good way to tell whether your peach has been poached properly is to try to peel the skin. If the skin doesn't pull off easily with your fingers, then the peach needs further cooking. If it peels off easily, it's ready. I like to poach the peaches a couple of days in advance, then store them in the refrigerator to let all the flavours come together, or you can cook them in jars like the Bottled pears on page 166. The syrup is delicious, and you should serve this in equal measure with the raspberry coulis and lashings of vanilla ice cream. If you want to add crunch, serve it with slivered almonds, which complement the peach flavours nicely.

For the raspberry coulis, process the ingredients in a blender then pass them through a sieve into a bowl. Set aside.

For the peaches, put all the ingredients, except the peaches and ice cream, in a large saucepan over medium–high heat. Bring to the boil and cook for 5 minutes.

Score the peaches deeply enough to semi-release the stones, and add the peaches to the liquid. Simmer gently for 5 minutes then remove the pan from the heat and set aside.

When the peaches are done (they should look as if the skin will peel easily), remove them from the pan and leave them to cool on a tray.

Over high heat, reduce the liquid remaining in the pan by one-third. Allow to cool then strain the liquid over the peaches. (Store in the refrigerator.)

Serve with a scoop of ice cream and a drizzle of the raspberry coulis.

Peaches contain vitamin A and flavonoids that help the eyes filter UV light efficiently. They also have good levels of vitamin C, vitamin E (which neutralises unstable molecules that can damage cells) and B complex vitamins, which prevent plaque forming in the arteries. They also contain potassium and fluoride, which encourage strong bone formation.

Pineapple, mint and kombucha iceblocks

SERVES 6–8

1 pineapple (about 1.2 kg/
  2 lb 10 oz), coarsely chopped
20 g (¾ oz/1 cup) firmly packed
  mint leaves
200 ml (7 fl oz) Kombucha
  (page 68)
iceblock (popsicle/ice lolly)
  sticks

Kombucha is a probiotic drink made by fermenting green tea with sugar. The recipe for this is on page 68, but you can also buy it in bottled form from most health food stores. This is such a refreshing way to cool down on a sunny day.

Juice the pineapple and mint in a cold-press juicer or blender (strain if blending and discard the solids). Add the kombucha and pour the mixture into 100 ml (3½ fl oz) iceblock moulds. Half-freeze for 1–2 hours, then insert the iceblock sticks. Freeze completely for another 2–3 hours.

To serve, dip the moulds briefly in hot water to unmould.

Note: You can also pour the mixture into a shallow tray to make granita. Allow it to semi-set in the freezer, then scrape with a fork every 30 minutes to form separated ice crystals.

MEDICINAL
MUSCLES,
BONES & JOINTS
BENEFIT

Pineapple contains an enzyme called bromelain that digests food by breaking down protein. Regular consumption of it helps fight arthritis and can relieve indigestion. Pineapple is an excellent source of vitamin C, required for collagen synthesis; collagen is the main structural protein in the body and required for maintaining blood vessels, skin, organs and bones. The fruit also contains vitamin A for healthy skin and sharp vision, folates for cell reproduction, and potassium for balancing body fluids. Mint contains essential oils that have calming, anti-inflammatory and antimicrobial properties and that also promote weight loss. The probiotics in the kombucha will be talked about under the making of kombucha (page 68).

68

Kombucha

MAKES 3 LITRES (101 FL OZ/ 12 CUPS)

3.5 litres (118 fl oz/14 cups) hot water (hot enough to steep the tea, but not boiling – about 80°C/176°F)

230 g (8 oz/1 cup) caster (superfine) sugar

2 tablespoons green tea leaves

500 ml (17 fl oz/2 cups) kombucha (buy a bottle from the health food store)

Kombucha has been called the elixir of life. It's a probiotic drink made by fermenting green tea with sugar. If this is your first time making it, and you have no 'scoby' (symbiotic culture of bacteria and yeast), you need to grow your own from scratch by using a bottle of store-bought kombucha. This is done by fermenting the kombucha with water, sugar and tea, allowing the scoby to form naturally and grow thick and strong enough. When you remove it from the jar, you can start to make the drinking kombucha. Your first batch won't be good to drink, but it will be suitable for the starter and scoby. Discard the rest. Your next batch, using the scoby and the starter you produced, will be ready to drink within about a month. (If you don't have the patience to grow a scoby from scratch, as explained in this recipe, see if you can find one online or get one from a friend.) Kombucha is great served chilled at the beginning of the day to get your gut moving, and also great as a base for cocktails or for the iceblocks on page 67.

Combine the hot water and sugar in a saucepan and stir until the sugar dissolves. Remove the pan from the heat, add the tea leaves to the sugar water and allow the tea to steep. Cool to room temperature. (This will probably take most of the day.)

Add the bottled kombucha to the cooled tea, then strain it into a jar, being careful not to let it touch any steel. Cover the jar tightly with muslin (cheesecloth) and secure with elastic bands, so the mixture can breathe. Leave the jar in a dark place for 10 days to 1 month, depending on the ambient temperature – the hotter the temperature, the faster it will ferment.

When it's ready, the kombucha starter will taste slightly acidic and will have grown a scoby on top. You can now remove the scoby and split it in half to make double the kombucha, or give half the scoby to a friend.

Keep at least 500 ml (17 fl oz/2 cups) of the liquid; you'll use this starter, poured into a jar with your scoby, for your next batch of kombucha. Ferment it, as above. Strain the liquid into bottles and keep it in the refrigerator. Serve chilled.

Something of a 'wonder' drink, kombucha increases the good bacteria in the gut via the many probiotics, enzymes and acids it contains. One of these, glucaric acid, aids in liver detoxification. Compounds in kombucha called glucosamines help lubricate joints. Kombucha, extremely rich in antioxidants, is also thought to have antibiotic qualities.

Lilly pilly Champagne cocktail

SERVES 4

8 dashes Angostura bitters
4 sugar cubes
60 ml (2 fl oz/¼ cup) Lilly pilly cordial (see below)
40 ml (1¼ fl oz) brandy
360 ml (12 fl oz) Champagne

LILLY PILLY CORDIAL

460 g (1 lb/2 cups) caster (superfine) sugar
1 teaspoon tartaric acid
2 lemons, zested and juiced
300 g (10½ oz/2 cups) lilly pillies, halved

A Champagne cocktail is a very elegant aperitif. The brandy and bitters with the sugar cube give this drink a lovely twist, and the forever-bubbling sugar cube at the bottom of the glass looks spectacular. This recipe calls for beautiful pink cordial made from the lilly pilly, an Australian native fruit. If you can't find lilly pilly, try using crabapples – when ripe, the lovely small apple is sharp and will give a very similar finish to the lilly pilly. The cocktail will look almost like a kir royale, but will have the flavour of the slightly tannic lilly pilly cordial. Try to find dark-coloured lilly pillies, as this means they are ripe. It's important to add only a small amount of cordial and not to overplay its delicate flavour. It's there to stain the Champagne, not overpower it. You may be concerned about the amount of cordial you've made against the amount you actually use. The reason you make a large amount is that the lilly pilly is very seasonal and is only at its peak for a number of weeks. So I say make hay while the sun shines!

For the lilly pilly cordial, in a large saucepan over medium heat, bring the sugar and 750 ml (25½ fl oz/3 cups) water to the boil. Add the tartaric acid and lemon zest and stir to dissolve. Add the lilly pillies to the pan and simmer over low heat for 10 minutes or until all the colour has been extracted from the fruit and it has softened.

Remove the pan from the heat, add the lemon juice and squash the fruit against the side of the pan. Allow to sit for 5 minutes off the heat.

Pour the fruit through a sieve, or strain it through muslin (cheesecloth) into a bowl, to yield a deep-red syrup. Discard the fruit. Pour the cordial into a sterilised 500 ml (17 fl oz) bottle and keep sealed in the refrigerator.

To serve, in each glass soak a sugar cube in 2 dashes Angostura bitters. Pour the cordial and brandy over the sugar cube, and top up gently with chilled Champagne.

Note: *Tartaric acid is derived from grapes and is very sharp and sour. It's not the same as cream of tartar, which is used for baking. I would use citric acid if you can't find tartaric acid, but add a little more to make up for it not being so intense.*

MEDICINAL
GUT, SKIN
BENEFIT

Lilly pilly, otherwise known as riberry, is an evergreen rainforest plant with glossy green leaves and fruit the size of a large cherry. An Australian native, it contains a high concentration of antioxidants, amino acids and vitamins A, E and C. Indigenous Australians use lilly pilly for its antibacterial properties. It also has astringent qualities that work to improve the firmness of the skin.

SHAVED PERSIMMON, PRESERVED LEMON

CHIA AND ALMOND MILK PUDDING WITH COCONUT
YOGHURT AND STEWED RHUBARB
— MUSHROOM OMELETTE WITH
NORI AND SESAME —
**BUCKWHEAT CRÊPES WITH RAW CHOCOLATE—
HAZELNUT SPREAD AND CRÈME FRAÎCHE**
Lamb burek, dill pickles and yoghurt
Sweetcorn soup with garlic and ginger butter
CELERIAC AND APPLE SOUP WITH WALNUTS AND CLOVES
Shaved persimmon, preserved lemon and capers
Asian greens slaw with lime and sesame dressing
NASHI PEAR, SHAVED FENNEL, PARMESAN, RAISINS AND PINE NUTS
Plum, radish, lemon thyme and green pistachio nuts
ROAST PUMPKIN WITH CHAI SPICE AND BUTTERMILK

AUTUMN/FALL

72-119

POTATO, LEEK AND THYME GALETTE
— ASIAN RATATOUILLE —
Sweet potato and red cabbage gratin
Mike's steak bordelaise in a hurry
SLOW-COOKED PORK SHOULDER WITH CHIMICHURRI
— COQ AU VIN BLANC —
MUSSELS IN CIDER WITH APPLES AND SORREL
Red mullet, café de Paris butter and cured roe
Crab cakes with red mayonnaise
QUEEN OF PUDDINGS
ZUCCHINI AND MARMALADE CAKE
Green pistachio jelly with persimmons in rose syrup
— POMEGRANATE AND APEROL SPRITZ —
Rhubarb and strawberry fizz

MEDICINAL
EAR, NOSE &
THROAT
• BENEFIT •

GARLIC

MEDICINAL
MUSLCES,
BONES & JOINTS
• BENEFIT •

MUSSELS

MEDICINAL
HEART, SKIN
• BENEFIT •

SWEET POTATOES

MEDICINAL
GUT, SKIN
BENEFIT

YOGHURT

MEDICINAL
GUT
BENEFIT

GINGER

MEDICINAL
EAR, NOSE &
THROAT
BENEFIT

LEMON

Autumn arrives in a flash. Suddenly, days are cooler and just a
tad shorter. Our bodies crave the nourishment the shifting
season demands and, luckily, these months give up some of the
year's best, most varied bounty – persimmons, apples, celeriac,
fennel and zucchini, for starters. It's still not too late for salads,
but it's time for galettes, gratins, soups and cakes too.

Chia and almond milk pudding with coconut yoghurt and stewed rhubarb

SERVES 4

625 ml (21 fl oz/2½ cups) almond milk (see page 238)

1½ teaspoons honey

150 g (5½ oz) chia seeds, plus 1 tablespoon extra for sprinkling

500 g (1 lb 2 oz) rhubarb

100 g (3½ oz) caster (superfine) sugar

¼ lemon, juiced

200 g (7 oz) coconut yoghurt

This dish needs some soaking time, so it's best to make it the day before you want to serve it. You can use coconut water instead of the almond milk if you have a nut allergy. Don't be stressed if you can't find coconut yoghurt, as any good-quality dairy yoghurt would also be delicious. The fruit can be interchanged throughout the year to suit the season – try chopped fresh mango in summer, baked quince in winter, or lovely new-season berries in spring.

Pour the almond milk into a bowl and stir in the honey until fully dissolved, then fold in the chia seeds. Cover and refrigerate overnight to allow the chia seeds to expand.

Wash and trim the rhubarb and cut it into 3 cm (1¼ in) lengths. Toss the rhubarb with the sugar and lemon juice and allow it to steep for several hours (overnight if possible) or until the juices bleed from the fruit.

The next day, bring the rhubarb to the boil in a heavy-based saucepan over medium heat and simmer gently until the rhubarb is soft (but try to maintain its shape). Remove the rhubarb pieces from the pan and simmer the juice until it reduces and forms a syrup. Fold the rhubarb back through the syrup and store in the refrigerator until ready to serve.

To serve, divide the chia pudding between four glasses or bowls, or place it in one large bowl to share. Spoon over half the coconut yoghurt followed by the rhubarb, then top with the remaining coconut yoghurt. Finish with a sprinkling of chia seeds.

Chia seeds are gluten-free and a great source of B complex vitamins, which help keep blood cholesterol levels in check. They also contain omega-3 fatty acids, which are anti-inflammatory and aid in lowering blood pressure. Rhubarb is high in vitamin K, which helps the body utilise calcium for building bones.

Mushroom omelette with nori and sesame

SERVES 4

250 g (9 oz) assorted Asian mushrooms, such as shiitake, shimeji, enoki, abalone, oyster or king oyster

1½ tablespoons rice bran oil

1 garlic clove, crushed

1 teaspoon finely diced fresh ginger

1 French shallot, finely diced

8 eggs

1 tablespoon soy sauce

½ teaspoon sesame oil

1 small pinch caster (superfine) sugar

1 teaspoon freshly toasted sesame seeds

90 g (3 oz/1 cup) bean sprouts, to serve

2 nori sheets, to serve

There are two types of omelette – the Spanish type, which is flat, and the French, which is rolled. I will let you choose which you want to make, as this recipe suits both. If you can't find assorted Asian mushrooms, button mushrooms or large field mushrooms also work a treat. If you can't find rice bran oil, use grapeseed oil or a mild olive oil.

In a large frying pan over medium heat, sauté the mushrooms in 2 teaspoons of the rice bran oil. Start with the largest mushrooms first, slowly adding more as you go and finishing with the enoki (the smallest). When you are a minute away from finishing, add the garlic, ginger and shallot to heat through for 1 minute. Your mushrooms should be a lovely golden colour. Remove the pan from the heat and allow to cool to room temperature.

In a bowl, whisk the eggs with the soy sauce, sesame oil, caster sugar and toasted sesame seeds.

This is where you need to decide which path you want to take with your omelette. If you are going to France, put 1 teaspoon of rice bran oil per omelette in a frying pan over medium heat and add a quarter of the egg mix, stirring it across the pan and shaking the pan every 10 seconds. Continue shaking until the egg mix starts to come together in the centre. Allow the egg to fully set on the bottom.

When the underside is golden, sprinkle the mushrooms down the centre of the egg, tip the pan and roll the egg mixture over itself. Tip the omelette straight onto a plate. Repeat with the remaining omelettes. Serve with a handful of fresh sprouts and some nori, cut with scissors, over the top.

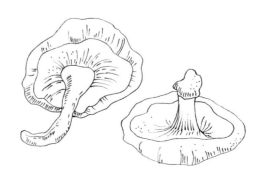

To go to Spain, preheat the oven to 180°C (350°F). Warm a large ovenproof frying pan over medium heat and add 1 tablespoon of rice bran oil and the cooked mushrooms, stirring until they become hot. Add all the egg mixture and stir the ingredients a little to combine and warm them. (You can make four individual omelettes if you prefer.) When the egg begins to firm up, transfer the pan to the oven to set the top, about 5 minutes. If the oven is too hot the omelette will soufflé and this will cause it to be tough, overcooked and shrunken.

Remove the omelette from the oven and let it rest in the pan for 5 minutes. Place the omelette on a chopping board, scatter with the bean sprouts and nori, cut with scissors, and slice the omelette into wedges to serve.

MEDICINAL
BRAIN
BENEFIT

An egg a day literally keeps your metabolism burning. Along with fish and seaweed, eggs are one of the few foods that naturally contain iodine, essential for the healthy functioning of the thyroid gland, which produces the hormones needed to control the metabolism. Eggs are also a good source of B complex vitamins, important for keeping our metabolic and nervous systems healthy. Mushrooms contain selenium, an anti-inflammatory that plays a role in liver enzyme function and so helps detoxify the body.

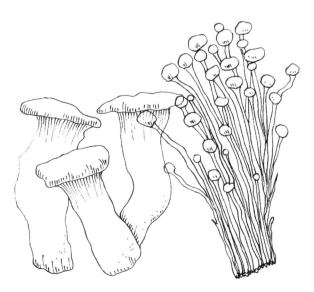

Buckwheat crêpes with raw chocolate–hazelnut spread and crème fraîche

SERVES 4

120 ml (4 fl oz) full-cream (whole) milk

2 eggs, beaten

15 g (½ oz) butter, melted, plus an extra 20 g (¾ oz) for greasing the crêpe pan

10 g (¼ oz) coconut sugar

65 g (2¼ oz) sprouted buckwheat flour

20 g (¾ oz) sorghum flour (if you can tolerate gluten, you can substitute 120 g/4½ oz plain/all-purpose flour)

1 quantity Raw chocolate–hazelnut spread (page 245)

crème fraîche or Labne (see page 181), to serve

The important thing about crêpes is that they should be thin, so make sure your crêpe batter is runny enough so when it hits the pan, it runs freely around to coat the bottom in a very thin layer. For this crêpe recipe I have given an option to use sorghum flour if you are gluten-intolerant, but you can use plain (all-purpose) flour if you can tolerate gluten.

For the crêpe batter, whisk together the milk and eggs until smooth, then whisk in the melted butter. Gradually whisk the sugar and flours into the milk mixture, whisking constantly so there are no lumps. Allow to rest for 30 minutes.

Heat a large non-stick frying pan over medium heat. Wipe the pan with some paper towel dipped in the extra melted butter. When the pan is hot, spoon about 2 tablespoons of batter into the middle of the pan, tilting the pan to thinly coat the base. Gently tap the pan once onto the burner to knock out any air bubbles and also to get an even spread of crêpe batter over the pan. Cook the crêpe for 1 minute. When bubbles start to rise up through the centre of the crêpe, flip it and cook the other side for 10 seconds. When firm, remove each crêpe from the pan and set aside in a stack.

To serve, add some raw chocolate–hazelnut spread and a spoonful of crème fraîche to each crêpe, then fold the crêpes into quarters.

Besides being gluten-free, buckwheat is high in rutin, a flavonoid that helps thin the blood and improve circulation. The raw chocolate–hazelnut spread is full of powerful ingredients – cacao (high in the phenolic antioxidants that help reduce the appearance of ageing), hazelnuts (which contain selenium for regulating thyroid hormone activity) and coconut oil (a rich source of vitamin D for maintaining normal blood levels of calcium). It also has phosphorus to help strengthen bones.

82

Lamb burek, dill pickles and yoghurt

SERVES 4

200 g (7 oz) brik or filo pastry
100 g (3½ oz) Clarified butter
  (page 234), melted
4 teaspoons sumac
2 teaspoons sesame seeds
120 g (4½ oz) yoghurt, to serve
400 g (14 oz) Dill pickles
  (page 240), to serve

FILLING

1½ teaspoons ground cumin
1 teaspoon ground ginger
1 teaspoon ground coriander
1½ teaspoons ground cinnamon
1 teaspoon ground cardamon
2 tablespoons olive oil
2 garlic cloves, crushed
1 brown onion, finely diced
400 g (14 oz) minced (ground)
  lamb
2 tablespoons pine nuts
1 lemon, juiced
1 bunch mint, leaves picked
  and chopped

I have fond memories of travelling through Eastern Europe and having a burek from the market early in the morning. It would often be served with sharp things, such as yoghurt and lemon to squeeze over, but I enjoy it with pickles. I like the crunch of the small cucumber with the rich lamb, and the creamy yoghurt brings the flavours together. This is also delicious with the Vegetable kraut on page 241.

For the filling, in a large frying pan over medium heat, cook the spices in the oil until they are aromatic. Add the garlic and onion and sauté until translucent. Add the lamb and pine nuts and cook for 10 minutes, until all the moisture has evaporated and the lamb is brown and sizzling in the oil. You will need to stir the meat regularly to stop the lamb from cooking in large lumps. Once the lamb is cooked and dry, remove the pan from the heat. Add the lemon juice and mint and season with salt and freshly ground black pepper.

Preheat the oven to 220°C (430°F). Line a large baking tray with baking paper.

On a clean work surface, lay out four sheets of brik pastry (one per burek). Brush each sheet with the clarified butter and scatter with sumac.

Divide the lamb filling between the four piles of pastry. Roll them up into a kebab shape, tucking the ends underneath. Alternatively, you can place the filling in a pile in the centre of your pastry layers, then gather the pastry up towards the centre to form a round parcel and then twist the top. Place the burek on the baking tray.

Brush the tops of the burek with more melted clarified butter and scatter with sesame seeds. Bake for 15 minutes or until golden. Serve with yoghurt for dipping and pickles to refresh the palate.

A high-quality protein, lamb is a very good source of vitamin B3 (niacin), which helps convert food into energy, and vitamin B12, which helps in the production of red blood cells. Both the lacto-fermented dill pickles and the yoghurt provide probiotics ('good' bacteria) for gut health. There are five main benefits of probiotics: they boost the immune system; they prevent and treat urinary tract infections; they improve digestive function; they help inflammatory bowel conditions like irritable bowel syndrome; and they help in managing and preventing eczema.

Sweetcorn soup with garlic and ginger butter

SERVES 4

1 brown onion, roughly diced

1 garlic clove, finely chopped

50 g (1¾ oz) butter

5 corn cobs, kernels removed from the cob using a sharp knife

25 ml (¾ fl oz) thickened (whipping) cream

1 quantity Garlic and ginger butter (page 235), chilled

This lovely soup will brighten your day. It's also delicious, and slightly more rustic, if you only blend half the corn and leave the rest of it whole. Mussels, clams, crabmeat and chicken breast are also nice additions.

In a large saucepan over medium heat, sweat the onion and garlic in half the butter until translucent. Add the corn kernels, top the pan up with about 500 ml (17 fl oz/2 cups) water and simmer for 10 minutes or until the corn is tender.

Remove the pan from the heat. Using a hand-held blender, process the mixture until smooth. Strain the mixture through a sieve into a bowl. Return the strained mixture to the pan and bring back to the boil with the cream and the remaining butter. Stir well until smooth. Season to taste with salt and freshly ground black pepper.

To serve, cut the garlic and ginger butter into 1 cm (½ in) thick discs. Ladle the warm soup into bowls, float the chilled butter discs on top and serve.

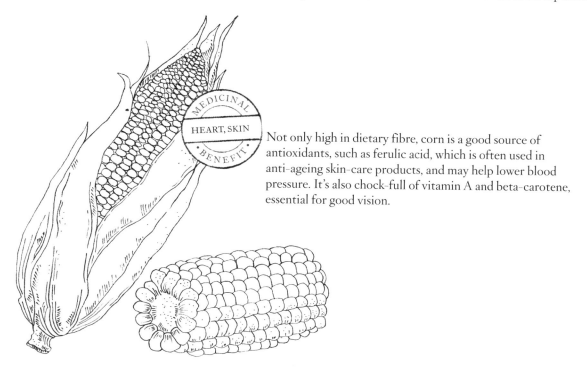

Not only high in dietary fibre, corn is a good source of antioxidants, such as ferulic acid, which is often used in anti-ageing skin-care products, and may help lower blood pressure. It's also chock-full of vitamin A and beta-carotene, essential for good vision.

84

Celeriac and apple soup with walnuts and cloves

SERVES 4

250 g (9 oz) granny smith apples, peeled, cored and cut into into 3 cm (1¼ in) dice

1 kg (2 lb 3 oz) celeriac, peeled and cut into 3 cm (1¼ in) dice

1 tablespoon extra-virgin olive oil

2 teaspoons caster (superfine) sugar

2 teaspoons chardonnay vinegar

about 2 litres (68 fl oz/8 cups) boiling water

35 g (1¼ oz) Clarified butter (page 234)

4 cloves

40 g (1½ oz) activated walnuts (see page 237), roughly chopped

This is a hearty vegetable soup, but you can refine it by processing it in a high-speed blender to give it a slightly thinner texture. It's nice to serve it in a mug so you can sip it. However, as you can see in the photograph, I like it chunky.

Preheat the oven to 180°C (350°F).

In a large saucepan over medium heat, sauté the apple and celeriac in the olive oil for 5 minutes until golden. Add the sugar and toss to coat the apple and celeriac. When the sugar dissolves and turns glossy, add the vinegar and cook for 2 minutes until it has evaporated. Add the boiling water and simmer for 20 minutes until the ingredients are very soft. You can use a fork or the side of a whisk to break up the solids to form a rustic soup. Season with salt and freshly ground black pepper. Ladle the soup into serving bowls.

In a small frying pan over medium heat, melt the clarified butter and fry the cloves and walnuts for 1 minute until fragrant. Spoon this mixture over the soup and serve.

Celeriac is a great source of B complex vitamins, which help convert food to energy, and vitamin C for bolstering the immune system and preparing the body for cold weather. Walnuts are high in omega-3 fatty acids and the antioxidant vitamin E. Cloves are the largest source of eugenol, a potent anti-inflammatory, antioxidant and antibacterial compound and a natural anaesthetic.

86

Shaved persimmon, preserved lemon and capers

SERVES 4

2 firm persimmons

1 preserved lemon

½ garlic clove, chopped

1 handful marjoram leaves, roughly chopped

2 teaspoons salted capers, rinsed and drained well

80 ml (2½ fl oz/⅓ cup) olive oil

1 lemon, juiced

½ bunch flat-leaf (Italian) parsley, leaves picked

This is a great recipe for using persimmons at the beginning of their life, when they are firm. Slice them thinly to enjoy their sweet flavour and celebrate the firm texture. If the parsley leaves are not young and soft, I recommend you tear or chop them before garnishing your salad, as this dish is about the texture of the persimmon not the parsley. A nice addition to the dressing is a sliver of chilli.

Slice the persimmons very thinly using a mandoline or sharp knife and arrange them on a platter.

Cut the preserved lemon into quarters. Remove the flesh from the centre by scraping it out with a spoon. Roughly chop the skin and place it in a mortar. Add the garlic, most of the marjoram (reserving some for a garnish) and half the capers. Grind with the pestle to form a paste, adding the olive oil when needed to turn it into a dressing. Add fresh lemon juice to give it some pep, then spoon the dressing over the persimmon.

Garnish with the remaining capers and marjoram leaves and some parsley. Finish with a grinding of black pepper.

Persimmons contain plenty of vitamin C to boost the immune system. They also contain folic acid for new cell creation, potassium to balance the fluids in the body, and manganese to help in bone formation and metabolising amino acids, cholesterol and carbohydrates.

88

Asian greens slaw with lime and sesame dressing

SERVES 4–6

½ Chinese cabbage (wombok), shaved with a mandoline or sharp knife

1 bok choy (pak choy), leaves cut into strips

6 spring onions (scallions), cut into thin strips

1 bunch coriander (cilantro), leaves and stems picked

1 Lebanese (short) cucumber, cut with a mandoline into strips

6 shiitake mushrooms, thinly sliced lengthways

1 tablespoon toasted sesame seeds

½ lime, juiced, if needed

SESAME DRESSING

15 ml (½ fl oz) sesame seed sauce

1 tablespoon light soy sauce

3 teaspoons rice wine vinegar

10 g (¼ oz) fresh ginger, finely chopped

½ garlic clove, finely chopped

½ teaspoon caster (superfine) sugar

60 ml (2 fl oz/¼ cup) sesame oil

I like to place all the slaw ingredients on a serving platter and then dress them, so I don't bruise the ingredients. However, if you prefer you can toss everything together in a bowl and serve it like a regular slaw. You can find sesame seed sauce in most Asian grocery stores.

For the sesame dressing, mix all the ingredients together in a bowl. Set aside.

Arrange all the slaw ingredients, except the sesame seeds and lime juice, separately on a large platter. Drizzle over the dressing and sprinkle on the sesame seeds. Add a squeeze of lime juice if you feel it needs a sharper flavour.

Cabbage is a good source of vitamin K, which activates the proteins and calcium essential for proper blood clotting. It also contains potassium, which besides helping balance bodily fluids, is essential for muscle contractions, such as a steady heartbeat. Sesame seeds, being rich in a monounsaturated fatty acid called oleic acid, help lower 'bad' cholesterol and increase 'good' cholesterol.

Nashi pear, shaved fennel, parmesan, raisins and pine nuts

SERVES 4

50 ml (1¾ fl oz) chardonnay
    vinegar or apple-cider vinegar
150 ml (5 fl oz) olive oil
1 large fennel bulb, shaved with
    a mandoline or knife
½ bunch watercress, leaves
    picked
4 radicchio leaves, torn into
    pieces about the size of a
    parsley leaf
½ bunch dill, leaves picked
½ bunch mint, leaves picked
1 nashi pear
60 g (2 oz/⅓ cup) small black
    olives
4 dates, pitted and chopped
    into eighths
2 tablespoons plump organic
    raisins from the vine
15 g (½ oz) activated pine nuts
    (see page 237)
20 g (¾ oz) parmesan

This salad is about the texture of the pear and not the crunch of the fennel, which is there only for flavour. If nashi pears are not available, use a crisp corella or beurre bosc pear. Lovely, plump organic raisins are sometimes hard to find, so you could substitute the Raisins in tea on page 143. Pecorino cheese, instead of the parmesan, would be a nice twist with its salty flavour, but something creamy like mozzarella or burrata would make this salad a much heartier meal.

To make a dressing, whisk together the vinegar and olive oil and season to taste with salt and freshly ground black pepper.

Place the shaved fennel in a bowl with a pinch of salt and massage them together with your hands. Set aside for 30 minutes, to allow the fennel to soften slightly.

Once the fennel has softened, rinse it briefly in water and pat it dry. Put the fennel in a bowl and add the watercress, radicchio, dill and mint – I like to leave the herb leaves whole to show off the beautiful colours and shapes. Mix to combine, then arrange this mixture on a serving plate.

Shave the nashi pear over the top of the salad using a mandoline.

In a bowl, mix the dressing, olives, dates, raisins and pine nuts and spoon this mixture over the salad.

Using a peeler or mandoline, shave the parmesan over the salad and finish with a good grinding of black pepper.

Pears contain phytosterols, which are known to help lower cholesterol. They also contain folic acid, vital for cell reproduction, and vitamin C to help boost the immune system. The mineral copper is also found in pears, and this plays an important role in iron metabolism and the production of red blood cells.

92

Plum, radish, lemon thyme and green pistachio nuts

SERVES 4

8 victoria plums, stoned and halved

1 bunch breakfast radishes, leaves rinsed, patted dry and reserved

2 handfuls dandelion leaves, well washed

1 handful basil leaves

1 tablespoon green pistachio nuts, shelled

GREEN PISTACHIO NUT DRESSING

1 tablespoon green pistachio nuts, shelled

1 teaspoon lemon thyme leaves

1 lemon, juiced

60 ml (2 fl oz/¼ cup) extra-virgin olive oil

If you can't find green pistachio nuts (as they have quite a short season), you can use very good-quality, unsalted pistachio nuts. The lovely, fresh juicy plum works well to balance the flavours in this dish. Dandelion leaves have a lovely bitter flavour and a great crisp-textured stem. A good greengrocer would stock them in the lettuce section. However, a nice substitute would be wild rocket (arugula), or a bitter green like chicory (endive).

You can either leave your plums in half or tear them in half again. By tearing, you will release a nice amount of juice to add to your dressing.

For the green pistachio nut dressing, grind the pistachio nuts and lemon thyme in a mortar and pestle before adding the lemon juice. Add the olive oil and mix to create a dressing. Combine with any juice from the plums.

Cut the breakfast radishes thinly lengthways, put them in a bowl with the dressing and toss to combine.

Place the dandelion leaves on a platter. Tumble the radishes onto the dandelion, reserving the dressing in the bowl.

Place the plums on the dandelion and radishes, along with the basil leaves. Spoon over the dressing and add the radish leaves. To finish, roughly slice the green pistachio nuts and scatter them over the salad.

Radishes are a good source of sulforaphane, a compound that reduces inflammation, fights unhealthy bacteria and protects against carcinogenic toxins. Plums are full of dietary fibre, vitamins A, B complex and C. Thyme is antimicrobial, and can be gargled for a sore throat (chop fresh leaves and make a tea), as well as being antihypertensive, meaning it can lower blood pressure. Thyme's essential oils contain carvacrol, which can help lift your mood.

94

Roast pumpkin with chai spice and buttermilk

SERVES 4

½ jap pumpkin (squash), skin on, cut into wedges, seeds left in

2 tablespoons extra-virgin olive oil, for drizzling

1 teaspoon ground cinnamon

1 pinch sea salt

½ bunch coriander (cilantro), leaves picked

1 lime, cut into wedges

DRESSING

125 ml (4 fl oz/½ cup) buttermilk

1 tablespoon sticky chai tea (see Note)

125 g (4½ oz/½ cup) plain yoghurt

Leaving the seeds attached and the skin on pumpkin brings fantastic textures and nutritional benefits to any dish. The skin and seeds also allow you to bake the pumpkin that little bit longer to increase its colour and sweetness – without them the pumpkin would just cook to a pulp. I love the sharp flavour of the buttermilk, but the dressing can be made with any milk – try it with one of the nut milks on page 238.

For the dressing, pour the buttermilk into a saucepan and bring it to the boil. Remove the pan from the heat and add the sticky chai tea. Leave for 5 minutes to infuse, then strain the mixture into a bowl. Allow to cool for 5 minutes, then stir in the yoghurt to complete the dressing. Set aside.

Preheat the oven to 220°C (430°F). Line a baking tray with baking paper.

Place the pumpkin, skin side down, on the baking paper. Drizzle with the olive oil to coat, then sprinkle the cinnamon and sea salt over. Bake for 25 minutes or until the pumpkin is light brown and soft with burnt tips. Serve the pumpkin with the dressing drizzled over, a scattering of coriander leaves and the lime wedges on the side.

Note: *Sticky chai tea, also known as wet chai, is a mixture of raw chai tea ingredients combined with honey to give it a sticky, thick texture.*

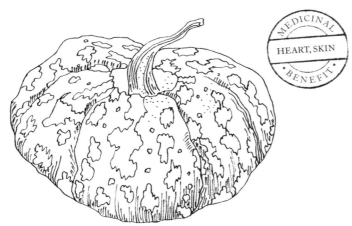

MEDICINAL
HEART, SKIN
· BENEFIT ·

Pumpkin is rich in vitamin A and beta-carotene, which are essential for good vision. The seeds are high in protein and iron, which aid in the production of haemoglobin in red blood cells. Buttermilk is a source of calcium, which builds and protects bones, and the cinnamon contains eugenol, a potent anti-inflammatory, antioxidant and antibacterial compound.

96

Potato, leek and thyme galette

SERVES 6

40 g (1½ oz) unsalted butter

5 leeks, halved lengthways

2 garlic cloves, thinly sliced

¼ bunch thyme, leaves picked

200 g (7 oz) crème fraîche or sour cream

100 g (3½ oz/¾ cup) grated gruyère

1 large raw nicola potato or other waxy variety of potato, thinly sliced

1 quantity Gluten-free pastry dough (page 244), chilled

This galette is delicious served warm from the oven, or at room temperature for a picnic. When the pastry cools it firms up and it's then easier to hold firmly in your hand. Due to the pastry being gluten-free, you will need to work it slowly when folding the edges in, using the paper to support the pastry, as it's very weak and may crumble if you are rough. Don't be too discouraged by its rustic appearance as this just adds to its personality. Other interesting fillings to try would be spinach and goat's cheese, or blue cheese with walnuts and radicchio.

Melt the butter in a large frying pan over medium heat. Add the leek, garlic, thyme and 2 tablespoons water. Bring to a simmer, then cover and cook, stirring every 5 minutes, for 20 minutes or until tender. Remove from the heat.

Transfer the leek mixture to a large bowl. Add the crème fraîche, gruyère and potato slices. Season with salt and freshly ground black pepper and stir to combine. Chill for 1 hour or until cool.

Meanwhile, place the chilled pastry dough between two sheets of baking paper and roll it out to a 35 × 25 cm (14 × 10 in) rectangle. Slide the pastry base, still on the bottom piece of baking paper, onto a baking tray. Refrigerate for 10 minutes to firm up. Preheat the oven to 180°C (350°F).

Remove the pastry from the refrigerator. Top the pastry with the leek mixture, leaving a 4 cm (1½ in) border around the edges without any filling. Using the baking paper to help, fold the bare pastry edges over the topping. Bake for 40 minutes or until the pastry is cooked through and golden. Transfer to a wire rack to cool slightly, then slice and serve.

Potatoes are packed with vitamins A and B complex (to convert food to energy), vitamin C (to bolster the immune system) and minerals like iron and phosphorus (to help build bones). Leeks contain a compound called allicin, which is antifungal, antiviral, antibacterial and boosts immunity. You'll know it by its pungent smell, which it has in common with garlic, onions and chives.

Asian ratatouille

SERVES 4

500 g (1 lb 2 oz) tomatoes

150 g (5½ oz) eggplants
(aubergines), seeds removed,
diced, salted in a colander over
the sink for 30 minutes and
drained

150 g (5½ oz) zucchini
(courgettes), diced, salted in
a colander over the sink for
30 minutes and drained

90 ml (3 fl oz) extra-virgin olive
oil

150 g (5½ oz) brown onions,
finely diced

150 g (5½ oz) red capsicums
(bell peppers), finely diced

150 g (5½ oz) green capsicums
(bell peppers), finely diced

180 g (6½ oz/2 cups) bean sprouts

¼ bunch spring onions
(scallions), cut into thin strips

1 bunch coriander (cilantro)
sprigs

SAUCE

2 teaspoons chilli flakes

1 tablespoon sichuan pepper

1½ tablespoons extra-virgin
olive oil

75 g (2¾ oz) fresh ginger, peeled
and crushed

75 g (2¾ oz) garlic, peeled and
crushed

150 g (5½ oz) palm sugar (jaggery)

75 ml (2½ fl oz) soy sauce

200 ml (7 fl oz) Chinese vinegar

75 ml (2½ fl oz) chilli oil

This ratatouille is delicious served with steamed fish, but equally good
with chicken, or with lamb chops from the barbecue. You can cut the
vegetables as chunky or as fine as you like, depending on the effect you
are looking for. I find that if they're cut small this dish goes better with
delicate textures like fish. However, if they're chunkier, you can roast
this in the oven and it's heartier for serving with chicken or lamb.

For the sauce, in a large frying pan over medium heat, sauté the chilli flakes
and sichuan pepper in the oil for 1 minute. Add the ginger and garlic and
stir-fry until fragrant. Add the palm sugar, soy sauce and Chinese vinegar and
stir well to dissolve the palm sugar. Remove the pan from the heat, stir in the
chilli oil and set aside until needed.

For the vegetables, peel the tomatoes and remove the seeds, reserving the
juice to use later. Dice the tomato flesh and set aside.

In a large ovenproof frying pan over medium heat, fry the eggplant and
zucchini in the oil for 5 minutes until golden. Add the onion and capsicum
and sauté for a further 10 minutes until tender. Add the tomato and simmer
for another 2 minutes, before pouring in the reserved tomato juice and adding
some freshly ground black pepper. Simmer for 5 minutes to reduce.

From here you can choose to reduce it down even more on the stove top to
form a very thick jam or, if you have cut the vegetables larger, you can bake
it at 225°C (435°F) to cook it down and caramelise it.

Once cooked down and thick, fold through the sauce, garnish with the bean
sprouts, spring onion and coriander and serve.

Asian ingredients are packed with medicinal benefits.
Sichuan peppercorns, for example, are rich in vitamin B6
(called pyridoxine), which influences cognitive abilities and
immune function. Ginger contains gingerol, a potent anti-
inflammatory compound. Coriander (cilantro) is full of
compounds called polyphenols, which have both antioxidant
and anti-inflammatory properties.

100

Sweet potato and red cabbage gratin

SERVES 4, OR 6 AS A SIDE

2 large sweet potatoes, peeled
  and cut into 1 cm (½ in) thick
  discs
600 ml (20½ fl oz) pouring
  (single/light) cream (35% fat)
1 whole nutmeg

BRAISED RED CABBAGE

1 red cabbage, finely shredded
25 g (1 oz) duck fat or butter
125 g (4½ oz) brown onions,
  diced
5 g (¼ oz) caraway seeds
4 cloves
2 g (⅛ oz) juniper berries
2 bay leaves
250 ml (8½ fl oz/1 cup) red
  wine
100 ml (3½ fl oz) apple juice
100 g (3½ oz) desiree potatoes,
  grated
50 g (1¾ oz) honey, or to taste
125 g (4½ oz) unsalted butter

This is the perfect vegetable dish to serve in the middle of the table, hot and sizzling straight from the oven. I really like the strong red cabbage and wine flavours with the spices, which play against the sweet potato and cream. Of course you can try using white cabbage and, instead of red wine, verjuice. You will be surprised by the effect of adding the grated white potato to the cabbage – the starch really does make the juice into a lovely velvety sauce. If the cream you use is too heavy, it will split in the oven during cooking and give you a layer of fat on top of your gratin. Pouring cream is best, but if you have thickened (whipping) cream, add a little milk to it to make it thinner.

Preheat the oven to 170°C (340°F).

For the braised red cabbage, put the cabbage in a colander, sprinkle it with 1 tablespoon salt then leave for 1 hour. Rinse the cabbage.

Melt the duck fat in a large ovenproof frying pan over medium heat. Add the onion, caraway seeds, cloves, juniper berries and bay leaves and sweat until the onion is translucent. Add the cabbage, wine and apple juice to the pan. Cover with baking paper, transfer to the oven and bake for 1 hour until most of the liquid has evaporated. Add the potato and cook for another 30 minutes – the potato will give the cabbage a creamy texture.

Remove from the oven and stir in the honey. Season with salt and freshly ground black pepper. Stir the butter through the hot cabbage mixture. Increase the oven temperature to 180°C (350°F).

Add the braised cabbage to the frying pan and place the discs of sweet potato on top. Pour the cream over slowly, so it works its way into the cabbage and gradually covers the sweet potato. Grate over some nutmeg and season with salt and freshly ground black pepper. Bake for 30–45 minutes or until golden and bubbling. Serve hot.

Sweet potatoes are packed with vitamins A (for good vision), B complex (for healthy skin and hair), C (to boost immunity) and K (to help with blood clotting). They also contain potassium, which helps balance the body's fluids and lower blood pressure.

Mike's steak bordelaise in a hurry

SERVES 2

4 French shallots, finely diced

40 g (1½ oz) butter

500 ml (17 fl oz/2 cups) good-quality red wine, preferably bordeaux, cabernet or merlot

2 teaspoons red-wine vinegar

white peppercorns

2 stems of bone marrow (ask your butcher)

2 flank (bavette) steaks, at room temperature, cut 2 cm (¾ in) thick, or Scotch fillet

1 teaspoon olive oil

1 tablespoon chopped flat-leaf (Italian) parsley, to garnish

Steak bordelaise is delicious made with most cuts of steak. One of my favourites is flank steak, otherwise known as bavette. It has a lovely grain, good marbling and is very well priced, as it's considered a second-class cut of beef. The trick with flank is that it can't be too rare and it certainly cannot be cooked past medium or it becomes chewy. The cooking times I have given will work well if you use steaks that have been cut across the grain into 225 g (8 oz) portions before cooking. I'm sure your butcher would be happy to help you with the cutting. You'll notice that the recipe calls for 500 ml (17 fl oz/2 cups) of good-quality red wine, preferably bordeaux. This allows you to share the remainder of the bottle between two glasses to drink and enjoy with your steak.

In a small saucepan over medium heat, sweat the shallots in half the butter until translucent. Add the red wine and reduce to a glaze consistency. It should be a glossy, shiny sauce, not like watery wine. Add the red-wine vinegar, a pinch of salt and a grinding of white pepper. Set aside.

Preheat the oven to 180°C (350°F). Place the bone marrow stems in an ovenproof frying pan. Sprinkle with salt, place the pan in the oven and bake for 10 minutes until the bone marrow is soft. Remove from the oven, transfer to a plate and keep warm (reserve the bone marrow fat in the pan).

Allow your steaks to sit at room temperature for 1 hour before cooking. Season the steaks on both sides with salt.

In the same ovenproof frying pan over medium heat, warm the remaining butter and the olive oil with the bone marrow fat. Pan-fry the steak for 3 minutes on the first side, then 2 minutes on the second side. Transfer the steaks to the plate with the bone marrow to rest in a warm place for 5 minutes.

Place each steak on a warm plate with a piece of bone marrow next to it. Tip the steak juices from the resting plate into the shallot and wine glaze and add a spoonful of the cooking fat from the pan. Stir and spoon over the steak. Garnish with the parsley and serve. Provide a lobster pick or a thin fork to pick out the bone marrow.

As opposed to grain-fed beef, grass-fed beef has more omega-3 fats (heart-healthy fats), more antioxidant vitamins, such as E, and more conjugated linoleic acid (CLA), which increases metabolic rates, boosts the immune system and keeps cholesterol levels in check. Try to source the very best-quality grass-fed beef you can find, and reap the benefits.

104

Slow-cooked pork shoulder with chimichurri

SERVES 10

350 g (12½ oz) salt

1 whole pork shoulder on the bone with skin (about 3.5 kg/7 lb 12 oz)

1 tablespoon Old Bay seasoning

20 g (¾ oz) smoked sweet paprika

1 tablespoon ground coffee beans

250 ml (8½ fl oz/1 cup) dry cider, or ale or stout

250 ml (8½ fl oz/1 cup) prepared espresso coffee

3 fresh bay leaves

5 juniper berries, bruised

1 whole savoy cabbage

½ quantity Chimichurri (page 239), to serve

200 g (7 oz) wholegrain mustard, to serve

For the very best result, start this recipe a day ahead by brining your pork shoulder overnight to release the flavour and maintain the moisture. Any leftovers are delicious served with baked beans, or try them with Baked eggs with piperade and sorrel (page 184). Old Bay seasoning is available from most good grocery stores. However, if you can't find it, the main flavours are mustard, paprika, celery salt, bay leaves, black pepper, chilli flakes, mace, cloves, allspice, nutmeg, cardamom and ginger.

The day before, make a brine by dissolving the salt in 7 litres (236 fl oz/28 cups) cold water. Place the pork shoulder in a non-reactive container that will hold it snugly, then pour the brine over until the pork is covered. Leave to soak overnight in the refrigerator – you may need to weigh the pork down with a plate or similar to keep it submerged.

The next day, preheat the oven to 120° C (250°F).

Remove the pork from the brine, pat it dry and rub it with the Old Bay seasoning, smoked sweet paprika and ground coffee beans. Place the pork in a casserole dish, skin side up. Pour in the cider and prepared espresso coffee and add the bay leaves and juniper berries. Cover the casserole dish well with baking paper, then with aluminium foil – or use a lid. Slow-cook the pork in the oven for 8 hours until the meat is falling off the bone.

Remove the pork from the oven, tip the clear cooking liquid into a saucepan and let it simmer for a few seconds. Adjust the seasoning with salt and freshly ground black pepper.

To serve, shave the cabbage finely into a serving bowl and season it with a little salt and freshly ground black pepper. Peel the skin back from the pork, tear the flesh from the bone and place large shards of meat with the cabbage in the bowl. Pour over some of the hot pan juices to cover the bottom of the bowl and wilt a little of the cabbage. Dollop with chimichurri and serve with the wholegrain mustard on the side.

Pork shoulder is a great cut of meat to serve whole, as the fat layer surrounding the flesh is easy to remove after cooking, so you can offer lean meat to those who prefer it. The chimichurri is jam-packed with medicinal benefits. Thyme and oregano, for example, contain thymol, an antimicrobial; sage contains rosmarinic acid, good for the memory; and parsley contains eugenol, a potent anti-inflammatory, antioxidant and antibacterial compound.

106 Coq au vin blanc

SERVES 4

250 g (9 oz) French shallots, diced

50 g (1¾ oz) butter

250 g (9 oz) bacon, cut into thin strips

250 g (9 oz) button mushrooms

1.5–1.6 kg (3 lb 5 oz–3½ lb) chicken, cut into 8 pieces

375 ml (12½ fl oz/1½ cups) port

750 ml (25½ fl oz/3 cups) white wine

750 ml (25½ fl oz/3 cups) chicken stock

2 fresh bay leaves

¼ bunch fresh flat-leaf (Italian) parsley, finely chopped

¼ bunch fresh tarragon leaves

crusty bread, to serve

Everybody knows coq au vin is chicken cooked in red wine, but I really enjoy the lighter flavours of cooking it in white wine. It's rare to find a rooster, which is traditional for this recipe, so I've adjusted the recipe to use chicken. Traditionally coq au vin is cooked for a long time in a Dutch oven to break down the tough rooster meat. However, my method of cooking the ingredients individually for their own correct times, returning them to the pan, then poaching on the stove top, enables you to cook your chicken perfectly rather than overcook it. You can ask your butcher to cut your chicken into primal cuts – two drumsticks, two thighs, two chicken wings with some breast attached, and two chicken breast pieces. For the wine, choose a white burgundy or chardonnay to cook with and, as always, it really should be the same wine you choose to drink with the chicken.

In a large frying pan over medium heat, cook the shallots for 5 minutes in the butter until caramelised. Add the bacon and fry for another 5 minutes until crisp. Remove the shallots and bacon and set aside.

Add the mushrooms to the pan and sauté for 5 minutes until tender. Remove the mushrooms and set aside.

Add the chicken pieces to the pan and cook for 10 minutes, turning to cook on all sides, until firm and golden. Remove the chicken from the pan and set aside with the other cooked ingredients.

Pour the port and wine into the pan and cook for 30 minutes or until reduced by half. Add the chicken stock, shallots, bacon and bay leaves and simmer for 30 minutes to reduce to a light sauce consistency. Return the chicken pieces to the pan and poach them gently for 15 minutes, removing them when just cooked. Add the mushrooms and simmer the sauce for 5 minutes, adjusting the seasoning with salt and freshly ground black pepper, and reduce to a lovely light gravy. Return the chicken to the pan and scatter over chopped parsley and tarragon. Serve straight from the pan with crusty bread.

Cooking meat on the bone not only makes it taste better, it also makes it better for you. Slow, deep cooking softens the collagen in meat (which is highly beneficial for joints), making it highly nutritious and more digestible.

Mussels in cider with apples and sorrel

SERVES 4

40 ml (1½ fl oz) extra-virgin
  olive oil

80 g (2¾ oz) French shallots,
  peeled and finely diced

1 garlic clove, peeled and finely
  chopped

½ large fennel bulb, finely
  chopped

1 granny smith apple, finely
  chopped

1 tablespoon dill, chopped

400 ml (13½ fl oz) dry cider

2 kg (4 lb 6 oz) mussels

300 g (10½ oz) butter

1 bunch sorrel, leaves picked

1 lemon, juiced

1 bunch flat-leaf (Italian)
  parsley, leaves picked and
  chopped

crusty bread, to serve

For me, this recipe brings back fond memories of my trip to Normandy in France, where the cider is second to none. If you don't have cider, use white wine rather than beer, which would be too strong. The granny smith apples work well due to their tart flavour as well as their firm texture, which doesn't go too soft when cooked. The sorrel adds a lovely sharp flavour to the sauce. However, if you can't find it, you can use baby English spinach leaves instead and add another shot of lemon juice to increase the acidity.

Warm the olive oil in a 5 litre (169 fl oz/20 cup) saucepan over medium heat. Add the shallots, garlic, fennel, apple and dill and sauté for 2 minutes until tender. Increase the heat to medium–high and add the cider. When the cider is boiling, add the mussels and put the lid on the pan. Keep the pan covered and cook for about 1 minute, shaking the pan occasionally. Remove the lid and check to see if the mussels have opened. If not, put the lid back on for a moment longer until they are ready.

Transfer the mussels to a bowl with a slotted spoon. If there are any mussels that have not opened, I suggest discarding them.

Reduce the stock in the pan by half. Add the butter and sorrel and cook until the sorrel is just wilted. Adjust the flavour with a squeeze of lemon juice and a good grinding of black pepper. (If the mussels are very fresh they'll be holding a lot of seawater so you won't have to add salt.)

Return the mussels to the pan and toss them through the sauce. Scatter with parsley and serve with lots of crusty bread.

Note: *If you want the dish to be a little richer, fold in some crème fraîche while the pan is off the heat before returning the mussels to the pan.*

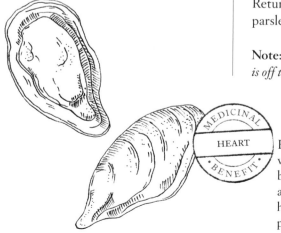

MEDICINAL HEART BENEFIT

Eating mussels is good for blood and bones. Mussels are high in vitamin B12, which aids in lowering homocysteine levels in the blood. If these get too high they can contribute to heart disease and stroke. Mussels also contain high levels of iron (which helps boost the haemoglobin in red blood cells), manganese, phosphorus, potassium, selenium and of zinc, which frees vitamin A stored in the liver.

108

Red mullet, café de Paris butter and cured roe

SERVES 4

15 g (½ oz) butter

15 ml (½ fl oz) extra-virgin olive oil

½ lemon, juiced, plus lemon wedges to serve

3 teaspoons white wine

800 g (1 lb 12 oz) red mullet fillets

200 g (7 oz) Café de Paris butter (page 237)

20 g (¾ oz) bottarga (dried mullet roe) (optional)

The dish is garnished with a small grating of bottarga (dried mullet roe) to give an intense taste of the sea. This is optional but certainly adds that little extra something. You can pan-fry the fish in foaming butter instead of 'wet baking', particularly if you prefer to use small whole fish. However, I find that the wet baking helps keep thin fillets moist, especially when they have such delicate-textured flesh. This dish is delicious served with Cumin-scented carrots (page 205). The Café de Paris butter recipe on page 237 makes more than you'll need here. Keep the excess in the freezer and use it for melting on seafood or steak.

Preheat the oven to 210°C (410°F). Line a baking dish with baking paper.

For the fish, melt the butter with the olive oil in a saucepan then pour the mixture into the prepared baking dish along with the lemon juice and wine. Place the fish fillets in the dish, skin side down, to coat the skin. Then turn the fish skin side up and bake for 5 minutes without turning – or place under a grill (broiler) to give a blistered skin. Remove the fish from the oven and allow to rest while you make a sauce.

Pour the juice from the dish into a saucepan and bring to the boil. Whisk in half the café de Paris butter. When fully absorbed, add the remaining café de Paris butter, whisking again to combine and form a thick butter sauce.

Transfer the fish to serving plates and spoon over the sauce. Finely grate over the bottarga, if using. Serve with lemon wedges.

Butter or margarine, you ask? For me, there's no contest. Butter is completely natural and contains calcium, omega-3 fats (heart-healthy fats) and antioxidant vitamins, such as E. Margarine is a science experiment of preservatives and stabilisers.

110

Crab cakes with red mayonnaise

SERVES 4

800 g (1 lb 12 oz) cooked
   crabmeat

4 eggs

60 g (2 oz/¼ cup) mayonnaise

40 g (1½ oz/2 cups) flat-leaf
   (Italian) parsley, leaves picked
   and chopped

1 tablespoon dijon mustard

140 g (5 oz) spring onions
   (scallions), sliced

300 g (10½ oz) water crackers,
   crumbled

1 lemon, zested and juiced, plus
   lemon wedges to serve

1 pinch cayenne pepper

flour for dusting

2 tablespoons Clarified butter
   (page 234) or oil for shallow
   frying

RED MAYONNAISE

75 g (2¾ fl oz) mayonnaise

125 g (4½ oz) Romesco sauce
   (page 239)

This is a quick and easy recipe for crab cakes, which can be made from very few ingredients. The pleasure is that the crabmeat is already cooked, so the cooking time is just as long as it takes to colour and warm the cakes through. You can adjust the recipe slightly if you have a gluten intolerance by using gluten-free crackers in the cakes and dusting with polenta instead of flour. American in style, the crab cakes can be enhanced by adding a sprinkling of Old Bay seasoning to give them that authentic Maryland crab cake flavour. However, we are in Spain here and therefore serving ours with romesco sauce.

Preheat the oven to 200°C (400°F).

For the red mayonnaise, mix together the mayonnaise and romesco sauce. Refrigerate until needed.

For the crab cakes, combine all the ingredients – except the flour and clarified butter – in a bowl and divide the mixture into even-sized patties.

Dust each crab cake in flour, then shallow-fry them in a frying pan in the clarified butter over medium–high heat for 3 minutes on each side, until golden brown. (Remember that the crabmeat is already cooked so you are only pan-frying it for colour and heat.) Serve with lemon wedges and red mayonnaise to dip.

Crab is a great source of protein, omega-3 fatty acids and of selenium, an antioxidant that helps regulate thyroid hormone activity. Crab is also rich in vitamin B2 (riboflavin), which helps in converting food into energy and is also essential for healthy skin, hair, blood and the brain. It also contains minerals like copper (to help produce red blood cells) and phosphorus (to build and protect bones).

Queen of puddings

SERVES 4

800 ml (27 fl oz) full-cream (whole) milk

15 g (½ oz) butter

150 g (5½ oz) fresh breadcrumbs

75 g (2¾ oz) caster (superfine) sugar

1 lemon, zested

3 eggs yolks

75 g (2¾ oz) raspberry jam

icing (confectioners') sugar for sprinkling

MERINGUE TOP

3 egg whites

150 g (5½ oz) caster (superfine) sugar

Like most traditional English puddings, there are very few ingredients in this recipe. Queen of puddings is simple and delicious using any jam. However, I particularly enjoy it with raspberry jam, as the sharp flavour works well with the sweet meringue. If you have a dairy allergy, you can replace the milk with one of the nut milks on page 238. You can also use the meringue recipe from Pavlova with raspberries in vinegar (page 61) instead. If you can't make fresh breadcrumbs, then dry ones will work, but only use two-thirds of the amount as they will absorb more milk.

Preheat the oven to 180°C (350°F). Grease a baking dish with butter.

In a medium saucepan over medium heat, scald the milk (heat it to just below boiling). Add the butter, breadcrumbs, half the sugar and the lemon zest. Remove the pan from the heat and let the mixture cool and swell for 30 minutes.

Beat the egg yolks with the remaining sugar and add to the cooled milk mixture. Pour the custard into the prepared baking dish and bake for 15 minutes or until just set. Remove from the oven and allow to cool.

Melt the jam in a small saucepan over a low heat and spread it over the set bread custard.

For the meringue top, using an electric mixer, beat the egg whites with half the sugar at high speed for 3 minutes, until the sugar has dissolved and the meringue has formed stiff peaks. While the mixer is still running, add the remaining sugar slowly and whisk for another 3–5 minutes until the stiff peaks are very shiny and when you lift the whisk the mixture forms long licks of glossy meringue.

Top the pudding with the meringue, sprinkle with icing sugar and bake for 10 minutes or until the tips of the meringue turn golden brown. Dust with more icing sugar and serve.

MEDICINAL
MUSCLES,
BONES & JOINTS
BENEFIT

Full-cream (whole) milk is nutrient-dense and full of vitamins A, D and E. It also contains less lactose than skim and light milks because these often have milk solids added back into them.

Zucchini and marmalade cake

SERVES 8

270 g (9½ oz) plain (all-purpose) flour

½ teaspoon baking powder

½ teaspoon bicarbonate of soda (baking soda)

1 teaspoon ground cinnamon

2 eggs

155 ml (5 fl oz) vegetable oil

150 g (5½ oz) caster (superfine) sugar

215 g (7½ oz) Seville orange marmalade

285 g (10 oz) zucchini (courgettes), coarsely grated

115 g (4 oz) walnuts, toasted and chopped

1 quantity Buttercream (page 245)

I think this nutritious vegetable cake rivals any carrot cake. I am a purist when it comes to marmalade, and wait the whole year until I can find Seville oranges (traditional bitter oranges used for marmalade). The sharp, bitter flavours of the orange rind and the sweetness from the sugars are a match made in heaven. These flavours go perfectly with the buttercream, and almost remind me of eating marmalade with lots of butter on toast. This recipe would also work very well using carrot if you don't have any zucchini (courgettes).

Preheat the oven to 175°C (350°F). Grease and line a 20 x 28 cm (8 x 11 in) loaf (bar) tin.

Sift the flour, baking powder, bicarbonate of soda and cinnamon into a large mixing bowl.

In a separate bowl, using an electric mixer, beat together the eggs, oil, sugar and 115 g (4 oz) of the marmalade. Add the zucchini and ½ teaspoon salt and beat to combine. Add the flour mixture and beat until just combined, then fold through the nuts. Pour the batter into the prepared tin and smooth the surface. Bake for about 1 hour or until a skewer inserted into the centre of the cake comes out clean. Leave for 20 minutes to cool in the tin, then transfer to a wire rack to cool completely.

Spread the top of the cake with the buttercream and garnish with the remaining marmalade.

Zucchini (courgettes) are rich in folates, important for new cell production. They are also full of vitamin C, which not only bolsters the immune system, but also helps make collagen, the connective tissue that knits together wounds and supports blood vessel walls. They also contain vitamins A and B for good vision and healthy skin. Walnuts are high in omega-3 fatty acids, and vitamin E antioxidants, which neutralise free radicals that can damage other cells.

116

Green pistachio jelly with persimmons in rose syrup

SERVES 4

2 ripe persimmons, cut into chunks

1 tablespoon Rose syrup (page 244)

GREEN PISTACHIO JELLY

250 g (9 oz) green pistachio nuts, shelled

200 ml (7 fl oz) buttermilk

200 ml (7 fl oz) soy milk

4 g (¼ oz) titanium-strength gelatine leaves

80 g (2¾ oz/⅓ cup) caster (superfine) sugar

300 ml (10 fl oz) thickened (whipping) cream

Pistachio nuts picked from the tree are known as green nuts, not just because of their colour, but also due to their soft and waxy texture and their pure, fresh flavour. They don't need to be activated as they are fully hydrated and packed full of nutrients, so just peel them from their shell and use them. If you can't find fresh raw nuts from the tree, you can use organic pistachio kernels instead and activate them (see page 237). Source the ripest persimmons you can find, as these beauties are truly sweet and delicious and will only need a little rose syrup drizzled over them. Firmer persimmons will need to be cut and poached in the rose syrup to soften before serving. I set my jelly in a large mould, but you can set it in individual cups or moulds. To unmould, dip the mould in boiling water for a few seconds and release the side of the jelly by running a knife around the rim.

For the green pistachio jelly, blitz the green pistachio nuts with both milks in a blender and chill for 1 hour in the refrigerator. Strain the mixture through muslin (cheesecloth) into a bowl, squeezing to extract all the liquid.

Soak the gelatine in cold water to soften, then squeeze out the excess water.

In a saucepan over low heat, warm half the pistachio milk with the sugar, stirring to dissolve the sugar and taking care that the mixture doesn't boil. Add the softened gelatine and stir to dissolve. Remove the pan from the heat and whisk in the remaining pistachio milk to combine.

Whip the cream to medium peaks. Gently fold the pistachio milk into the whipped cream then pour the mixture into the moulds. Cover and refrigerate for 3 hours or until set. To serve, unmould your jelly onto a platter and put it back in the refrigerator.

For the persimmons, if they are very ripe, simply cut them and toss them in a little bit of rose syrup and scatter them around your jelly. However, as mentioned above, if they are not ripe, poach the persimmon pieces in the syrup until soft. Allow them to cool and serve them around the jelly.

Pistachio nuts are high in oleic acid and antioxidants, which can help lower cholesterol. Persimmons are rich in fibre and manganese, and have a high concentration of anti-inflammatory and antioxidant tannins.

118

Pomegranate and Aperol spritz

SERVES 4

ice
juice of 2 pomegranates
180 ml (6 fl oz) Aperol
1 litre (34 fl oz/4 cups) soda
   water (club soda), to top each
   glass up to three-quarters full
1 orange, thinly sliced, to
   garnish

If you want to juice a pomegranate, the quickest way is to cut the fruit in half crossways then, using a citrus juicer, squeeze the halves like an orange to remove all the pods. Another way is to surgically remove the little pomegranate pearls and pulse them in a blender in order to rupture the cell membranes and release the juice. Be sure to strain the juice, though, as the seeds can be rather chalky and not very pleasant in a drink. Look for the darker pomegranates, as they are often riper and ready to juice. Usually in our spritz we would use vermouth, but here we use Aperol to let the pomegranate flavour sing.

Place a handful of ice in each glass and divide the pomegranate juice between them. Pour 45 ml (1½ fl oz) of Aperol into each glass and top up with the soda water. Garnish with orange slices.

MEDICINAL
EAR, NOSE &
THROAT
BENEFIT

Pomegranates are rich in vitamin C, which makes them great for boosting the immune system. Just as importantly, they are rich in antioxidant tannin compounds, which occur in the juice and peel. These tannins are so powerful that pomegranate juice has been found to have three times the antioxidant activity of red wine and green tea.

Rhubarb and strawberry fizz

MAKES 1.8 LITRES (61 FL OZ)

200 g (7 oz) rhubarb, sliced

20 g (¾ oz) sugar

1 granny smith apple, grated

125 g (4½ oz) strawberries, sliced

½ bunch mint, leaves picked and roughly chopped

½ vanilla bean, seeds scraped

½ lemon, sliced

½ orange, sliced

1.5 litres (51 fl oz/6 cups) sparkling mineral water

This is such a refreshing drink and probably one of the quicker fermented drinks to make. Once you get to know the recipe, the flavour combinations and adjustments are endless. Try replacing the mint with basil as your first experiment. For a cheeky aperitif, add a nip of vodka or gin to get the party started.

Toss the rhubarb and sugar together in a bowl and leave for 1 hour to allow all the lovely rhubarb juices to seep out.

Combine all the remaining ingredients, except the mineral water, in a bowl. Add the rhubarb before setting the mixture aside at room temperature, covered, overnight.

The next day, strain the mixture through muslin (cheesecloth). Divide between six glasses and top up with mineral water. Serve chilled.

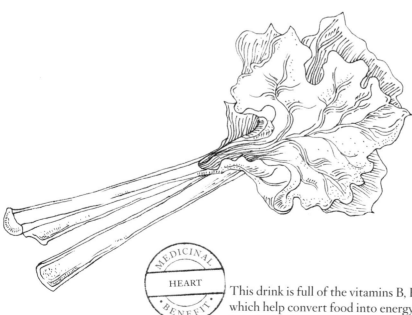

MEDICINAL · HEART · BENEFIT

This drink is full of the vitamins B, B1 (thiamine), B2 (riboflavin) and B3 (niacin), which help convert food into energy and help in the production of red blood cells. It is also high in B5, B6 and B7, which also assist in the production of red blood cells as well as in lowering the homocysteine levels in the blood – if these get too high, they can contribute to heart disease and stroke.

BAKED WHOLE CAULIFLOWER WITH INDIAN SPICES,
MINT AND YOGHURT *page 143*

PINK GRAPEFRUIT WITH CHILLI SALT AND HONEY

Quinoa porridge with pomegranate and macadamia milk

Sprouted buckwheat bread with vegetable kraut and goat's curd

— KEDGEREE —

BORSCHT WITH HORSERADISH CREAM

Parsnip, kale and white bean soup

BEETROOT, QUINOA, RHUBARB AND PONZU

Salted kale with chickpeas and green tahini

Stuffed baby artichokes with olive, citrus and herb salad

SHREDDED BRUSSELS SPROUTS, LENTILS, SPECK AND PARSLEY

BROCCOLINI WITH WALNUT AND ROSEMARY TARATOR

Baked whole cauliflower with Indian spices, mint and yoghurt

Roast Jerusalem artichokes, soffritto and hazelnuts

WINTER
120-175

— BRAISED QUINCE AND WITLOF —

BAKED MUSHROOMS 'SAINT-JACQUES' STYLE

CORNISH PASTIES

Freekeh-stuffed duck with saffron, olives and preserved lemon

Daube of beef oyster blade

Roasted whole John Dory with vanilla and saffron

Octopus braised in red wine with lemon and oregano

GRILLED MACKEREL WITH BLOOD ORANGES AND DILL

— CUMQUAT SUSSEX POND —

BOTTLED PEARS

Mont Blanc

Alastair's caramelised oranges with toasted almonds

LEMON DRIZZLE CAKE

BEETROOT KVASS

— GINGER BEER —

MEDICINAL · BENEFIT · BRAIN, HEART, SKIN — FISH

Less of the sun's rays means greater risk of sniffles and viruses. I like to fortify my family's immunity by preparing foods that are extra rich in vitamins and minerals. It's time for the porridge pot, the borscht pan and for braises, bakes and daubes. Citrus, antioxidant-rich herbs, slow-cooked meats and plenty of cold-weather veg (cauliflower, broccoli and cabbage) get us through to spring.

MEDICINAL
MUSCLES,
BONES & JOINTS
• BENEFIT •
MUSHROOMS

MEDICINAL
GUT, HEART,
SKIN
• BENEFIT •
EGGS

MEDICINAL
BRAIN, GUT,
SKIN
• BENEFIT •
MILK

124

Pink grapefruit with chilli salt and honey

SERVES 4

2 pink grapefruits
Chilli salt (page 232)
80 ml (2½ fl oz/⅓ cup) honey,
  or use maple syrup or treacle
  (molasses)
2 tablespoons roughly chopped
  toasted pecans, walnuts or
  hazelnuts

Pink grapefruit is a wonderful citrus to eat for breakfast as its mild bitterness helps you get started. Instead of pink grapefruit you could use pomelo, a large citrus fruit similar to a grapefruit, with extremely large segments. Or try a regular white grapefruit – but you'll need a little more honey. Meyer lemons would work well too.

Run a knife around each grapefruit segment to make it easier for the person eating to remove the flesh. Serve each grapefruit half on plate, and let each person sprinkle on their own chilli salt and honey. Crumble over some nuts for crunch.

MEDICINAL
EAR, NOSE &
THROAT
· BENEFIT ·

Citrus fruits are rich sources of immune-boosting vitamin C, a powerful natural antioxidant that plays a vital role in collagen synthesis, wound healing and antiviral and anticancer activity. It can also help prevent neurodegenerative diseases, arthritis and colds. Raw honey is different from average honey: it hasn't been heated or processed in any way and therefore retains nutrients. Not only is it full of minerals, vitamins, enzymes and antioxidants, it has antibacterial and antifungal properties, too. Honey has even more benefits if it's local (made within a 5 km/3 mile radius of where you live), as it contains pollens specific to your area. These can help with seasonal allergies. It's said that eating a spoonful of raw local honey every day, 1–2 months before allergy season hits, is a great way to temper pollen-related allergies.

Quinoa porridge with pomegranate and macadamia milk

SERVES 4

300 g (10½ oz/1½ cups) quinoa

1 pomegranate

1 quantity macadamia nut milk
  (see page 238)

brown sugar, honey or maple
  syrup, for sprinkling

I love the juxtaposition of hot and cold, so I serve this quinoa porridge steaming hot with cold milk. It's best to make the macadamia milk the night before and keep it chilled in the refrigerator so you can pour it over cold. But you can also stir the milk through in the porridge pan, making a creamier, milkier porridge. If the pomegranate is sour, I suggest you add a little pomegrante molasses instead of brown sugar, honey or maple syrup. But any of these would taste delicious.

Soak the quinoa in cold water overnight. The next day, rinse it well until the water runs clean.

Place the quinoa in a saucepan with 750 ml (25½ fl oz/3 cups) water and a pinch of salt. Over medium–low heat, slowly bring the mixture to the boil, skimming the quinoa regularly until no more scum rises to the surface. Once it starts to boil, stir it occasionally to prevent it from catching on the bottom of the pan. As it gets thicker, stir constantly until the mixture has the texture of porridge.

To remove the pomegranate seeds, score the skin of the fruit into quarters, making sure not to cut into the flesh. Twist the pomegranate and the quarters will break off in your hand, maintaining the pearl structure inside – rather than a knife cutting through the precious pearls. Do this over a bowl to catch any juice. With a latex glove on, flick the jewels out of the pith of the pomegranate into the bowl with the juice (the pith is very bitter). Serve the hot quinoa with the cold macadamia milk and sprinkle with brown sugar. Scatter with pomegranate seeds and pour over any remaining juice.

MEDICINAL
GUT, HEART, SKIN
BENEFIT

Quinoa is a particularly rich source of dietary fibre. Fibre binds to toxins, aiding in their excretion from the gut and helping protect from colon cancer. It also contains B complex vitamins (to help the body convert food into energy), as well as essential fatty acids. These help in the formation of cells, help with thyroid and adrenal gland activity, maintain healthy blood pressure, help with the breakdown of cholesterol, as well as with blood clotting and maintaining healthy hair and skin. Quinoa is also an excellent source of vitamins A and E, and minerals like iron, copper, calcium, potassium, manganese and magnesium. Copper and iron are required for the production of red blood cells. Magnesium is known as the 'relaxation' mineral, as it has a positive effect on depression, insomnia and headaches.

Sprouted buckwheat bread with vegetable kraut and goat's curd

SERVES 4

4 slices Sprouted buckwheat sourdough (page 242)

180 g (6½ oz) goat's curd or a very young goat's cheese

280 g (10 oz) Vegetable kraut (page 241)

20 g (¾ oz) alfalfa sprouts

¼ bunch mint, leaves picked

40 ml (1¼ fl oz) argan oil (see Note)

Living in Australia has changed my breakfast habits, due both to the climate and the Aussie emphasis on healthy living. My wife, Joss, is very passionate about living food and wholefoods, and has heavily influenced the way I eat and the food I serve. This is a nice light breakfast to eat before the tyranny of the kids' early morning Saturday sport begins, but it's equally perfect as a Sunday brunch item. It's also cracking with a poached egg (see page 180).

Toast the bread and smear it with the goat's curd.

Combine the vegetable kraut, alfalfa sprouts and mint in a bowl to make a little salad and dress it with half the argan oil.

Place a pile of salad on each slice of toast, drizzle with a little extra argan oil and a good grinding of black pepper and serve.

Note: *Be certain to look for edible argan oil in a health food store, as many cosmetic companies use argan oil but often add other inedible ingredients.*

MEDICINAL · GUT, HEART · BENEFIT

Buckwheat contains amino acids, the building blocks of the protein that builds muscle tissue and gives muscle strength. It's also high in rutin, a flavonoid which helps thin the blood and improve circulation. The assorted seeds add plant-based omega-3 fats, zinc to support the immune system, and magnesium for regulating blood pressure. Cabbage is full of essential vitamin C for boosting the immune system, and vitamin K for activating the proteins and calcium essential for blood clotting. It also contains potassium, which balances fluids in the body and helps maintain steady muscle contractions and nerve impulses. It's thought that a diet high in potassium may lower blood pressure. Lacto-fermented vegetables contain beneficial *Lactobacillus* bacteria – more than occur in live yoghurt. Its benefits are:

- It increases healthy flora in the intestinal tract
- It lines the intestinal wall with friendly bacterial flora, which prevents yeast, and other pathogenic organisms overgrowing
- It boosts the immune system
- It detoxifies and cleans the colon and helps with constipation
- It helps balance the pH (acidity/alkalinity) of the intestinal tract. (This is important, as eating too many acidic foods can lead to too much acid in the blood, causing bone thinning and inflammation.)

128 Kedgeree

SERVES 4

4 eggs

80 g (2¾ oz) French shallots, finely diced

60 g (2 oz) unsalted butter, plus a little extra for finishing

35 g (1¼ oz/¼ cup) pistachio nuts

1 tablespoon currants

2 tablespoons curry powder

200 g (7 oz/1 cup) basmati rice

20 g (¾ oz) plain (all-purpose) flour

320 ml (11 fl oz) water or fish stock

80 ml (2½ fl oz/⅓ cup) thickened (whipping) cream

1 lemon, juiced, plus lemon wedges to serve

500 g (1 lb 2 oz) hot-smoked ocean trout or salmon, flaked

1 handful flat-leaf (Italian) parsley leaves, shredded

This is my ideal Sunday-morning brunch dish to share with friends and family. Its history is steeped in the Raj, and I love the meeting of cultures. The Indian curry-flavoured rice served with the English ingredients of smoked trout and eggs is such a good match. Leftovers are fantastic the next day with assorted lettuce leaves to make a rice salad.

Place the eggs in a saucepan with cold water over medium–high heat. Once the water comes to the boil, cook the eggs for 6 minutes. Immediately refresh the eggs in iced water to make sure they stop cooking. Peel the eggs and set them aside to serve with the rice.

Preheat the oven to 180°C (350°F).

In a large ovenproof saucepan (with a tight-fitting lid) over medium heat, sweat one-third of the butter until translucent. Add the pistachio nuts, currants, half the curry powder and the rice. Add another one-third of the butter and mix to coat. Add 375 ml (12½ fl oz/1½ cups) water and bring to the boil. Cover the pan tightly with the lid, transfer to the oven and bake for 20 minutes.

Meanwhile, make the sauce by heating the remaining butter and the flour with the remaining curry powder in a saucepan over medium–high heat, stirring continuously until the mixture resembles soft sand. Slowly add the water or fish stock, stirring continuously until smooth. Simmer for 15 minutes, then add the cream and season to taste with a squeeze of lemon juice and some salt and freshly ground black pepper. Keep warm until serving.

By this time the rice should be ready. Remove the pan from the oven and rest for 10 minutes before removing the lid.

Fork half the smoked fish and a little extra butter through the rice. Pile the rice onto a platter or into a bowl with the remaining fish and the halved eggs on top. Drizzle over some of the sauce, scatter over the parsley and serve with a lemon wedge and more of the lovely sauce on the side for extra helpings.

Trout is a good source of omega-3 fats, which help in the formation of cells, and with thyroid and adrenal activity, blood pressure, the breakdown of cholesterol, blood clotting and maintaining healthy hair and skin. The components of curry powder, such as curry leaves, mustard seeds, chilli, fennel, cumin and turmeric, all have benefits well known in Ayurvedic medicine. They're packed with potent compounds that have calming, anti-inflammatory, antimicrobial and anti-stress properties. Vitamins such as A, B, C and E are also present.

Borscht with horseradish cream

SERVES 8

800 g (1 lb 12 oz) oxtail, cut into joints

1 duck, cut into 6 pieces (you can ask your butcher to do this for you)

140 g (5 oz) white cabbage, finely shredded

140 g (5 oz) brown onions, finely chopped

140 g (5 oz) carrots, finely chopped

140 g (5 oz) leeks, finely chopped

1 celery stalk, finely chopped

½ fennel bulb, finely chopped

500 g (1 lb 2 oz) beetroot (beets), washed and cut into large wedges

extra-virgin olive oil for cooking

3 litres (101 fl oz/12 cups) veal stock

2 bay leaves

3 rashers (slices) bacon, cut into batons

Many believe borscht is just beetroot (beet) soup, but it's truly so much more. Some borscht recipes call for the meats to be picked from the bones after cooking and made into dumplings called piroshki, which are served with the soup in its broth form. This recipe serves both meats within the soup, making it very hearty. Traditionally you would use beef shin but I have used oxtail – it's more readily available and has a slightly sweeter flavour. If you find the broth a little flat, a dollop of tomato paste (concentrated tomato purée) and a splash of red-wine vinegar will lift the mix. If you want to maintain the sour cream tradition, use it instead of the mascarpone.

Preheat the oven to 200°C (400°F).

Tumble the oxtail and duck pieces into a large roasting tin and brown them in the oven for 20 minutes.

In a large, deep ovenproof saucepan (with a lid) over medium heat, sweat the shredded and chopped vegetables and one-third of the beetroot in a splash of olive oil until tender.

Remove the oxtail and duck from the oven and add them to the pan, followed by the stock and bay leaves.

Reduce the oven temperature to 140°C (275°F).

Cover the pan with a lid and transfer it to the oven to bake slowly for 3 hours until the oxtail is fully cooked and starting to fall off the bone.

Meanwhile, put half the remaining beetroot in a saucepan over medium heat, with water to cover, and poach it for 30 minutes until tender. Remove the pan from the heat and leave the beetroot to cool.

Pass the oxtail broth through a sieve, reserving the meat. Chill the broth in the refrigerator in order to solidify the fat on the surface, so you can easily skim it off.

Drain, peel and slice the poached beetroot. Pick the meat from the oxtail into nice chunks and slice the duck breast. Set the meats aside. ➤

HORSERADISH CREAM
(MAKES 250 G/9 OZ)

125 g (4½ oz) fresh horseradish, peeled, washed and grated

2 teaspoons white wine

2 teaspoons dijon mustard

2 teaspoons caster (superfine) sugar

½ teaspoon sea salt

150 g (5½ oz) mascarpone

In a small frying pan over high heat, lightly fry the bacon until crisp.

Bring the broth back to the boil and season with salt and freshly ground black pepper if needed.

Peel, chop and process the remaining beetroot in a blender with a little water to form a juice. Pass the juice through a sieve.

For the horseradish cream, combine all the ingredients, except the mascarpone, in a bowl and allow the mixture to infuse for 30 minutes. Lightly fold through the mascarpone and give it a quick whisk to thicken. Refrigerate to set.

Divide your garnishes – oxtail, duck, crisp bacon pieces and sliced beetroot – between bowls. Reheat the broth over medium heat. When it comes to the boil, remove it from the heat and add the beetroot juice. Pour this over the garnish in the bowls. Serve with a dollop of horseradish cream on the side.

MEDICINAL
GUT, HEART, SKIN
· BENEFIT ·

This soup is nutrient-dense and very rich in protein, from the slow, deep cooking of the duck and oxtail. Beetroot (beet) contains an amino acid that can lower the homocysteine levels in the blood, reducing the chance of heart disease and stroke caused by arterial plaque build-up. High levels of folates help in the creation of new cells, and there is vitamin A too, which is essential for good vision and the maintenance of skin and body tissue. B complex vitamins help convert food into energy, and vitamin C boosts the immune system. Beetroot is also rich in potassium to balance body fluids, help maintain a steady heartbeat and regulate blood pressure. Horseradish root contains many volatile compounds that have antioxidant and detoxification functions. Phytochemical compounds in the root stimulate salivary, gastric and intestinal digestive enzymes. It's also high in vitamin C, folates and B complex vitamins.

Parsnip, kale and white bean soup

SERVES 4

450 g (1 lb) pork belly, minced (ground)

1 small swede (rutabaga), peeled and diced

1 brown onion, peeled and diced

2 small or 1 large carrot, peeled and diced

1 large leek, washed and diced

150 ml (5 fl oz) olive oil, plus 1 tablespoon extra

200 ml (7 fl oz) white wine

125 g (4½ oz) cannellini (lima) beans, soaked in water overnight (see recipe introduction)

1 bay leaf

1 litre (34 fl oz/4 cups) chicken stock, plus extra as needed

350 g (12½ oz) parsnips, peeled and chopped into large chunks

200 g (7 oz) kale, stems chopped and leaves shredded

¼ bunch flat-leaf (Italian) parsley, chopped

1 large garlic clove, crushed

2 marjoram sprigs, chopped

2 teaspoons sea salt flakes

freshly ground white pepper

500 g (1 lb 2 oz) sourdough bread

I make this soup with chicken stock but, for a vegetarian base, you can use water or a nice vegetable stock and omit the pork belly from the recipe. You can use the gluten-free Sprouted buckwheat sourdough on page 242 instead of the sourdough bread in the recipe, if you prefer. A good tip with a pulse like cannellini (lima) beans, is to soak them overnight with a pinch of bicarbonate of soda (baking soda) in the water. The next day rinse and drain the beans well and simmer them very slowly in water or stock. The bicarbonate of soda will make the skin supple, enabling the beans to expand slowly without splitting and losing their shape.

In a large, heavy-based saucepan over medium heat, sauté the pork and diced vegetables in the oil until lightly coloured. Add the wine and cook until reduced by half. Add the beans and bay leaf and top up with stock to cover by 2 cm (¾ in). Simmer gently over low heat for 2 hours or until the beans are tender, adding more stock if needed.

Add the parsnip, kale and parsley and simmer for another 30 minutes until just cooked. Add the garlic and marjoram and season with the sea salt and white pepper.

Allow to stand, off the heat, for 20 minutes before serving, so all the vegetables and beans can continue to soak up the stock. Serve the soup poured over a slice of sourdough bread with a generous drizzle of olive oil.

Kale is a rich source of flavanoids, such as beta-carotene, which have strong antioxidant and anticancer attributes. It contains vitamin K (essential for blood clotting) and vitamin C (for an immune boost). The nutrients in kale offer protection from vitamin A deficiency, osteoporosis, iron-deficiency anaemia, and are believed to protect from cardiovascular disease. Parsnips are rich in anti-inflammatory, antifungal and anticancer antioxidants. They also contain generous amounts of the vitamins B, C, K and E.

134

Beetroot, quinoa, rhubarb and ponzu

SERVES 4

170 g (6 oz) mixed white and red quinoa, rinsed and soaked

1 kg (2 lb 3 oz) mixed beetroot (beets), such as regular, baby, golden

100 ml (3½ fl oz) extra-virgin olive oil

250 g (9 oz) rhubarb, sliced very thinly diagonally, using a mandoline

1 pinch sugar

1 fennel bulb, thinly sliced

¼ bunch coriander (cilantro), leaves picked

½ bunch watercress, leaves picked

YUZU PONZU DRESSING

125 ml (4 fl oz/½ cup) Ponzu (page 234)

25 ml (¾ fl oz) yuzu juice (see Note)

75 ml (2½ fl oz) extra-virgin olive oil

25 ml (¾ fl oz) seasame oil

This salad is so colourful and full of texture. It's this simple method of cooking beetroot that enables you to keep their integrity and colour and also allows you to peel them after they have been cooked. It's best to wear a pair of gloves if you don't want to stain your hands. The rhubarb in this salad adds a lovely tart flavour and is a nice way to serve something in its raw state. The curing from the salt and sugar helps break down the texture.

For the yuzu ponzu dressing, combine all the ingredients in a glass jar and shake well. Set aside.

Put the quinoa and 375 ml (12½ fl oz/1½ cups) water in a saucepan over medium–high heat and bring to the boil. When it starts to boil, turn the heat to the lowest setting and place a lid on the pan. Cook as for steamed rice for 10 minutes then turn off the heat, not opening the lid at all during this time. Leave it resting with the lid on for another 10 minutes. Remove the lid, fluff up the quinoa with a fork and leave to cool.

Preheat the oven to 180°C (350°F).

Toss the beetroot in the olive oil, season with a little salt and freshly ground black pepper and place them in a roasting tin. Cover the tin tightly with aluminium foil and bake for 30 minutes. Remove the tin from the oven and open the foil. Test the smaller beetroot first to see if they are done – they are cooked when the skin rubs off with your finger. Remove any beetroot that are cooked, cover the tin again with the foil and cook for another 15–20 minutes. Test again and remove the beetroot that are ready. When the beetroot are cool, rub the skin off and cut the beetroot into your desired shapes.

Toss the rhubarb in a bowl with the sugar and a pinch of salt and leave for 10 minutes.

Arrange the quinoa, beetroot, fennel and rhubarb on a serving platter and garnish with the coriander and watercress. Pour over the dressing, adjust the seasoning and serve.

Note: *Yuzu is a Japanese lime that tastes like a sour mandarin. You should find fresh yuzu or bottled yuzu juice in Asian grocery stores. If you can't find it, use lime instead.*

Beetroot (beet) contains an amino acid that can lower homocysteine levels in the blood, which means lowering the risk of heart disease and stroke. They also contain folates, for new cell creation. Rhubarb is rich in vitamin A, B complex vitamins and in vitamin K, for maintaining healthy bones and for blood clotting.

Salted kale with chickpeas and green tahini

SERVES 4

1 generous handful activated
  walnuts (see page 237)

½ lemon, juiced

1 bunch young kale

200 g (7 oz) cooked chickpeas
  (garbanzo beans), drained

1 handful coriander (cilantro)
  leaves

1 handful mint leaves

1 tablespoon thinly sliced spring
  onion (scallion)

1 tablespoon each of black and
  white sesame seeds, toasted

seeds from ½ pomegranate

1 tablespoon extra-virgin olive
  oil

½ quantity Green tahini
  (page 238)

1 pinch sumac

When making this salad always look for the youngest kale possible, as old kale is tougher and harder for the body to digest. You can make tougher kale more digestible by sprinkling over some salt and lemon juice or apple-cider vinegar and letting it sit for 15 minutes before eating.

Dehydrate the walnuts until crisp. I'm very lo-fi at home, and we don't have a dehydrator, so I dehydrate or toast the nuts in the oven at 70°C (160°F) until crisp – usually overnight works best. If you want to season the nuts, simply soak them in salted water so when they dehydrate they have a nice salty bloom on the surface.

Massage the lemon juice and a pinch of salt into the kale, then let it sit for 15 minutes. Remove the kale from the curing bowl and it will be ready to use. Reserve the juice in the bowl.

In another bowl, toss all your ingredients together, except the tahini and sumac. Add the juice from the curing bowl for more acidity if needed. (If you find lemon too sharp, winter is brimming with lovely citrus to choose from, so perhaps try blood orange juice.)

Smear the green tahini on a serving platter to make a shallow pool. (I find that if you toss the green tahini through the salad, it is too heavy and will crush your lovely leaves.) Place the dressed ingredients on top, sprinkle with the sumac and serve.

MEDICINAL · BRAIN, HEART · BENEFIT

Kale has been hailed as a superfood and it's not hard to see why (see page 133). Chickpeas (garbanzo beans), an ancient food, also have many health-giving attributes. They're a good source of plant-based amino acids (the building blocks of protein), and are high in fibre, as well as vitamins C and B6 and potassium, which are all supportive of heart health. They're rich in selenium, which can detoxify cancer-causing compounds in the body, and contain choline, which can help with sleep, learning and memory. Sesame seeds are particularly rich in the monounsaturated fatty acid oleic acid, which helps lower LDL ('bad' cholesterol) and increase HDL ('good' cholesterol) in the blood. They are excellent sources of B complex vitamins such as niacin, which also helps reduce LDL-cholesterol levels in the blood. Niacin enhances GABA (a calming neurotransmitter) activity in the brain, which in turn helps reduce anxiety.

Stuffed baby artichokes with olive, citrus and herb salad

SERVES 6–8 AS A STARTER OR SIDE

16 small globe artichokes

1 lemon, juiced

2 fresh bay leaves

½ teaspoon white peppercorns

20 g (¾ oz) flat-leaf (Italian) parsley, leaves finely chopped, stalks reserved

20 g (¾ oz/1 cup firmly packed) mint leaves, finely chopped

40 g (1½ oz) salted baby capers, rinsed, drained well and finely chopped

3 garlic cloves, finely chopped

400 ml (13½ fl oz) dry white wine

sea salt

250 ml (8½ fl oz/1 cup) extra-virgin olive oil

OLIVE, CITRUS AND HERB SALAD

1 orange, segmented

1 ruby grapefruit, segmented

1 lemon, segmented

95 g (3¼ oz/½ cup) kalamata olives

½ bunch mint, leaves picked

¼ bunch basil, leaves picked

¼ bunch dill, leaves picked

¼ bunch salad burnet, leaves picked

60 ml (2 fl oz/¼ cup) Mint oil (page 232)

This recipe is perfect for small, tender artichokes. However, if you can only find large ones, I suggest you cut the top 2 cm (¾ in) off each artichoke, then cut the artichoke in half and remove the choke and some of the tough outer leaves. The artichoke cup that is left will be perfect for the stuffing. The cooking method will be the same, but they may take a little extra time to cook through. A good way to test is to pull one of the outer leaves off and see whether it is soft enough to eat easily.

Preheat the oven to 120°C (250°F).

Working with one artichoke at a time, trim off the top third, then trim off the centre leaves and remove the hairy choke with a teaspoon. Trim the stems. Peel off the thick outer leaves to reveal the bright, tender flesh, then place the artichokes in a bowl of cold water with lemon juice added to prevent discolouration.

Put the bay leaves, peppercorns and parsley stalks in the base of a non-reactive baking dish large enough to hold the artichokes snugly in a single layer.

In a bowl, combine the mint, parsley leaves, capers and garlic. Season to taste with salt and freshly ground black pepper and mix well.

Drain the artichokes and stuff each one with a little of the herb mixture. Arrange the artichokes in the baking dish, sitting them on their bases and packing them tightly so they remain upright. Pour over the wine and 300 ml (10 fl oz) cold water. Season to taste with sea salt, drizzle with the olive oil and cover tightly with baking paper. Cover tightly with aluminium foil and braise in the oven until tender, 1¾–2 hours.

For the salad, combine the fruit, olives and herbs in a bowl and dress with the mint oil.

To serve, drain the artichokes from the cooking liquid and arrange them on a platter. Serve the olive, citrus and herb salad on the side and spoon it over before eating.

Artichokes are high in folates to help with cell creation, antioxidant vitamin C to boost the immune system, vitamin B to help convert food to energy, and vitamin K, which helps in the activation of proteins and calcium, essential for strong bones.

Shredded brussels sprouts, lentils, speck and parsley

SERVES 4

2 red onions, unpeeled

60 ml (2 fl oz/¼ cup) extra-
   virgin olive oil, plus extra for
   drizzling

370 g (13 oz/2 cups) black or
   green lentils, soaked in water
   overnight

200 g (7 oz) speck, sliced into
   small batons

1 tablespoon sherry vinegar

16 brussels sprouts

1 lemon

¼ bunch flat-leaf (Italian)
   parsley, leaves picked, plus
   extra to serve

MEDICINAL
HEART
BENEFIT

Brussels sprouts contain
good amounts of flavonoid
antioxidants, which can help
protect against prostate and
colon cancers. They're also an
excellent source of vitamin C
and other antioxidant vitamins
like A and E, which help protect
the body from harmful free
radicals. Vitamin A is essential
for healthy mucous tissue
and skin, and for eye health.
Brussels sprouts also contain
vitamin K (for bone health and
blood clotting), B complex (to
help convert food to energy),
potassium (for balancing bodily
fluids) and iron (essential for the
production of red blood cells).

It's a good idea to get into the habit of soaking grains and legumes overnight before you use them. Once soaked, the lentils can be steamed perfectly while keeping them loose and light. Once you've cooked them this way, you'll never go back. Brussels sprouts, being raw cruciferous vegetables, are a lot easier to digest if they have been cured with some sort of acid and salt.

Preheat the oven to 180°C (350°F). Line a baking tray with baking paper.

Holding the top and bottom of the onions with your thumb and index finger, cut the onions in half crossways (not from sprout to core). Leaving the skin on, place the onions, cut side down, on the prepared tray. Drizzle with a little extra olive oil and bake for 1 hour, until the onion is extremely soft. Remove the onions from the oven and allow to cool.

Meanwhile drain the lentils. Place them in a steamer and cook for 25 minutes or until tender. If you don't have a steamer, cook the lentils in a saucepan of barely simmering water for about 15 minutes until just done. Drain the lentils and separate them with a fork.

Cook the speck slowly in a frying pan over medium–low heat, until it renders down and becomes crispy. Remove the pan from the heat and fold the speck through the lentils, leaving the fat in the pan. For the dressing, add the olive oil and sherry vinegar to the fat in the pan and stir well, scraping any solids from the bottom.

Shred the brussels sprouts with a mandoline or sharp knife. Put the sprouts in a bowl with a generous pinch of salt and a squeeze of lemon juice. Break down the tough fibres of the sprouts by massaging the salt and lemon juice into them and allowing the sprouts to sit for 15 minutes to cure and soften the leaves. Add the parsley to the bowl, along with the speck and lentils. Spoon in some of the dressing in order to coat the ingredients.

Take the onions and remove the dried skin layer by squeezing the onion gently and pulling up the skin to reveal a glossy, soft inner onion. Pick each layer of onion out and add it to the lentils and brussels sprouts. Toss together with a little more dressing and serve.

142

Broccolini with walnut and rosemary tarator

SERVES 4

3 bunches broccolini, or more,
depending on what you are
serving the dish with

1 bunch rosemary, sprigs picked

60 ml (2 fl oz/¼ cup) new-
season extra-virigin olive oil

½ quantity Rosemary tarator
(page 240)

1 long red chilli, sliced (seeded
for less heat)

crushed walnuts, to serve
(optional)

Broccolini is delicious simply steamed or lightly boiled in salty water. But for this dish it's best grilled on the barbecue or baked in a very hot oven. If it's going to be used as a side to a meat dish, a couple of sprigs per person will do. However, if this is a stand-alone dish, maybe served with a poached egg as a small meal, a bunch of broccolini each is a nice amount. If you have dairy allergies you can use any of the nut milks on page 238 when making the tarator.

Heat a barbecue or chargrill pan to hot (or preheat the oven to 250°C/480°F).

To keep the broccolini green, give it a quick blanch in boiling, salty water for a few seconds and then plunge it into a large bowl of iced water to stop it from cooking any further.

Lightly coat the broccolini and rosemary sprigs in 1 tablespoon of the olive oil and season with salt and freshly ground black pepper. Grill for 2 minutes until tender or bake for 5 minutes until the florets are lightly charred. Toss with the remaining olive oil and the rosemary tarator and scatter over the chilli. For texture, serve the dish with the crushed walnuts, if desired.

MEDICINAL
EAR, NOSE &
THROAT
· BENEFIT ·

Broccolini is rich in vitamin C, a powerful natural antioxidant and immunity booster that helps fight flu viruses. It's also high in vitamin A, essential for healthy eyesight and to help prevent macular degeneration of the retina. Broccolini leaves (the green tops) are an excellent source of carotenoids and vitamin A. Broccolini is also rich in vitamin K and B complex vitamins, and the florets contain some omega-3 fatty acids. The phytonutrient compounds in broccolini have anticancer properties. Walnuts are high in omega-3 fatty acids and vitamin E antioxidants; these neutralise unstable molecules that can damage other cells. Rosemary is not only a good source of vitamins A and C, it also contains rosmarinic acid. This has antioxidant, anti-inflammatory and antimicrobial properties and helps prevent cell damage. Rosemary is also said to be good for the memory.

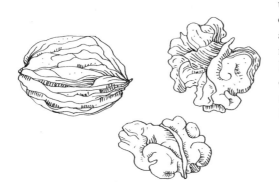

Baked whole cauliflower with Indian spices, mint and yoghurt

SERVES 4

1 small cauliflower

125 g (4½ oz) Clarified butter (page 234)

1 teaspoon fennel seeds

1 teaspoon cumin seeds

1 teaspoon black mustard seeds

2 tablespoons Indian spice mix (page 232)

1 lime, juiced

60 ml (2 fl oz/¼ cup) Curry oil (page 233), to serve

1 handful coriander (cilantro) leaves, to serve

SALTWATER BRINE

2 litres (68 fl oz/8 cups) water

100 g (3½ oz) sea salt

RAISINS IN TEA (MAKES 120 G/4½ OZ)

2 teaspoons Darjeeling tea leaves

500 ml (17 fl oz/2 cups) boiling water

60 g (2 oz/½ cup) raisins

Ideally you want to brine your cauliflower overnight, but even a couple of hours in brine will work wonders. Look for a small cauliflower and trim only a couple of the outside leaves as you want as many as possible to help protect the cauliflower while it cooks – plus the leaves make great eating. My Indian spice mix is a personal favourite, but you can choose any spices you like. You'll find many varieties in Asian grocery stores. Try using different yoghurts, too. I love buffalo milk yoghurt for its light texture, and coconut yoghurt works very well if you have dairy allergies. If this is the case you can also replace the clarified butter with olive oil. Additions of sliced fresh chilli to add heat and mint for a menthol hit are great twists.

For the saltwater brine, combine the salt and water, stirring to fully dissolve the salt.

Place the cauliflower in a non-reactive, snug-fitting container with a lid. Pour over the brine to fully submerge the cauliflower and leave in the refrigerator overnight.

For the raisins in tea, brew the tea leaves in the boiling water for 3 minutes. Strain the tea over the raisins in a bowl and allow them to swell for 30 minutes before using. (They keep well in the refrigerator until needed. Any type of tea works well, depending on your taste and what you're using the raisins for.)

The next day remove the cauliflower from the brine and pat it dry.

Preheat the oven to 190°C (375°F). Line a heavy-based roasting tin with baking paper. ➤

<

YOGHURT DRESSING

1 teaspoon grated fresh ginger
1 crushed garlic clove
1 handful mint leaves, finely
   shredded
300 g (10½ oz) yoghurt

Place the cauliflower in the tin, cut side down, so it sits upright. Pour the tea from the raisins over the cauliflower so it hydrates the vegetable and forms a puddle in the tin.

Melt the clarified butter in a frying pan over medium heat. When it starts to warm up, add the fennel seeds, cumin seeds and mustard seeds. Cook for 1 minute until the seeds start to pop in the pan and become aromatic. Brush the clarified butter and seed mixture over the cauliflower and then dust it with the Indian spice mix. Cover the tin with aluminium foil and place it in the oven. Bake for 30 minutes, undisturbed. Remove the foil and baste the cauliflower with the clarified butter and tea liquid sitting in the bottom of the tin. Bake for another 30 minutes, basting regularly with the clarified butter–spice mix.

After the cauliflower has been cooking for 1 hour, insert a skewer or knife into the base. If it's tender, remove it from the oven and rest it in the tin for 15 minutes. If it's not tender, cook it for a few more minutes and check again.

Squeeze the lime juice into the baking tin to mingle with the pan juices and create a lovely dressing.

For the yoghurt dressing, fold the ginger, garlic, mint and a pinch of salt through the yoghurt.

Serve a wedge of the cauliflower, like a piece of cake, with a few spoonfuls of the pan juice vinaigrette, a dollop of yoghurt dressing, the tea-soaked raisins and a drizzle of curry oil. Scatter the fresh coriander leaves over to finish.

Cauliflower is full of phytochemical, and other, compounds that can work to inhibit cancer cell growth. A 100 g (3½ oz) serve of cauliflower gives 80 per cent of the daily recommended intake of vitamin C, a proven agent in the fight against harmful free radicals and infections. Cauliflower also contains good amounts various B complex vitamins and vitamin K, all required for fat, protein and carbohydrate metabolism. The Indian spices have essential oils that activate both the salivary glands, to aid with digestion, and the glands that secrete bile in the stomach and intestine. Antioxidant essential oils in spices have antimicrobial, anti-inflammatory and anti-stress effects. They're also anticoagulant (i.e. they prevent blood clotting) and carminative, which means they relieve intestinal gas, thereby improving digestion and appetite.

Roast Jerusalem artichokes, soffritto and hazelnuts

SERVES 4

1 kg (2 lb 3 oz) Jerusalem
  artichokes

60 ml (2 fl oz/¼ cup) extra-
  virgin olive oil

½ lemon, thinly sliced, plus
  ½ lemon, juiced

1 handful activated hazelnuts
  (see page 237)

1 handful rocket (arugula) leaves

SOFFRITTO
(MAKES 250 G/9 OZ)

60 ml (2 fl oz/¼ cup) extra-
  virgin olive oil

1 large brown onion, chopped

5 garlic cloves, roughly chopped

4 red capsicums (bell peppers),
  roughly chopped

3 fresh long red chillies

3 purple shallots, roughly
  chopped

50 g (1¾ oz) tinned piquillo
  peppers

2 teaspoons caster (superfine)
  sugar

2 tablespoons sherry vinegar

Jerusalem artichokes come in lots of odd shapes, so you may need to cook them in different ways. If they are shaped like an egg, you'll want to cut them in half. If they are the little knobbly ones that look like ginger, break the nodules from each other and leave them as they are. The soffritto keeps well in the refrigerator for up to 1 week. It is also delicious with a fried egg for breakfast or as a dip with some nice crusty bread.

For the soffritto, warm two-thirds of the olive oil in a large frying pan over medium heat. Add the onion, garlic, capsicum, chillies and shallots and fry for about 5 minutes until golden. Keep stirring the mixture for another 5 minutes until it starts to caramelise. Add the piquillo peppers – the temperature shock will release the caramelisation from the bottom of the pan. Add the sugar and stir until the mixture is a dark crimson. Add the vinegar to stop the cooking process. Remove the pan from the heat and add the remaining olive oil. Season to taste with 2 pinches salt and set aside.

Preheat the oven to 200°C (400°F).

Place the artichokes in a roasting tin and drizzle them with half the olive oil, tossing to coat. Add a generous sprinkling of salt and place the tin in the oven. The skin will start to blister and become crisp, while the inside will become soft and buttery. After 10 minutes, add a scattering of lemon slices to the pan. Give the artichokes another 15–20 minutes or until, when you test them with a skewer, they are soft on the inside and beautifully caramelised on the outside. Remove the tin from the oven and allow the artichokes to sit for the flavours to develop.

Serve the artichokes warm from the oven or at room temperature with the soffritto, hazelnuts and the rocket, which has been tossed with the remaining olive oil and lemon juice.

Jerusalem artichokes contain inulin, a low-calorie type of fructan and inert carbohydrate, which isn't metabolised inside the body, making them ideal for diabetics. They also contain antioxidant vitamins such as vitamin C, vitamin A for good vision and vitamin E for neutralising unstable molecules that damage cells. They're rich in potassium, for balancing bodily fluids and for a healthy heartbeat.

148

Braised quince and witlof

SERVES 4

750 g (1 lb 11 oz) witlof
   (chicory), halved lengthways
2 quinces, cut into eighths, skin
   left on and seeds removed
50 g (1¾ oz) light soft brown
   sugar
50 ml (1¾ fl oz) extra-virgin
   olive oil
50 g (1¾ oz) unsalted butter
2 oranges, zested and juiced
2 star anise
100 ml (3½ fl oz) chicken stock
100 ml (3½ fl oz) balsamic
   vinegar

Quince is my favourite fruit and it's wonderful to use in a savoury way rather than always sweet as a dessert. You can speed this recipe up by cutting the quince into smaller pieces – however, larger chunks mean a longer cooking time and more flavour development, which is always better. Try using red witlof for colour contrast and blood orange for an even darker caramel colour. This is absolutely delicious served with all types of meat and strong-flavoured fish, such as mackerel, mullet, groper or tuna.

Preheat the oven to 180°C (350°F).

In a large flameproof casserole dish over medium heat, fry the witlof, quince and sugar in the olive oil and butter until lightly brown. Add the orange zest and juice, star anise and stock. Cover with baking paper and bake in the oven until tender, about 30 minutes.

Add the vinegar and, on the stove top, reduce the liquor down to a glaze, with everything in the pan, turning the witlof and the quince occasionally to give them a shiny finish.

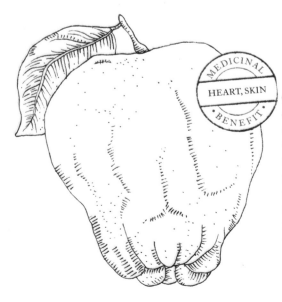

MEDICINAL
HEART, SKIN
BENEFIT

Quince contains certain tannins that bind to toxins in the colon, protecting from inflammatory bowel disease, cancers and diverticulitis. Quince is also high in immune-boosting vitamin C, which helps in the body's production of collagen, the connective tissue that knits together wounds and supports blood vessel walls. It also contains copper, a mineral that plays an important role in iron metabolism and the production of red blood cells. Witlof (chicory) is a good source of vitamin A, essential for healthy eyesight and maintaining tissue and skin. It also has B complex vitamins (for converting food into energy), folic acid (for building new cells) and manganese (to help in the breakdown of amino acids, cholesterol and carbohydrates).

150

Baked mushrooms 'Saint-Jacques' style

SERVES 4

250 g (9 oz) butter, melted gently in a pan

3 garlic cloves, finely chopped

¼ bunch flat-leaf (Italian) parsley, leaves picked and finely chopped

¼ bunch thyme, leaves picked and finely chopped

8 large portobello mushrooms

125 ml (4 fl oz/½ cup) white wine

250 g (9 oz) piece speck, cut into batons

120 g (4 oz/1½ cups) fresh breadcrumbs (made from stale sourdough bread – see Note)

lemon cheeks, to serve

I love coquilles Saint-Jacques – plump and juicy scallops baked or grilled in their shells, in garlic butter with bacon, parsley and a drizzle of wine, and that lovely breadcrumb top. The flat mushroom is also the perfect vehicle for all of these wonderful flavours – particularly when it's not scallop season. Look for the largest flat mushrooms you can find. Big portobello mushrooms, which are so juicy and fat, are perfect.

Put the warm butter, garlic, parsley, thyme and a pinch of salt in a bowl and mix to combine.

Preheat the oven to 250°C (480°F). Line a baking tray with baking paper.

Place the mushrooms, upside down, on the baking tray and remove the stalks. Drizzle each mushroom with a tablespoon of white wine, then scatter with the speck batons. Spoon some of the garlic butter mixture into each mushroom cap. Place the mushrooms in the refrigerator for a few hours – the butter will set on top of the mushrooms and hold everything together.

When you are ready to cook, scatter the mushrooms with the breadcrumbs and bake for 7–10 minutes until the mushrooms are tender and the breadcrumbs are golden and sizzling. Serve with lemon wedges and a good grinding of black pepper.

Note: *To make the fresh breadcrumbs, pop the bread in the freezer until hard, then grate it using a box grater. If you buy toasted breadcrumbs, when you bake your Saint-Jacques mushrooms they will toast too far and may catch and burn, while the fresh will just start to become golden and plump, absorbing all the lovely flavours.*

Mushrooms contain ergosterols, which are converted to vitamin D when exposed to sunlight after harvesting. Vitamin D is crucial for maintaining normal blood levels of calcium and phosphorus, which help strengthen bones. Mushrooms also have vitamins B2 and B3 (to help convert food into energy), selenium and potassium (to help balance bodily fluids), dietary fibre (for a healthy bowel) and phosphorus (to build bones and move nutrients into and out of cells).

152

Cornish pasties

SERVES 6

1 quantity Shortcrust suet pastry
  dough (page 244)

1 egg, lightly beaten

LAMB FILLING

500 g (1 lb 2 oz) lamb shoulder,
  finely diced

½ brown onion, diced

½ carrot, diced

1 swede (rutabaga), cut into
  1 cm (½ in) dice

1 small potato, diced

1 garlic clove, finely chopped

1 tablespoon thyme

1 tablespoon chopped flat-leaf
  (Italian) parsley

There are many ways to make a pasty, but there are two things that must always be in it – lamb and swede (rutabaga). These two ingredients give it a truly authentic flavour. The pasty is shaped like it is, with a thick, pleated crust because traditionally Cornish miners, with coal all over their hands, used to hold the pasty by the thick, crisp edge. Then they ate the inside and could just throw away the soiled crust. There is a great gluten-free pastry recipe on page 244, which will also work perfectly for these pasties. It's very delicate and I suggest you use the paper to help support the dough when you fold it over and make the shape. Remove the paper when you are ready to put the pasties in the oven. You can put them in the refrigerator to firm them up a little before taking the paper off.

Lamb shoulder has the perfect meat to fat ratio. It's where all the flavour is and it just so happens to be my favourite cut of meat. The problem is that the shoulder is a working muscle and therefore is tough, so it doesn't work well for cooking quickly. However, I suggest you cut it very finely with a knife into dice no bigger than 5 mm (¼ in). Alternatively you could mince (grind) it, but by far the best result comes from hand-cutting.

For the lamb filling, preheat the oven to 210°C (410°F).

Mix all the filling ingredients together in a bowl to combine. Set aside.

Roll the suet pastry dough out to a 5 mm (¼ in) thickness and cut it into 15 cm (6 in) circles – I always find a bread plate a good template.

Put a good amount of filling in the middle of each circle. Brush the egg over the rim, fold it over to form a semi-circle and crimp the edges with your fingers or a fork. Brush the top of the pasties with the egg and prick once with a fork to allow the steam to vent. Bake for 20 minutes, then reduce the temperature to 180°C (350°F) and bake for another 10 minutes until golden brown.

Grass-fed lamb can contain 25 per cent more omega-3 fatty acids than grain-fed lamb. It's also high in conjugated lineolic acid (CLA), found in the fat of ruminants and linked to various health benefits, in small amounts.

Freekeh-stuffed duck with saffron, olives and preserved lemon

SERVES 6–8

2 pinches saffron threads

2 pinches sea salt

1 red onion, diced

3 garlic cloves, finely chopped

90 ml (3 fl oz) extra-virgin olive oil, plus extra to serve

300 g (10½ oz/1½ cups) freekeh

1 teaspoon ground allspice

½ teaspoon ground cinnamon

½ teaspoon sumac

½ lemon, juiced

1 duck (about 1.9 kg/4 lb 7 oz)

200 g (7 oz) mixed olives, such as wild and green

rocket (arugula), to serve

Pot-roasting is a good way to cook a duck. It's gentle enough to keep it moist, which means you can cook it as a whole bird, breast and legs together. Roasting a duck conventionally quite often means the breast is overcooked by the time the legs are done, so this is the perfect solution. Although freekeh is a green wheat, don't be scared. It's a lovely grain that is good for you and it has a nice waxy texture. If you can't find freekeh, use barley or quinoa.

Preheat the oven to 100°C (210°F).

Place the saffron in a bowl with 125 ml (4 fl oz/½ cup) warm water and half the sea salt and set aside to infuse for 30 minutes.

Meanwhile, sauté the onion and garlic in 60 ml (2 fl oz/¼ cup) of the olive oil with the remaining sea salt over medium heat until tender and translucent, 5–6 minutes. Add the freekeh and spices and stir to toast for 1 minute. Remove from the heat, add the lemon juice, season to taste with salt and freshly ground black pepper and set aside to cool.

Stuff the freekeh mixture into the duck cavity and leave to stand for about 30 minutes.

Heat the remaining oil in a large flameproof casserole dish or roasting tin over medium–high heat and cook the duck, breast side down, until well browned, 4–5 minutes per breast. Turn the duck onto its back and pour the saffron and its liquid over the breasts. Add the olives to the pan, cover with a lid or aluminium foil and transfer to the oven to braise until the duck is very tender, 2½ hours.

When the duck is cooked, rest it for 15 minutes, then drain the pan juices into a jug to use as a gravy, and reserve the olives separately.

Carve the duck and serve it with the olives and stuffing spooned out onto the plate. When everyone is nearly finished, serve the rocket to help mop up the juices and cleanse the palate.

MEDICINAL

MUSCLES,
BONES & JOINTS

BENEFIT

Duck is high in omega-6 fatty acid (linoleic acid), which can help stimulate skin and hair growth and maintain bone health. Freekeh is high in protein and also rich in fibre, and foods like this help you feel full for longer. Freekeh also has good quantities of calcium (to build and protect bones), zinc (for the immune system, taste and smell) and iron (for producing haemoglobin in red blood cells, to help transport oxygen throughout the body).

156

Daube of beef oyster blade

SERVES 4

4 beef cheeks

salt flakes

100 g (3½ oz/⅔ cup) plain (all-purpose) flour

100 g (3½ oz) butter, plus extra for finishing

3 onions, chopped

10 garlic cloves, thinly sliced

2 bay leaves

3 thyme sprigs, leaves picked

3 savory sprigs, leaves picked (see Note)

200 g (7 oz) button mushrooms, roughly chopped

2 celery stalks, roughly chopped

2 large carrots, peeled and cut into sixths crossways

125 ml (4 fl oz/½ cup) intense red wine (cabernet or bordeaux)

1 handful flat-leaf (Italian) parsley leaves, roughly chopped

A 'daube' is actually the dish that this French stew is traditionally cooked in. It's usually made from terracotta and has a lid to hold in the moisture. In this recipe I use a flameproof casserole dish, which can be ceramic, enamelware or the traditional terracotta. However, if you have none of these, an ovenproof, heavy-based stainless steel pot will work just fine. This recipe hails from Provence, so the herbs play a very important role in the stew. The other key ingredient, aside from high-quality beef, is good wine. I believe a very full-bodied red is what you need, such as a cabernet or a bordeaux and, as always, if you're serving wine you should be drinking the same one that you cooked with. This dish is best served with lovely creamy mashed potato.

Preheat the oven to 140°C (275°F).

Season the beef cheeks with the salt flakes and some freshly ground black pepper. Dust the beef in the flour, shaking off any excess.

Melt one-third of the butter in a large flameproof casserole dish, with a lid, over medium–high heat until sizzling. Brown the meat evenly in batches for about 5 minutes each side, adding the remaining butter between batches.

Reduce the heat to medium–low and add the onion, garlic, bay leaves, thyme, savory, mushrooms, celery and carrot. Slowly sweat the vegetables until translucent, then add the red wine and simmer for 2 minutes. Return the beef cheeks to the pan, nestling them among the vegetables, then cover with baking paper and the lid. Transfer to the oven to slow-braise for 3 hours or until the beef cheeks are tender. Stir through the parsley and a generous knob of butter for richness, then serve.

Note: *Savory is a herb that looks like tarragon but it has a little spice in it, which gives things a nice kick. If you can't find it, use tarragon or flat-leaf (Italian) parsley.*

So-called 'secondary' cuts of meat are usually taken from hardworking parts of the animal. They contain large amounts of collagen, which require long, slow cooking in order to break down into gelatine. Gelatine contains glycine (which can reduce inflammation associated with diseases like arthritis) and proline, another amino acid important for good immune function and warding off infection. Consumption of gelatine helps boost natural keratin levels, essential for healthy nails and hair. Minerals such as selenium, phosphorus and copper found in gelatine help maintain strong bones and increase bone density, to defend against osteoporosis.

Roasted whole John Dory with vanilla and saffron

SERVES 4

1 pinch saffron threads

125 ml (4 fl oz/½ cup) hot fish stock

80 g (2¾ oz) butter

2 tablespoons olive oil

2 kg (4 lb 6 oz) John Dory

1 vanilla bean, split and seeds scraped

1 splash medium vermouth

1 lemon, juiced, plus lemon cheeks to serve

Generally speaking, 400 g (14 oz) of fish per person is the right amount. However, a John Dory has a very large head and a lot of bones so you won't end up with much fish per person. Therefore I would increase the amount to 500 g (1 lb 2 oz) per person. If you don't have a pan large enough to fit the whole fish, ask your fishmonger to chop the head off and gut the fish for you. If they're not too busy, they may also cut the fins off for you (with scissors) so you are left with a sort of obtuse triangle of John Dory. Vanilla can really complement and enhance a savoury dish. We expect it with sweets and so when you taste the vanilla with this fish, it takes you by surprise.

Preheat the oven to 180°C (350°F).

Soak the saffon threads for 30 minutes in the fish stock until the stock is a gorgeous deep-yellow colour. Set aside and keep hot.

In a heavy-based ovenproof frying pan, melt half the butter with the olive oil. When the butter is foaming, add the fish. Once the fish is in, make sure you shake the pan to ensure that the fish is not sticking. Add the vanilla seeds and bean with the saffron-infused fish stock. Continue to fry the fish for 4 minutes on one side, before you turn it and give it one more minute on the other side. Transfer the pan to the oven and cook for a further 5 minutes.

Remove the pan from the oven and add the vermouth. Place the fish on a plate to rest for 3–4 minutes.

While the fish is resting, return the pan to the stove top and add the remaining butter. Over high heat, allow the butter to sizzle, making sure not to let it darken. Add a good squeeze of lemon juice to stop the butter from cooking further and set aside to keep warm. ➤

<

If you have cooked a whole fish, put the fish on a platter and take it to the table, as it makes a wonderful centrepiece. To serve, slide a spatula under the fish fillet along the top of the bone – the top fillet should slide off the bone. Hold onto the tail and lift it up, using the bone to free the flesh from the spine. You will be left with two lovely fillets. Pick out the remaining bones and put the fillets back together on the serving plate. Spoon over the butter, vanilla and vermouth mixture and serve with the lemon cheeks.

Note: *A nice touch is to foam the butter. (Whisk the butter continuously as it melts. Before it browns, take it off the heat and continue whisking until a foam forms.) Then, to finish, add some lovely green leaves. I find things like turnip tops, beetroot (beet) tops or cavolo nero are good light vegetables that wilt quickly and add a nice balance to the dish..*

We all know that fish provides omega-3 fatty acids, essential to our body and helpful in lowering 'bad' cholesterol. But saffron and vanilla also pack a nutritional punch. Saffron is full of vitamin A carotenoids, which are antioxidants that protect against cataracts in the eyes. It also has B complex vitamins, to help transform food into energy, and immune-boosting vitamin C and potassium, to help with muscle contractions. Vanilla is very rich in the B complex vitamins that are so essential for healthy skin, healthy blood cells and the proper functioning of the nervous system.

Octopus braised in red wine with lemon and oregano

SERVES 4

100 g (3½ oz) brown onions, finely diced

100 g (3½ oz) carrots, finely diced

60 g (2 oz) leeks, finely diced

60 g (2 oz) fennel, finely diced

60 g (2 oz) celery stalks, finely diced

40 g (1½ oz) garlic cloves, sliced

2 bay leaves

100 g (3½ oz) small black olives

½ bunch oregano, leaves picked, plus extra to serve

200 ml (7 fl oz) extra-virgin olive oil

¼ bunch flat-leaf (Italian) parsley, leaves picked and stems finely chopped

1 lemon, zested

600 ml (20½ fl oz) red wine

1 kg (2 lb 3 oz) large octopus

crusty bread, to serve

Strong, bold flavours, such as those in this dish, make you feel warm in winter. Large octopus has a really delicious flavour and texture. If you can't find any, then baby octopus will cook the same way, but you may need to reduce the cooking time – try checking after 20 minutes. It's nice to leave the pits in the olives as they add to the tannins but, if you're concerned about breaking your teeth, I suggest removing them. This is delicious served as a sauce with plain pasta, but I suggest cutting the octopus into bite-sized chunks. Good types of pasta to use would be the larger kinds that hold sauce well, such as shells and penne.

Preheat the oven to 200°C (400°F).

In a large, cast-iron, heavy-based ovenproof frying pan over medium heat, sauté the vegetables, garlic, bay leaves, olives and oregano in the olive oil for 5 minutes until fragrant and soft. Add the parsley stems, 1 teaspoon of the lemon zest and the red wine and let the mixture sizzle for a minute before adding the octopus. Stir gently to coat the octopus.

Cover the pan with a lid and cook over very low heat for 1 hour. Test to see whether the octopus is tender by removing one of the tentacles and slicing it with a knife. If it's to your liking, remove the octopus and simmer the liquid a little longer to form a glossy black sauce.

Place the octopus on a platter and drizzle over the sauce. Scatter over the extra oregano, the parsley leaves and the lemon zest. Serve with the crusty bread to soak up the sauce.

MEDICINAL
EAR, NOSE &
THROAT
BENEFIT

Octopus is a nutritious lean protein, packed with vitamins B12 and B6, plus the minerals selenium, iron and copper. Oregano has antifungal, antimicrobial and anti-inflammatory effects, and its essential oils are believed to alleviate the symptoms of respiratory ailments like colds and flus.

162

Grilled mackerel with blood oranges and dill

SERVES 4

25 g (1 oz) fresh ginger

1 blood orange, rind reserved and flesh segmented

2 teaspoons rice wine vinegar

olive oil for brushing

four 350 g (12½ oz each) whole mackerel, gutted

1 bunch dill, chopped

SUGAR SYRUP

30 ml (1 fl oz) water

1½ tablespoons sugar

BLOOD ORANGE BUTTER SAUCE

1½ tablespoons vegetable stock

1 blood orange, zested and segmented

1 tablespoon olive oil

1 handful coriander (cilantro) leaves, chopped

80 g (2¾ oz) unsalted butter

lemon juice, if needed

Intense citrus is perfect for cutting through the somewhat oily texture of mackerel, and the barbecue coals add a lovely smoky charred flavour. Dill is a great herb to serve with this, but tarragon, flat-leaf (Italian) parsley or oregano would also be delicious.

To make the sugar syrup, bring the water to the boil in a small saucepan, add the sugar and remove the pan from the heat, stirring to dissolve the sugar.

For the blood orange butter sauce, in a saucepan over medium heat, bring the stock to a simmer with the zest and then add the orange segments. Whisk until the segments disintegrate, then mix in the olive oil, coriander and butter. Season with salt and freshly ground black pepper and add a little lemon juice if the sauce is too sweet. Set aside.

To make a garnish, cut the ginger and the orange rind into thin strips. Bring a small saucepan of water to the boil and blanch the ginger and orange rind for 10 seconds. Immediately refresh in iced water. Repeat twice.

In a small saucepan over medium heat, warm the sugar syrup with the blanched rind and ginger and simmer for 15 minutes. Add the vinegar for a sweet and sour taste then remove the pan from the heat. Add the butter sauce and set aside.

Heat a barbecue or chargrill pan to hot. Lightly brush a little olive oil on the mackerel and grill it for 3 minutes on each side. Remove the fish and rest it for 2 minutes on a plate.

To serve, place the fish on a serving plate and spoon over the butter sauce. Garnish with the orange segments. Add a good grinding of black pepper and garnish with lots of chopped dill.

Mackerel is very rich in omega-3 fatty acids, which help regulate blood sugar levels and can help control diabetes. They also play a role in preventing heart disease, by lowering 'bad' cholesterol. Mackerel contains anti-inflammatory compounds, which help with arthritis, and coenzyme Q10, which can help get rid of cancerous agents that attach to cells. Like other oily fish, it's high in protein, to help build and repair muscle, and the vitamins A, B3, B12, D, E, folate and K, as well as minerals such as calcium, potassium, selenium and magnesium.

Cumquat Sussex pond

SERVES 4

100 g (3½ oz) unsalted butter

100 g (3½ oz) caster (superfine)
sugar

10–12 cumquats

150 g (5½ oz) thickened
(whipping) cream, to serve

PUDDING DOUGH

350 g (12½ oz/2⅓ cups)
self-raising flour

100 g (3½ oz) caster (superfine)
sugar

½ teaspoon fine salt

150 g (5½ oz) suet

1 egg, lightly whisked

iced water

'Sussex pond' is a classic British pudding usually made with a whole lemon inside, but my version is made with cumquats. This pudding was first recorded in Sussex, hence the name, and the pond is the gooey syrupy substance that forms in the centre of the pudding while steaming. It is crucial that you keep this boiling at all times, as a slight drop in temperature will cause your pudding to sink. Also, be very quick when you are turning it out, so the 'pond' will stay contained until you cut the pastry and allow it to flood the plate. If you wish to try it with lemon, I suggest you cut the lemon into eighths to speed up the cooking time, as it can take a long time to soften a whole one.

For the pudding dough, blitz the flour, sugar, salt and suet in a food processor to form a texture like breadcrumbs. Stir the whisked egg into the flour mixture. Add a few drops of iced water and bring the dough together by hand. Tip the contents of the bowl onto a work surface and knead the dough until it's firm and smooth. Grease a 12 cm (4¾ in) pudding basin (mould) with butter.

Roll out the dough to a 5 mm (¼ in) thickness and line the basin. Re-roll the remaining pastry and cut a lid large enough to fit across the top of the basin, and be crimped to seal.

For the cumquats, cream the butter and sugar using an electric mixer.

Prick the cumquats all over and mix them in a bowl with the creamed butter and sugar. Pile the mixture high in the pastry-lined basin as it will shrink during cooking. Place the dough lid on top and crimp the edges to seal the pastry. Cover with a buttered piece of baking paper and then some aluminium foil, and tie with string around the basin to secure. Cover again with foil.

Place the basin in a large saucepan, sitting on a trivet. Fill the pan with boiling water to reach two-thirds of the way up the side of the basin. Place the lid on the pan and steam for 2½–3 hours, with the water boiling constantly.

Unmould the pudding straight from the steamer onto a serving plate while it's piping hot, or it will sink. Spoon it into bowls and serve with cream.

Cumquats are rich in a variety of antioxidant, anti-inflammatory and antimicrobial essential oils. They're also full of vitamin C, which performs many essential biological roles, such as collagen production and wound healing; it's also a powerful antiviral. Such is the power of vitamin C that it can help prevent conditions such as neurodegenerative diseases, arthritis and even diabetes, by removing oxidant free radicals from the body.

166 Bottled pears

MAKES 12 PEARS

12 ripe pears, peeled and cored
(or halved if large)
2 kg (4 lb 6 oz) caster
(superfine) sugar
2 litres (68 fl oz/8 cups) warm
water
1 teaspoon citric acid

There is much to be said for bottled fruit. The Europeans hold them in high esteem and usually only the finest fruit is kept for this purpose, presented in syrup set in stunning tall jars. When fruit is out of season, this is as close as it gets to eating fruit that still tastes its very best. Any orchard fruit works well, and you can adjust the syrup according to your palate. For a slightly sweeter version, use 60 per cent sugar to 40 per cent water. Or, for a more natural-flavoured syrup, use 40 per cent sugar and 60 per cent water. Syrup choice also depends on the fruit. I find sharper fruit, such as plums and quince, work well in the heavier 60/40 sugar–water syrup while, in this recipe for pears (as well as apples, peaches and nectarines) the standard, medium 50/50 syrup works nicely.

Pack the pears into a 3 litre (101 fl oz/12 cup) capacity sterilised jar.

Combine the sugar, warm water and citric acid in a bowl and stir until the sugar dissolves. Pour the liquid over the pears until they are fully submerged. Secure the jar with a lid, but not too tightly.

Place the jar in a large stockpot with enough water to come three-quarters of the way up the jar and bring the pot to the boil over high heat. Reduce the heat to medium and boil gently for 1 hour. Remove the jar from the pan and immediately secure the lid tightly – using a tea towel (dish towel) to help (as it's hot) – to form a vacuum. Leave to cool.

Once cool, tap the lid to see if it clicks. This means that the lid has been sucked down by the vacuum and it makes the clicking sound as the metal changes direction. The lid will now look slightly concave instead of convex. If not, give it another 15 minutes in a pot of rapidly boiling water. Unopened, the pears will keep for up to 1 year in the pantry. Once open, your pears will keep for up to 1 month in the refrigerator.

Pears are among the least allergenic of all fruits; reactions to them are rare. They are full of the antioxidant vitamins A and C (to protect the body), and minerals such as copper, potassium, manganese and magnesium, which may help stabilise blood pressure. Pears are also a good source of insoluble fibre, which acts as a mild laxative. It's believed it could help protect against cancer-causing toxins by binding to them in the colon.

168 Mont Blanc

SERVES 4

4 meringues (see page 61)
  10 cm (4 in) in diameter
1 quantity Chantilly cream
  (page 245)
4 chestnuts in syrup (from a jar)

CHESTNUT PURÉE

400 g (14 oz) chestnuts
½ vanilla bean, seeds scraped
500 ml (17 fl oz/2 cups)
  full-cream (whole) milk
2 tablespoons icing
  (confectioners') sugar, sifted

Traditionally this dessert is supposed to resemble the famous snow-capped peak of Mont Blanc. However, I always find it a little difficult to eat on a plate and it doesn't look appealing, so I decided to serve it in a glass. You can stack the layers in whichever order you wish. This is a dessert you can prepare easily in advance. See Pavlova with raspberries in vinegar (page 61) for the meringue recipe.

Preheat the oven to 160°C (320°F).

For the chestnut purée, shell the chestnuts by cutting across them, through the skin, to expose the flesh. Bake them for 30 minutes until the skin hardens and peels off the chestnut flesh. Place the flesh in a saucepan with the vanilla seeds and bean and the milk. Simmer over medium–low heat until very soft. Pass through a fine-mesh sieve for a very smooth texture. Fold through the icing sugar to give a glossy sheen.

Crumble a meringue into each of the four serving glasses. Top with chestnut purée, followed by chantilly cream and then a chestnut in syrup.

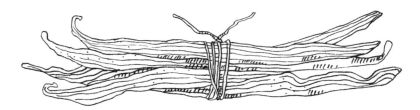

Chestnuts, unlike other nuts, are high in a starch similar to that found in sweet potato and corn. A good source of dietary fibre, which helps lower cholesterol, they're also rich in immune-boosting vitamin C and folates, which help create new cells in the body. They also contain vitamin B3 for converting food into energy, and are a source of the monounsaturated fatty acid that helps lower 'bad' cholesterol. And they contain potassium, useful in helping to lower blood pressure.

Alastair's caramelised oranges with toasted almonds

SERVES 4

40 g (1½ oz) activated almonds
  (see page 237)
4 oranges, peeled and sliced
230 g (8 oz/1 cup) caster sugar
crème fraîche or plain yoghurt,
  to serve

When we were living in London, every Sunday we were invited to lunch by my father-in-law, Alastair. It was often the highlight of my week, especially when we had small kids, as Alastair is a phenomenal cook. It was such a pleasure to be the one reading the Sunday papers instead of standing over the stove. This recipe of his was and always will be a favourite – simple but just divine. It works well with both blood oranges and regular oranges (I like Seville). For the nuts I like toasted almonds, but you can use pistachio nuts or activated walnuts.

Preheat the oven to 170°C (340°F). Put the nuts on a baking tray and roast them in the oven for 5 minutes until they are light golden brown. Remove them from the oven and allow to cool.

Top and tail the oranges. Sit them on a work surface and, using a sharp paring knife, peel them lengthways down the fruit, so the knife removes the skin and pith of the orange. Slice the oranges into approximately 1 cm (½ in) thick rounds – not too thin or they will break. While you are slicing, be certain to reserve the juice that falls from the oranges, as you will use that in the caramel.

Put 2 tablespoons of water and the sugar in a large, heavy-based pan over high heat. Cook to caramelise the sugar, swirling the pan occasionally, but not stirring (as this will make the mixture crystallise).

Continue swirling the pan until the sugar starts to become crimson – the centre of your swirling vortex will be a deep caramel and the edges will be lighter. Make sure to pull the pan off the stove just before the caramel is about to burn. Add 2 tablespoons of the juice from the oranges and swirl the pan until the caramel absorbs the juice and stops the cooking. Allow the caramel to cool to a thick syrup. If it starts to firm up, add a little more juice. It needs to be the consistency of molasses.

Arrange the sliced oranges on a platter in a single layer. Spoon over the caramel syrup and scatter with the almonds. Serve in bowls with crème fraîche or yoghurt.

Oranges are a well-known source of immune-boosting vitamin C, as well as fibre and pectin. Pectin is a soluble fibre that can help lower cholesterol and slow the rate of sugar absorption. Oranges contain vitamin A for vision, B for converting food into energy, and minerals such as potassium and calcium, which build and protect bones, help with muscle contraction and relaxation, blood clotting and maintaining healthy blood pressure.

170

Lemon drizzle cake

SERVES 8

4 eggs

90 ml (3 fl oz) vegetable oil

230 g (8 oz/1 cup) caster (superfine) sugar

130 ml (4½ fl oz) thickened (whipping) cream

2 lemons, zested and juiced

230 g (8 oz) self-raising flour

2 teaspoons baking powder

LEMON ICING

150 g (5½ oz) icing (confectioners') sugar

1½ tablespoons lemon juice

I like to use oil in most cake recipes to replace some or all of the butter or lard, especially when I'm baking at home, as I find the cake will keep for longer. (Although with three young boys around, trying to get the cake to 'keep' isn't really an issue.) The oil also ensures a lovely moist texture to the crumb of the cake.

Preheat the oven to 190°C (375°F). Grease and line a 20 x 28 cm (8 x 11 in) loaf (bar) tin with baking paper.

In a large mixing bowl, either using a wooden spoon or an electric mixer, beat all the ingredients, except the flour and baking powder, until well combined and slightly pale. Fold through the sifted flour and baking powder.

Spoon the mixture into the prepared tin and bake for about 45 minutes or until the cake springs back when pressed gently on top. Turn the cake out onto a wire rack to cool.

For the lemon icing, sift the icing sugar into a bowl and add two-thirds of the juice, mixing to form a paste. Add as much more juice as you need to make a runny icing. Drizzle the icing over the cooled cake and serve.

MEDICINAL

EAR, NOSE &
THROAT

· BENEFIT ·

Lemons are notably high in vitamin C, which boosts the immune system and helps produce collagen, a connective tissue that knits together wounds and supports blood vessel walls. Lemon's flu- and cold-fighting abilities are well documented. They also contain good levels of vitamin A, essential for healthy eyesight, and B complex vitamins for the conversion of food into energy. They're also a good source of potassium to help balance body fluids, maintain a steady heartbeat and lower blood pressure.

172

Beetroot kvass

**MAKES 3 LITRES
(101 FL OZ/12 CUPS)**

1.25 kg (2 lb 12 oz) beetroot
  (beets)
2½ teaspoons Himalayan salt

This would have to be the easiest probiotic drink I know of, or certainly the most easily accessible. It's a lacto-fermented drink, which is believed to be cleansing for the blood. It's delicious served ice-cold from the refrigerator. The chunks of beetroot (beet) you have strained from the fermentation are also delicious served in salads, both grated and sliced. Try it grated through the Beetroot, quinoa, rhubarb and ponzu recipe on page 134.

Wash the beetroot and remove the dirt but don't peel them, as we want to embrace the friendly bacteria here. Roughly dice the beetroot into 3 cm (1¼ in) chunks or slices, being sure not to grate them or cut them too small, as the beetroot will ferment too fast and become alcoholic instead of lactic, which will spoil your drink.

Place the beetroot and salt in a 5 litre (169 fl oz/20 cup) glass jar and shake. Allow to sit at room temperature for 2 hours to draw the juices from the beetroot, which will dissolve the salt. Add 3.5 litres (118 fl oz/14 cups) water and shake the jar around really well to help dissolve the last of the salt. Make sure the lid is tight and keep in a place at a stable room temperature, agitating daily. Ferment for 1–2 weeks.

Give the jar a shake. If you notice bubbles rising gently up the glass, it's probably ready. If there are no bubbles it will need longer to ferment. Once bubbles are apparent, open the lid and you will hear a hiss from the escaping carbon dioxide and it will also start to fizz. Strain the kvass through a fine-mesh sieve into bottles and chill. It's best drunk ice-cold in a small glass. But remember that it's a probiotic and too much may give you the runs!

Beetroot (beet) is a great liver cleanser. It thins bile, which can ease the movement of gallstones out of the liver. Fermentation increases the already significant health benefits of beetroot by creating a greater bio-availability of easily absorbed nutrients. This recipe boosts the healthy bacteria in the gut, some benefits of which are:

- Strengthening the immune system and helping manage eczema
- Preventing and treating urinary tract infections
- Improving digestive function
- Helping inflammatory bowel conditions, such as irritable bowel syndrome.

Ginger beer

MAKES 1 LITRE (34 FL OZ/4 CUPS)

2 pinches salt

440 g (15½/2 cups) sugar

four 5 cm (2 in) pieces fresh ginger, peeled

250 ml (8½ fl oz/1 cup) freshly squeezed lemon juice

500 ml (17 fl oz/2 cups) ginger beer bug liquid (see method)

GINGER BEER PLANT

750 ml (25½ fl oz/3 cups) water

2 teaspoons ground ginger

2 teaspoons grated fresh ginger

2 tablespoons caster (superfine) sugar

1 teaspoon grated lemon zest

75 ml (2½ fl oz) lemon juice

75 g (2¾ oz) raisins (organic on the vine)

GINGER PLANT FOOD

60 g (2 oz) ground ginger

180 g (6½ oz) caster (superfine) sugar

MEDICINAL · GUT · BENEFIT

Ginger has anti-inflamatory, carminative and antimicrobial properties, and is very effective against *E. coli*-induced diarrhoea.

It's fun to make your own ginger beer, but you need to understand the terminology. First, 'ginger beer plant' refers to the solids that remain when you strain the fermentation. You can keep this and use it each time you make ginger beer. It's a living thing and full of healthy bacteria. Second, the liquid you squeeze out when you strain the ginger beer plant is called the 'ginger beer bug liquid', which is the natural fermented liquid that will make your ginger beer fizzy. You need to make the ginger beer plant first in order to make the ginger beer bug liquid. Every time you make ginger beer, you need to discard half the ginger beer plant. (I always try to give it to a friend, as it's already developed for them to start the recipe immediately from day four.) The beauty of this recipe is that the more times you make it, the stronger the ginger beer plant and ginger beer bug liquid become, and the less time you need to ferment your ginger beer. This is due to the ginger beer plant increasing its bacteria count. Try playing with the sugar content or even use different sweeteners to change the flavours. (I try to make sure my children don't eat too much sugar, so this recipe is conservative on the sugar front.)

For the ginger beer plant, mix all the ingredients in a bowl and cover with muslin (cheesecloth). Allow to ferment in a dark place at room temperature for 3 days.

On the fourth day, begin the feeding stage of the ginger beer plant. Add an eleventh of the ground ginger and an eleventh of the sugar from your ginger plant food. Stir vigorously to dissolve the sugar. Cover with muslin and leave in a dark place at room temperature for 24 hours. Repeat this feeding regime for the next 10 days.

On the eleventh day, strain the ginger beer plant through muslin and squeeze out the juice. This juice is the ginger beer bug liquid.

Place half of the ginger beer plant back in a bowl and start the recipe again from the day-four feeding stage. Discard the other half.

To make the ginger beer, in a large saucepan, bring 2 litres (68 fl oz/8 cups) water, the salt and sugar to the boil. Remove from the heat and add the fresh ginger. Allow to cool to room temperature. Add the fresh lemon juice and 500 ml (17 fl oz/2 cups) of the ginger beer bug liquid that you strained from the ginger beer plant and mix very well. Strain into flip-top bottles and leave sealed in a dark place at room temperature for 1 week. After a week, turn the bottles upside down and then the right way up again to see if there are any bubbles rising. If there are, then the ginger beer is carbonated and ready to go. If not, leave the bottles out, and test them every day until you see bubbles. Store in the refrigerator. The ginger beer will last at least a month until opened and will keep its fizz for about a day once opened. Serve chilled.

ASPARAGUS, PEAS AND CHAMOMILE
WITH RICOTTA *page 190*

Peas and mint on toast with a poached egg
Blueberry, celery and pecan salad with
lemon myrtle and labne
MAPLE-TOASTED BUCKWHEAT, NUTS AND SEEDS
WITH SMASHED BANANA AND ALMOND MILK
BAKED EGGS WITH PIPERADE AND SORREL
— CABBAGE, BREAD AND CHEESE SOUP—
CHILLED AVOCADO, TURMERIC AND CASHEW NUT SOUP
Asparagus, peas and chamomile with ricotta
Green beans, tangelo and nduja
CHOPPED SALAD OF ICEBERG, CORN AND JALAPEÑO
— SPRING TABOULEH —
Poached asparagus
Artichoke vinaigrette
STEAMED CHOKO WITH SORREL BUTTER
Cumin-scented carrots
GRILLED SPATCHCOCK MARINATED IN CRÈME FRAÎCHE

SPRING
176-229

Pot-roasted shoulder of lamb cooked in buttermilk
with roast pears and potatoes
STUFFED SPRING CABBAGE WITH PORK AND CHESTNUTS
Chargrilled sardines, nasturtiums,
oregano and chilli
BAKED WHOLE LEATHER JACKETS, MARJORAM,
CAPERS AND LEMON
Yabbies poached in chicken stock with
broad beans and basil
— STRAWBERRY SHORTCAKE —
LAVENDER SABLE BISCUITS
Mandarin and rosemary syllabub
Parsnip and ginger cake
PINEAPPLE TARTS
PINK GRAPEFRUIT BICICLETTA
— WHEY LEMONADE —

MEDICINAL
MUSCLES,
BONES & JOINTS
BENEFIT

WATERCRESS

MEDICINAL
GUT, HEART,
SKIN
BENEFIT

ONION

MEDICINAL
EAR, NOSE &
THROAT
BENEFIT

TURMERIC

MEDICINAL · GUT, HEART · BENEFIT

HONEY

Spring brings the hope of warmer weather to come. It signals delicious, snappy green vegetables like peas, beans, asparagus, snow peas and artichokes and it also brings ... allergies. Pollens and other irritants can wreak havoc at this time of year and I find the best plan of attack is to charge my cooking up with as much seasonal goodness as I can, reaping the benefits of nature's antihistamines.

180

Peas and mint on toast with a poached egg

SERVES 4

1 tablespoon extra-virgin olive oil

2 anchovies, very finely chopped

175 g (6 oz) French tinned peas, liquid reserved (see Note)

3 mint sprigs, small leaves picked and chopped

4 slices sourdough toast

POACHED EGGS

1 teaspoon organic, unfiltered apple-cider vinegar

4 eggs

Good-quality anchovies add a meaty, salty flavour and enhance the sweetness of the peas, giving the egg something intense to cling to. If you want to give this dish some bling, serve it with a little Basil oil (page 233) and a poached egg. If you want to luxe it up even more, treat yourself with a fried duck egg in place of a poached chicken egg.

In a heavy-based saucepan over medium heat, warm a drizzle of olive oil and cook the anchovies slowly so they melt. Tip the juice from the tin of peas into the pan first, and reduce it to a glaze, then add the peas and stir. Take the pan off the heat and add the mint. You can now serve it as is on sourdough toast, or you could add poached eggs.

To poach the eggs, bring a tall, deep saucepan with 1 litre (34 fl oz/4 cups) water to the boil and add the vinegar and 2 teaspoons salt. Taste to check whether the water is slightly acidic. Crack the eggs into individual small cups.

Reduce the heat to a gentle boil, so it is simmering, and stir in one direction to form a vortex of water. Tip the eggs in, one at a time, and allow them to slowly circle down to the bottom of the pan – I find the deeper the pan, the nicer the shape, as the egg forms a lovely tail and looks like a ghost.

The eggs will float to the top when they are ready, after about 2 minutes. They should feel like a balloon – soft with a slight spring. Remove them from the pan and transfer them to paper towel to drain, then place the eggs on your toast.

Note: If you can't find beautiful French tinned peas for this recipe, I suggest you look for young fresh spring peas. Simmer them in a small amount of water – just enough to cover the peas – and, by the time the water is reduced, your peas will be cooked. Add a knob of butter, swirl it around in the pan and this will thicken around the peas. Then squash the peas with the back of a fork.

Peas are a rich cocktail of folic acid (important in cell creation in the early stages of pregnancy), vitamins A (for eye health), B (for converting food to energy), C (which boosts the immune system) and K (which helps with blood clotting). Mint contains a whole pile of essential oils – menthol, alpha-pinene, linalool and limonen – which, as well as having calming, anti-inflammatory and antimicrobial properties, can help with weight loss.

Blueberry, celery and pecan salad with lemon myrtle and labne

SERVES 4

1 handful lemon myrtle leaves

500 ml (17 fl oz/2 cups) boiling water

1 young celery stalk, or a thin stalk from the middle of a bunch of celery

250 g (9 oz) blueberries

50 g (1¾ oz/½ cup) activated pecans (see page 237), sliced

2 teaspoons honey

LABNE

375 g (13 oz) pot-set yoghurt

I'm a big fan of breakfast salads. I like to eat light in the morning as I'm always quite busy and don't want to feel lethargic while trying to digest a heavy breakfast. If you don't have time to make labne or find it, yoghurt is a good substitute. Try to find strained yoghurt or a high-quality, pot-set yoghurt with no sugar added. If you do make labne, save the whey for the Whey lemonade on page 229.

To make the labne, line a strainer or fine colander with two layers of muslin (cheesecloth) and spoon in the yoghurt. Suspend the lined strainer over a large bowl in the refrigerator overnight to strain the whey. (The labne is the solids left in the muslin.)

Bruise the lemon myrtle leaves by holding them in your hand and clenching your fist a few times. Place them in a teapot and pour over the boiling water. Allow to steep for 30 minutes until cooled to room temperature. Strain and discard the leaves.

Shave the celery very thinly into serving bowls. Add the blueberries and pecans and mix to combine. Pour the tea into the bowls over the blueberry mix and place a nice dollop of labne on top. Drizzle with the honey and serve.

MEDICINAL
HEART
BENEFIT

Anthocyanidins are a type of antioxidant responsible for the red, blue and purple pigmentation we see in various fruits and vegetables such as blueberries. Anticarcinogenic, they also help to maintain good heart health. Blueberries also contain a substance called chlorogenic acid, which helps slow down fat absorption and speeds up the metabolism, which is handy for weight loss. Lemon myrtle leaves are rich in an essential oil called citral; it's antifungal, high in antioxidants and can provide an immune boost, plus help with muscle cramps and rheumatism.

182

Maple-toasted buckwheat, nuts and seeds with smashed banana and almond milk

SERVES 4

750 g (1 lb 11 oz) activated
  buckwheat kernels
  (see page 237)
125 ml (4 fl oz/½ cup) maple
  syrup
75 ml (2½ fl oz) grapeseed oil
250 g (9 oz) activated almonds
  (see page 237)
150 g (5½ oz) activated
  pistachio nuts (see page 237)
50 g (1¾ oz) ground cinnamon
125 g (4½ oz) linseeds (flax
  seeds)
125 g (4½ oz) pepitas (pumpkin
  seeds)
65 g (2¼ oz) sesame seeds
chopped dried fruits of your
  choice (see Note)
2 bananas, smashed with a fork,
  to serve
almond milk (see page 238),
  to serve

This recipe is made up of simple ingredients, so they all need to be as good as possible. Always look for organic varieties and for nuts and seeds that are whole and have been graded to the very highest standard. Avoid bags with broken nuts and crushed seeds. All nuts in this book are activated, so follow the recipe on page 237 or buy them activated.

Preheat the oven to 130°C (265°F).

Combine all the ingredients, except the dried fruit, bananas and milk, in a large bowl and stir well to combine. Spread on a baking tray and toast in the oven for 45 minutes to an hour until crisp and lightly golden. Remove from the oven and allow to cool before breaking the muesli (granola) up and transferring it to an airtight container.

To serve, dollop the smashed banana in the bottom of your bowl and scatter over the muesli as though it's a topping. Serve the chilled nut milk on the side to add your desired amount. I always like to mix it all together in the bowl so it turns into a thick, fruity muesli.

Note: *I like to chop a mixture of dried fruits to mix in with the muesli on the day, as sometimes if you don't eat muesli quickly enough and it has dried fruits stored in it, it goes soft. Try chopped fig, date and apricot or, for the warmer months, dried tropical fruits, such as mango, pineapple and peach. I add 1 tablespoon of chopped fruit per cup of muesli.*

Buckwheat contains amino acids, which are the basis of protein and vital for building muscle tissue and muscle strength. It's also high in rutin, a flavonoid that helps thin the blood and improve circulation. The seeds provide omega-3 fats, zinc to support the immune system and magnesium for regulating blood pressure. Nut milks, which are lactose-, cholesterol- and saturated-fat-free, contain vitamin E (good for the skin) and vitamin B for muscle growth.

184

Baked eggs with piperade and sorrel

SERVES 4

200 g (7 oz) brown onions,
   thinly sliced

1 tablespoon salted capers,
   rinsed and drained well

50 g (1¾ oz) garlic cloves, peeled
   and thinly sliced

200 ml (7 fl oz) extra-virgin
   olive oil

200 g (7 oz) red capsicums (bell
   peppers), cut into strips

200 g (7 oz) green capsicums
   (bell peppers), cut into strips

200 g (7 oz) yellow capsicums
   (bell peppers), cut into strips

100 ml (3½ fl oz) white wine

200 g (7 oz) cherry tomatoes

1 bunch basil, leaves torn

1 bunch flat-leaf (Italian)
   parsley, leaves chopped

red-wine vinegar or balsamic
   vinegar, if needed

1 large handful sorrel

4 eggs

toast, to serve

This is a traditional Basque dish made with lots of different capsicums (bell peppers). It's fantastic not just with eggs for breakfast, but also as a side for any meat or fish dish. A nice twist is to add a couple of anchovies to the piperade before it goes in the oven, or serve it with a couple of rashers (slices) of streaky bacon. If you can't find sorrel, use baby English spinach and add a squeeze of lemon juice when serving, to replicate the sharp flavour of sorrel.

In a large saucepan over medium heat, sweat the onion, capers and garlic in the oil until translucent. Add the capsicums and wine and cook down slowly for 5 minutes to a glaze. Add the tomatoes and stew slowly over a low heat for 20–30 minutes to form a thick sauce. Add the herbs and remove the pan from the heat. Season with salt and freshly ground black pepper. If you find the piperade a little sweet, you can acidulate it with red-wine vinegar or balsamic vinegar.

Preheat the oven to 150°C (300°F).

Transfer the piperade to a large, heavy-based ovenproof frying pan over medium heat – or divide it between four smaller frying pans for individual portions – and fold through the sorrel. Crack in the eggs and bake until the white is cooked but the yolk is lovely and runny. Serve with some toast.

Capsicums (bell peppers) have plenty of vitamin C antioxidants; these boost the immune system and help neutralise free radicals. They also contain vitamin A, which keeps skin healthy, and potassium, which balances body fluids and helps maintain low blood pressure. Sorrel is rich in iron, essential for ferrying oxygen around the body and keeping the extremities replenished and healthy. Eggs have more health benefits than I can possibly fit on a page: vitamin B2 to help convert food into energy, vitamin B12 for producing red blood cells, vitamin A for good eyesight, and vitamin E for preventing tissue and cellular damage.

186

Cabbage, bread and cheese soup

SERVES 4

1 savoy cabbage
1 brown onion, thinly sliced
¼ bunch thyme, leaves chopped
30 g (1 oz) duck fat or extra-
   virgin olive oil
125 ml (4 fl oz/½ cup) white
   wine (riesling)
1 loaf sourdough bread, cut into
   1 cm (½ in) slices
300 g (10½ oz) gruyère, grated
1 bunch savory
1.8 litres (61 fl oz) hot chicken
   stock
pinch cayenne pepper

At the beginning of spring there is still a bite in the air, which calls for a lovely hearty soup. This recipe works well with any white or green cabbage and can be made with vegetable stock instead of chicken, and oil or butter instead of duck fat, if you wish to make it vegetarian. Savory is a special herb that can be hard to find. It looks like tarragon but it has a little fire in it, which gives things a nice kick. If you can't find it, use tarragon or chopped parsley. The bread is obviously a very important part of the soup, so do your best to source the very best you can find. The soup will only work using sourdough, as any lighter-textured bread will fall to pieces and make the soup turn to a mush. This soup is delicious with a glass of riesling, hence my suggestion to use the same wine to cook with.

Preheat the oven to 180°C (350°F).

Separate the cabbage leaves and remove the ribs from the thin leaves. Shred the ribs and keep them separate. Shred all of the leaves.

In a large heavy-based ovenproof saucepan over medium heat, sweat the onion and thyme in the duck fat until translucent. Add the shredded cabbage ribs and sauté for 2 minutes. Add the wine and cook for another 2 minutes or until the wine has reduced and the ribs are soft. Add the shredded leaves and cook until wilted. Transfer from the saucepan into a bowl.

Cover the base of the saucepan with the slices of bread – I leave the crust on as I like the texture and flavour. Spoon over half the cabbage mixture, scatter with one-third of the cheese, sprinkle with some savory leaves and season with a little salt and freshly ground black pepper. Repeat the same layers again of bread, cabbage, cheese, savory, salt and pepper. Finish with a layer of bread slices.

In a separate saucepan, bring the hot chicken stock to the boil and slowly ladle three-quarters of it over the layered bread and cabbage. Leave for 15 minutes to rest, so the bread absorbs the stock. Slowly pour the rest of the hot stock on top, sprinkle the top with cheese and bake for 15 minutes, until the cheese blisters and the soup is hot. Remove the pan from the oven and give it a little sprinkling of cayenne pepper.

Place the pan in the middle of the table for everyone to serve themselves.

MEDICINAL

MUSCLES,
BONES & JOINTS

BENEFIT

Cabbage is incredibly good for us. It's full of vitamin C, essential for boosting the immune system, vitamin K to activate proteins, plus calcium, which is needed for blood clotting and strong bones. It also contains potassium, which helps balance fluids in the body and helps maintain steady muscle contractions and nerve impulses, such as the heartbeat. In common with all brassicas, cabbage is rich in sulphur, essential for proper cardiovascular function, among other things. Stock (bone broth) contains minerals, gelatine and a whole suite of amino acids, which can help with everything from boosting mental performance to sealing the lining of the gut.

Chilled avocado, turmeric and cashew nut soup

SERVES 4

2 avocados
600 ml (20½ fl oz) cashew
   nut milk (see page 238)
   or rice milk
1 teaspoon salt
½ lemon, juiced
1 teaspoon ground turmeric
¼ teaspoon ground cinnamon
freshly grated nutmeg
2 teaspoons pumpkin seed oil

This refreshing soup works well for breakfast to kick start your day, or as a light lunch. There are a number of varieties of avocados available in spring and they get better towards the end of the season. There is no right type to use for this soup, as they are all as good as each other. The only prerequisite is that the avocados must be ripe with a sweet flavour. Pumpkin seed oil can be found in most health food or good food stores. If you can't find it, try edible argan oil (see Note, page 126) or a simple drizzle of very good-quality extra-virgin olive oil. This recipe will also work well with any kind of nut milk, or you can use full-cream (whole) milk.

Pulse all the ingredients together in a blender or food processor and serve the soup chilled.

MEDICINAL · HEART, SKIN · BENEFIT

Avocado is high in monounsaturated fatty acids, as well as the omega-6 polyunsaturated fatty acid linoleic acid. A diet rich in these acids can help lower LDL, otherwise known as 'bad' cholesterol, and increase HDL, or 'good' cholesterol, helpful in preventing coronary artery disease. Avocados also contain vitamins A, K, E (great for skin) and B (for muscle growth). Cashew nuts contain monounsaturated fatty acids too, plus important micronutrients and minerals like manganese, potassium, copper, iron, magnesium, zinc and selenium. Turmeric root contains curcumin, a potent compound that not only imparts a deep orange colour, but can exhibit anti-tumour, antioxidant, anti-arthritic and anti-inflammatory attributes. Turmeric's phytonutrient profile is off the charts and its total antioxidant strength is one of the highest of all the herbs and spices.

190

Asparagus, peas and chamomile with ricotta

SERVES 4

20 asparagus spears
    (2–3 bunches), trimmed
extra-virgin olive oil
100 g (3½ oz) podded peas,
    or 200 g (7 oz) unpodded
2 handfuls snow pea
    (mangetout) tendrils
chamomile flowers and
    chamomile greens, to serve
    (optional)
200 g (7 oz) baked ricotta, or
    salted ricotta or regular ricotta

CHAMOMILE DRESSING

190 ml (6½ fl oz) grapeseed oil
1½ tablespoons loose-leaf
    chamomile tea
2 teaspoons honey
1 small lemon, juiced

Asparagus and peas are the most recognisable spring ingredients. You will find many different-shaped asparagus during this season, which give you great options. You can use the sprue (skinny) asparagus to eat raw, and use the larger, thicker ones to grill and blanch. Baked ricotta is available from most good delicatessens. If you can't find it, then try salted ricotta, which is a firm cheese that you can shave thinly over the top of the salad. Or you can just use plain ricotta. If you can't find chamomile greens or flowers, try using dandelion leaves, as they taste very similar. The chamomile flowers look wonderful and are delicious to eat, but are not essential to use, as enough flavour comes from the dry chamomile you use in the dressing.

Preheat the oven to 230°C (445°F).

For the chamomile dressing, warm the oil, tea and honey in a small saucepan to 60°C (140°F), using a thermometer to check the temperature. Transfer the mixture to a blender and blitz for 1 minute. Strain through a sieve lined with muslin (cheesecloth) into a bowl. Add the lemon juice for acidity and season to taste with salt and freshly ground black pepper.

For the salad, heat a chargrill pan over high heat. Drizzle one-third of the asparagus with olive oil and cook until tender and beginning to blister, 3–4 minutes. Set aside in a large bowl.

Blanch the peas and another third of the asparagus in a saucepan of boiling water until tender and bright green, 2 minutes. Drain, refresh, drain again and combine with the grilled asparagus.

Using a mandoline, thinly slice the remaining asparagus lengthways into the bowl. Add the snow pea tendrils, chamomile flowers and chamomile greens, and season to taste with salt and pepper. Crumble the ricotta over the salad and drizzle with the chamomile dressing.

Asparagus contain vitamins A, B complex, C and E, all anti-inflammatory. These help the body develop resistance to infectious agents, so they're great for immunity. It also contains vitamin K, which can help limit neuronal damage in the brain, useful with diseases like Alzheimer's. It also has high amounts of dietary fibre, which can decrease 'bad' (LDL) cholesterol levels. Chamomile is also an anti-inflammatory and is often used as a relaxing sleep aid, and as a treatment for fevers, colds and stomach ailments.

Green beans, tangelo and nduja

SERVES 4

1 heaped tablespoon nduja (see recipe introduction)

½ lemon, juiced

1 teaspoon red-wine vinegar

100 ml (3½ fl oz) extra-virgin olive oil

600 g (1 lb 5 oz) green beans, blanched and refreshed in iced water

2 tangelos, peeled and sliced

1 bunch mint, leaves picked

½ bunch spring onions (scallions), thinly sliced

50 g (1¾ oz) activated almonds (see page 237)

This salad is fantastic at the beginning of spring when the green beans are nice and young and the citrus is still in good shape. It's the perfect kind of salad to have on a cooler day as the spice of the nduja and the sweetness of the citrus are lovely and warming. Nduja is a cured pork sausage from southern Italy. It comes in the form of a paste and packs a real punch. If you like it milder or hotter, adjust the amount. Good Italian butchers will stock it. However, if you can't find it, buy some chorizo, remove the skin and process the meat in a blender to form a sausage paste and continue with the recipe. You can try other beans or peas, such as snow peas (mangetout), sugar-snaps, flat beans or roman beans. You can also use any sweet citrus in place of tangelo, such as tangerine, mandarin or orange.

In a frying pan over medium heat, cook the nduja for 2 minutes so it releases its lovely red oil and aroma.

Remove the pan from the heat and allow the nduja to cool for 2 minutes. Add the lemon juice and vinegar and mix well. Whisk in the olive oil to form a dressing (there's no need for salt as the nduja is cured in salt).

Put all the remaining ingredients in a bowl, pour over the dressing and mix to combine. Season with a pinch of salt if needed.

Note: *If you are vegetarian, you can omit the nduja and instead use a pinch or so of Spanish smoked paprika. It's best to mix the paprika, lemon juice and oil in a jar and give it a good shake before using.*

Citrus fruits are a rich source of vitamin C, which is antiviral and anticarcinogenic and can help prevent neurodegenerative diseases, arthritis, colds and fevers. The chilli in the nduja also contains vitamin C, as well as iron, which helps boost the haemoglobin in red blood cells as they carry oxygen through the body. If the nduja is of high quality, you may also receive valuable probiotic benefits from fermentation, which is the traditional process used to make it. Beans contain plenty of vitamin A for good vision, plus vitamin C to boost the immune system, folates for healthy cell creation and dietary fibre to help in lowering blood cholesterol and, of course, to keep the digestive system regular.

Chopped salad of iceberg, corn and jalapeño

SERVES 4

2 corn cobs

4 slices sourdough bread, cut into 1 cm (½ in) croutons

1 tablespoon extra-virgin olive oil

½ iceberg lettuce, cut into chunks

2 spring onions (scallions), chopped

1 Lebanese (short) cucumber, skin on, cut into dice the same size as the corn kernels

8 cherry tomatoes, halved

¼ bunch mint, leaves picked and torn

1 jalapeño, thinly sliced into rounds

¼ bunch coriander (cilantro), leaves picked and torn

½ green capsicum (bell pepper), cut into dice the same size as the corn kernels

½ red capsicum (bell pepper), cut into dice the same size as the corn kernels

2 sheets nori, toasted (flash them under a grill/broiler, or heat over a gas burner, for a second until they wrinkle)

DRESSING

175 ml (6 fl oz) buttermilk

15 g (½ oz) wholegrain mustard

1 tablespoon mayonnaise

1 spring onion (scallion), thinly sliced

1 pinch togarashi (Japanese seasoning – see Note)

The great thing about a chopped salad is that it's all meant to be eaten with a fork. Therefore, the best thing to do is to cut all the ingredients the same size. If you can't barbecue your corn, you can roast it in a hot oven to scald the kernels or just use it boiled. I grill it on the barbecue because I like a smoky flavour in the salad.

Preheat the oven to 180°C (350°F).

For the dressing, whisk all the ingredients together – the mixture should coat the back of a spoon. Season with salt and freshly ground black pepper.

In a large saucepan, blanch the corn cobs in boiling water for 2 minutes then remove and set aside.

Heat a barbecue or a chargrill pan to hot and cook the corn until it's blistered and a little charred on the outside. Remove from the heat and allow the corn to cool for 10 minutes. Run a knife down the length of the cob from top to bottom, shaving the kernels off the cob in one movement to keep them in clusters. Place them in a bowl and set aside.

Toss the croutons in olive oil and bake them on a tray in the oven for about 5–10 minutes, until golden and crisp. Season with a pinch of salt and allow to cool on some paper towel.

To serve, toss all the ingredients, except the nori, gently in a large bowl with the dressing. When everything is coated in the dressing, scatter the salad with torn or shredded pieces of nori.

Note: *You can buy togarashi from the Asian section of most grocery stores or from Japanese supermarkets. It's a mix of chilli powder, sesame seeds, Japanese pepper and ginger.*

The vitamin A antioxidants in lettuce keep tissue and skin healthy, while beta-carotenoids can help prevent cataracts. Then there's potassium for balancing body fluids, and manganese to help metabolise amino acids, cholesterol and carbohydrates. Corn is a source of ferulic acid, often used in anti-ageing skin products. Corn also contains vitamin A and beta-carotene for good vision. Chilli has plenty of vitamin C, as well as iron to help carry oxygen throughout the body.

Spring tabouleh

SERVES 4

150 g (5½) burghul (bulgur wheat)

125 ml (4 fl oz/½ cup) extra-virgin olive oil, plus 1 tablespoon extra

1 lemon, juiced

4 heirloom tomatoes, roughly chopped

2 bunches flat-leaf (Italian) parsley, shredded

½ bunch spring onions (scallions), thinly sliced

1 bunch green asparagus, thinly shaved lengthways

155 g (5½ oz/1 cup) fresh peas, blanched

200 g (7 oz) snow peas (mangetout), roughly sliced

1 fennel bulb, shaved, fronds reserved

¼ savoy cabbage, diced

1 broccoli head, shaved

2 tablespoons sumac, plus extra for sprinkling

The recipe is called spring tabouleh, but you can take the same approach using seasonal ingredients throughout the year. I've suggested ways to cut the vegetables, but you can dice them or cut them however you wish. If you're gluten-free, use cooked quinoa instead of the burghul. Pomegranate molasses is a nice touch in the dressing to add viscosity and a tart flavour. If you spot fresh pomegranates, the seeds are also nice little jewels to scatter through the salad.

Soak the burghul in boiling water (1:1 volume ratio of water to burghul), with a pinch of salt and the extra tablespoon of olive oil. Cover and allow to cool so all the liquid is absorbed.

Whisk the lemon juice and olive oil together to make a dressing.

Toss the burghul with all the remaining ingredients in a large bowl. The burghul will absorb the dressing, so only dress the salad when you're ready to serve. The sumac is good tossed through the salad along with a little more sprinkled on top.

MEDICINAL
EAR, NOSE &
THROAT
BENEFIT

Broccoli is a super-vegetable. It's a rich source of vitamin C, a powerful natural antioxidant and an immunity booster. It's also packed with vitamin A, vital for healthy eyesight and for preventing macular degeneration of the retina. Broccoli leaves are an excellent source of vitamin A as well as carotenoids, containing three times more than the florets. Broccoli also contains vitamin K and B complex vitamins; the florets even contain some omega-3 fatty acids. Certain compounds in broccoli can help protect against some cancers. Parsley is rich in all manner of potent antioxidant nutrients, including pro-vitamin A, beta-carotene, vitamins C, E and K and folates. It also contains a volatile oil called myristin, which has been shown to inhibit tumour formation, particularly in lung tissue.

198

Poached asparagus

Asparagus are such delicate vegetables that they can be easily overcooked. Here I present two cooking methods. One is for peeling them before you eat them hot, the other is for not peeling them in preparation for eating them hot or cold in salads. The great thing about an asparagus spear is that it tells you where it needs trimming. Take a spear and bend it and it will snap where the stem is dry.

SERVES 4

2 bunches asparagus, peeled
25 g (1 oz) butter
1 tablespoon white wine
½ lemon, juiced

Option 1

Break and trim the asparagus as discussed above.

Peel the asparagus from the bottom of the spear all the way up the stem. Place the raw asparagus in a frying pan to allow them to sit flat and not bunched. Add the butter, wine, a pinch of salt and 2 tablespoons water and cover with a piece of baking paper that fits the diameter of the pan. Bring quickly to the boil and simmer fast to evaporate the liquid, leaving the baking paper on top. During this time you should be swirling the pan in a circular motion to keep the asparagus moving. After 1 minute, remove the paper and add the lemon juice. Simmer for 1 more minute so the butter forms a glaze. Eat the asparagus straight from the pan.

SERVES 4

2 bunches asparagus, unpeeled

Option 2

Break and trim the asparagus as discussed above. Tie your bunch of asparagus together with kitchen twine.

Fill a tall, heavy-based saucepan with hot water and a pinch of salt and bring it to the boil. Stand your asparagus in the hot, salty water so the water comes up three-quarters of the length of the asparagus – you want the spears to stick out at the top, so the bottom cooks through while the tops gently steam. Use jars or ramekins to help keep your asparagus upright. Cover and simmer for 1–2 minutes. Remove the asparagus and cut the string. Serve as they are or plunge them into iced water to stop them from cooking further.

Asparagus contains the anti-inflammatory vitamins A, B complex, C and E, regular consumption of which can help develop resistance against infections. Asparagus also contains an important trace mineral called chromium, which helps insulin regulate blood glucose levels. It's also rich in glutathione, a detoxifying compound that's been shown to destroy some carcinogens.

TRIMMING

SIMMERING

BOILING

200 Artichoke vinaigrette

SERVES 4

4 whole globe artichokes

1 lemon, juiced

250 ml (8½ fl oz/1 cup) white wine

1 litre (34 fl oz/4 cups) water

60 ml (2 fl oz/¼ cup) extra-virgin olive oil

1 teaspoon white peppercorns

1 bay leaf

2 stems flat-leaf (Italian) parsley, stalks and leaves

½ leek

2 thyme sprigs

Walnut vinaigrette (page 234)

Globe artichokes are a type of thistle. They're traditionally peeled, trimmed and cooked in a court bouillon until tender. The artichokes can be served warm or cold on a plate with the walnut vinaigrette on the side. The way to eat them is to peel the leaves off one by one, dipping the fleshy part at the bottom of the leaves into the vinaigarette before scraping the delicious soft flesh off with your teeth. As you reach the centre, after eating the leaves, the choke will be exposed. This hairy-looking substance should be removed by scooping it out with your fork or a spoon before you eat the heart with your knife and fork.

Remove the stem and peel the lower, coarse leaves from around the base of the artichokes. Keep the artichokes in water with lemon juice added until ready to cook.

Put all the ingredients, except the artichokes and walnut vinaigrette, in a large, deep saucepan that will hold the artichokes snugly together, and bring to the boil. Lower in the artichokes, weigh them down with a plate and simmer for 20 minutes or until a knife penetrates the base without pressure. Serve the warm artichokes with the walnut vinaigrette on the side.

MEDICINAL
HEART
BENEFIT

Artichokes contain vitamin C for boosting the immune system, vitamin B for good cell function and vitamin K, which can potentially protect against osteoporosis. But the artichoke's most beneficial attribute is cynarine, a compound that increases bile excretion and improves how the body uses cholesterol, essential for cleansing and maintaining a healthy liver. Artichokes are also particularly high in folic acid, which is important for cell creation and preventing birth defects. As well, they're brimming with antioxidant compounds that help the body protect itself from harmful free radicals; these cause cell oxidation, which can compromise the body's ability to fight diseases and toxins.

202

Steamed choko with sorrel butter

SERVES 4

4 chokos (chayotes), halved or quartered

1 quantity Sorrel butter (page 235)

extra-virgin olive oil for drizzling

You don't see chokos (chayotes) very often, particularly on restaurant menus. They seemed to be popular in my grandparents' time and, as they served them to me a lot, I grew to like them. Quite often, given the huge number of chokos available, they were not just steamed but made into chutneys and pickles, as their generation wasted nothing. You can cut chokos in half or quarters depending on their size or, if you're boiling them, leave them whole and unpeeled to preserve their goodness from being tainted by the water.

Steam the chokos for 45 minutes to 1 hour. When they are ready, remove the seed, fill the cavities with sorrel butter, drizzle with olive oil, season with salt and lots of freshly ground black pepper and serve.

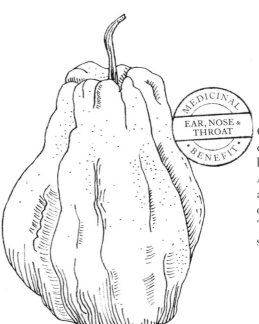

MEDICINAL
EAR, NOSE &
THROAT
BENEFIT

Chokos (chayotes) are a good source of folates (important for cell creation) and potassium (vital for maintaining a healthy heart rate and balancing bodily fluids). Sorrel is high in vitamin C, as well as vitamin A, necessary for maintaining healthy mucous membranes and skin; it's also essential for good eyesight. It's worth noting that sorrel contains oxalic acid, found to be useful in improving the condition of diabetics. Too much oxalic acid, though, can contribute to the growth of kidney stones, so don't overdo sorrel if you're at risk of these.

Cumin-scented carrots

SERVES 4 AS A SIDE

1 bouquet garni (parsley stalks,
   thyme stalks, coriander/
   cilantro stalks, celery stalk,
   1 bay leaf)
600 g (1 lb 5 oz) baby (Dutch)
   carrots, trimmed and
   scrubbed
1 teaspoon caster (superfine)
   sugar
10 g (¼ oz) cumin seeds
1 garlic clove, crushed
3 teaspoons extra-virgin olive oil
1 teaspoon sea salt flakes
1 orange, juiced, or your choice
   of citrus (use blood oranges if
   you're feeling fancy)
crusty bread, to serve
50 g (1¾ oz) butter

Baby (Dutch) carrots are delicious and have a lovely delicate shape. However, if you have garden carrots, they work just as well. I suggest you cut them into manageable shapes as the bigger they are the longer they will take to cook. The key thing about this recipe is cooking things fast in the pan and not having to add too much liquid. These carrots are delicious with fish and would make a perfect match for the Red mullet, café de Paris butter and cured roe (page 108) or with lamb.

Prepare your bouquet garni by tying the herb stalks and bay leaf together with string or wrapping them in a piece of muslin (cheesecloth) and securing the bundle with string.

Place the carrots, sugar, cumin seeds, garlic and oil in a large heavy-based saucepan over medium heat and stir well. Top the pan up with enough water to just cover the carrots. Add the salt and bouquet garni and bring to the boil.

Prepare a circle of baking paper, cut to fit the diameter of the pan. Pierce a few holes in it to allow the steam to escape and spread it with some butter. Place it on top of the pan, butter side down, to keep the carrots submerged during cooking. Simmer over low heat for about 10 minutes to reduce the water and cook the carrots. Test to see if the carrots are cooked with the end of a knife – if they're tender, remove the cartouche and bouquet garni. Add the orange juice and the butter and simmer for 2–5 minutes until it all has a nice sheen. Serve straight from the pan with crusty bread to mop up the juices.

Carrots are rich in beta-carotene, a powerful antioxidant that helps protect the body from harmful free-radical damage. It also carries out the functions of vitamin A, contributing to eye health, sperm production and tissue health. Carrots also contain good levels of vitamin C, and of vitamin B6, which helps make red blood cells. Cumin seeds' essential oils activate the salivary glands (aiding digestion) and the glands that secrete bile. The spice is also a calmative (it can help with insomnia), has detoxifying properties and is very rich in iron. It's great for breast-feeding mothers (who need more iron than others), and those with anaemia.

206 Grilled spatchcock marinated in crème fraîche

SERVES 4

2 spatchcocks (small chickens, size 10)

200 g (7 oz) crème fraîche

1 teaspoon sea salt flakes

extra-virgin olive oil

1–2 lemons, cut into cheeks, to serve

I had this dish once while travelling through France. It was elaborately served with a Sauternes sauce and was delicious. The essence of the dish is to use crème fraîche – the healthy bacteria in it tenderises the chicken and the curds caramelise during cooking. The squeeze of lemon juice is important as it balances the crème fraîche, which makes the chicken very rich.

To prepare the spatchcock, cut the bird down the backbone to open it out into a butterfly shape. Cut down the other side of the backbone and remove it entirely. Smother the spatchcocks in the crème fraîche and sea salt in a dish and cover. Leave to marinate overnight in the refrigerator.

Preheat the oven to 220°C (430°F).

In a large, ovenproof pan or baking tin over medium heat, heat a little olive oil and sear the spatchcock, skin side down, for 5 minutes. Turn the spatchcock skin side up and baste with the juices. Transfer to the oven and roast for 20 minutes until cooked through and crisp. You can also cook the spatchcock under the grill (broiler) or, even better, in a wood-fired oven. (These alternative cooking suggestions have a far more direct heat source and higher temperature, so would reduce the cooking time by about 5 minutes.) Rest the spatchcock for 5 minutes before serving it with the lemon cheeks.

Spatchcock is packed with good lean protein, essential for building muscle. It's also high in an antioxidant called selenium, which helps regulate thyroid hormone activity. Spatchcocks also contain plenty of vitamin B, which helps convert food into energy, as well as phosphorus and calcium to build and protect healthy bones. Crème fraîche is rich in calcium and, with its good live bacteria (similar to those found in natural yoghurt), also has probiotic benefits for the immune system.

Pot-roasted shoulder of lamb cooked in buttermilk with roast pears and potatoes

SERVES 4

10 garlic cloves, peeled

2 kg (4 lb 6 oz) lamb shoulder

1 litre (34 fl oz/4 cups) buttermilk

½ bunch thyme, leaves picked

2 fresh bay leaves

1.5 kg (3 lb 5 oz) roasting potatoes

ROAST PEARS WITH VANILLA, THYME AND VERJUICE

4 small pears (whatever is in season)

extra-virgin olive oil for brushing

100 ml (3½ fl oz) verjuice

2 vanilla beans, split lengthways and seeds scraped, or 1 teaspoon vanilla bean paste

1 bay leaf

4 thyme sprigs

1 teaspoon icing (confectioners') sugar

You can also use a leg of lamb for this recipe, but I do prefer the shoulder as it stays moist due to the fat coverage. I also find the leg can sometimes be a little stringy when cooked for a long period. Besides its probiotic values, buttermilk also helps to tenderise meat. The buttermilk will eventually curdle and separate during cooking. These curds, if left alone, can be gently spooned on top of the lamb during the final 30 minutes and then caramelised at a higher temperature – they will become little pillows of cream. The acidulated flavour from the whey is a perfect foil for the rich lamb, and the balance with the sweet young pear is a match made in heaven.

Preheat the oven to 220°C (430°F).

Place the garlic cloves in a large, heavy-based casserole dish. Season the lamb with salt and freshly ground black pepper and place it on top of the garlic. Roast the lamb in the oven, uncovered, for 10 minutes. Turn the lamb over and give it another 10 minutes on the other side. Remove the casserole dish from the oven.

In a saucepan over medium–high heat, bring the buttermilk to the boil. Add the thyme and bay leaves and pour the mixture over the lamb. Cover with a very tight-fitting lid or piece of aluminium foil. Reduce the oven temperature to 140°C (275°F). Return the casserole to the oven and bake until the meat is soft and tender (3–4 hours). Make sure to baste every 30 minutes with the pan juices during cooking.

While the lamb is cooking, prepare the pears by placing them in an ovenproof frying pan. Brush them with olive oil, pour in the verjuice, add the vanilla, bay leaf and thyme, and sprinkle the pears with salt and a dusting of icing sugar. ❯

‹

Peel the potatoes and halve them lengthways. Place one potato, cut side down, on a board and make thin, evenly spaced cuts at 1 mm ($^1/_{16}$ in) intervals, about two-thirds of the way through. Repeat with the remaining potatoes.

With 1 hour to go, add the potatoes, with the fins facing up, to the tray with the lamb and re-cover. In the final 30 minutes, remove the cover and turn the oven up to 220°C (430°F). Using a spoon, position the curds onto the lamb for them to caramelise for the rest of the cooking time. Baste the potatoes with the lamb juices and bake until crisp. This is also the time to place your pears in the oven. They will take about 30 minutes to bake until golden brown and soft.

After the final 30 minutes, check to see that everything is cooked. Remove the lamb from the pan and strain the whey sauce and caramelised buttermilk curd. Tear off a piece of lamb flesh for each serving, and include a couple of roast potatoes and a lovely roast pear. Spoon over some curd and a ladleful of whey to moisten.

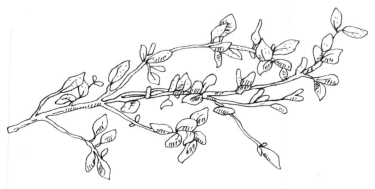

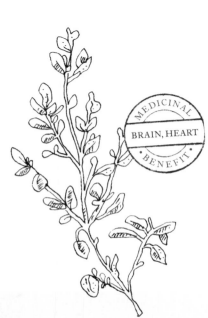

MEDICINAL
BRAIN, HEART
·BENEFIT·

Lamb is rich in vitamin B, which helps convert food into energy, and B12, essential for healthy nervous and digestive systems. Vitamin B12 is also crucial for energy production and for reducing an amino acid called homocysteine, which can potentially harm the heart. Lamb is high in selenium, a mineral that's vital for healthy cell division, cancer protection, thyroid health and general detoxification. It also contains zinc, used by more than a hundred different enzymes in the body. Being a red meat, lamb is also rich in iron, which helps transport oxygen around the body. Potatoes are packed with vitamins A, B and C, and with minerals, such as iron, potassium (essential for healthy nerves and maintaining healthy blood pressure) and phosphorus (to help build bones and convert food into energy).

212

Stuffed spring cabbage with pork and chestnuts

SERVES 4

1 large savoy cabbage

350 g (12½ oz) chestnuts, peeled

165 g (6 oz) pancetta, left in large chunks

3 fresh bay leaves

15 g (½ oz) fresh thyme, leaves picked

160 g (5½ oz) carrots, peeled and roughly diced

100 g (3½ oz) French shallots

400 ml (13½ fl oz) white wine

625 ml (21 fl oz/2½ cups) chicken stock

PORK STUFFING

375 g (13 oz) button mushrooms, sliced

30 g (1 oz) garlic cloves, peeled and crushed

90 g (3 oz) butter

45 ml (1½ fl oz) milk

45 g (1½ oz) breadcrumbs

225 g (8 oz) brown onions, finely chopped

1 handful flat-leaf (Italian) parsley leaves, chopped

1.125 kg (2½ lb) pork sausage, minced (ground)

1 teaspoon sea salt flakes

heart of the cabbage being used, shredded (see method)

2 eggs, lightly beaten

This is a great recipe to serve as a centrepiece. It looks very impressive turned out onto a plate and cut into wedges like a piece of cake. If time is of the essence, then a faster method is to blanch the cabbage leaves, spread them with the stuffing and roll the leaves up individually, securing them with string – or you can pack them tightly into an ovenproof dish so they can't unravel. They can be cooked the same way but with little preparation and a third of the cooking time. In my opinion, however, good things take time.

To prepare the cabbage, plunge it into boiling water and simmer slowly for 15 minutes. Lift it out carefully and drain on a wire rack for 10 minutes.

Place a clean tea towel (dish towel) on a work surface, then lay a large piece of muslin (cheesecloth) on top. Place the cabbage on top, stem side down. Slowly and gently open the cabbage from the top, like a flower. When you get to the heart, which is the size of a cricket ball, carefully remove it and finely shred it for the stuffing.

For the stuffing, in a medium frying pan over high heat, sauté the mushrooms with the garlic in half the butter and cook until all of the liquid has reduced, about 5 minutes. Transfer to a bowl.

In a separate large bowl, mix together the milk, breadcrumbs, onion, parsley and pork sausage.

In a frying pan over medium heat, sauté the shredded cabbage heart in the remaining butter until tender. Remove from the heat and set aside to cool slightly.

Add the cooled mushrooms and cooled cabbage to the bowl with the sausage mince and egg, mixing well, adding the sea salt and freshly ground black pepper to taste. (At this point you can fry a ball of stuffing in a little olive oil to check the seasoning.)

To stuff the cabbage, place a large cricket ball-sized lump of stuffing in the centre to replace the heart, and fold the leaves over the stuffing. Continue to pat a layer of stuffing in between each leaf and fold them back up. Do this so you have four layers of stuffing and three unstuffed layers of leaves around the outside to protect the cabbage while it cooks.

The cabbage should now somewhat resemble its original form. Take the diagonal corners of the muslin and tie them together to encase the cabbage. Slip a spoon through the knot to make a handle.

Preheat the oven to 150°C (300°F).

Put the chestnuts, pancetta, bay leaves and thyme in a deep, heavy-based ovenproof saucepan with a tight-fitting lid. Place the cabbage bundle on top of the chestnuts, scatter with the carrot and shallots and pour over the wine and chicken stock. Cover with baking paper and put the lid on. Bake for 3 hours. Remove the cabbage from the pan and drain on a wire rack set over a tray.

Simmer the cooking juices and season to taste with salt and pepper. Slice the cabbage into wedges and serve on a plate with a ladleful of juices.

Cabbage is a nutritional powerhouse. Its concentrations of vitamins, minerals and micronutrients make it effective for everything from improving mental function to general detoxification and regulating blood sugar. Vitamin C boosts the immune system and vitamin K help with blood clotting. Cabbage is particularly rich in sulfur, which can dry up acne, among other things, and is a key component of the protein called keratin, which hair, skin and nails are made of. Chestnuts contain monounsaturated fatty acids, B vitamins, vitamin C and plenty of minerals, such as phosphorus, which not only builds healthy bones and teeth, but helps shuttle nutrients into and out of cells.

Chargrilled sardines, nasturtiums, oregano and chilli

SERVES 6—8 AS A STARTER

12 whole sardines

65 g (2¼ oz) preserved lemon rind, rinsed and diced

60 g (2 oz) raisins, coarsely chopped

25 g (1 oz/½ cup) firmly packed mint leaves, finely chopped

15 g (½ oz/½ cup) flat-leaf (Italian) parsley leaves, finely chopped

20 g (¾ oz/½ cup) oregano leaves, finely chopped

1 large red chilli, thinly sliced

extra-virgin olive oil

nasturtium leaves, to serve

½ quantity Rosemary tarator (page 240)

LEMON DRESSING

50 ml (1¾ fl oz) extra-virgin olive oil

1½ lemons, juiced

Sardines are such tasty fish but, because of the bones, a lot of people are frightened of them. This recipes explains how to remove the bones so the fish is easier to eat. Nasturtiums are a common plant and I often find them while walking and foraging. The leaves have a far longer season than the flower. I look for smaller leaves, as the large ones can be a little tough. If you have a nut allergy, the Rosemary tarator recipe will still work very well without the nuts – but instead of tarator it will be a rosemary salsa verde.

For the lemon dressing, whisk the ingredients in a bowl, season to taste with salt and freshly ground black pepper and set aside.

To prepare the sardines, snip the backbones at both ends of the cavity and remove the ribs with your fingers – they lift out very easily. Combine the preserved rind, raisins, herbs and chilli in a bowl. Season to taste with salt and freshly ground black pepper, then stuff the mixture into the sardine cavities.

Heat a barbecue to high. Brush the sardines with olive oil and grill to just char and cook them through, 1–2 minutes each side. Transfer to a platter lined with nasturtium leaves, spoon the lemon dressing over and serve with the rosemary tarator on the side.

Sardines are a particularly rich source of omega-3 fatty acids, which help lower 'bad' cholesterol. They're also high in calcium, vitamin D and phosphorus. Calcium can prevent the loss of bone density and help heal broken bones. Rosemary is a good source of vitamins A and C and contains rosmarinic acid. This substance has powerful antioxidant, anti-inflammatory and antimicrobial properties; it can even aid in preventing cell damage. It also helps with poor concentration and memory, as well as with headaches and anxiety. Walnuts are high in fibre and antioxidants, and also have anti-inflammatory properties.

216

Baked whole leather jackets, marjoram, capers and lemon

SERVES 4–6

1 kg (2 lb 3 oz) leather jackets, black skin removed

75 g (2¾ oz/½ cup) plain (all-purpose) flour

extra-virgin olive oil for shallow-frying

50 g (1¾ oz) butter

2 tablespoons baby capers in vinegar, rinsed and drained well

1 bunch marjoram, leaves picked

squeeze of lemon juice, plus lemon cheeks to serve

Leather jackets are among the unsung heroes of Australian fish. They are often snared as a bycatch while the fishing boats are heading back to shore from an expedition. Other fish that would work well in this recipe are flat fish like John Dory, flounder or sole, or larger fish like halibut and turbot. They will just take a little longer to cook and I would add some white wine to the tray so they are not baking dry.

Preheat the oven to 250°C (480°F) and line a shallow roasting tin with baking paper.

Dust the fish with the flour and season with some salt and freshly ground black pepper.

In a large frying pan, heat a little olive oil and fry the fish for about 4 minutes on one side only. Remove the fish from the pan and place them, cooked side up, in the roasting tin.

While the pan is still hot, add the butter, capers, half the marjoram leaves and the lemon juice and sizzle for 2 minutes to form a burnt butter sauce. Pour the sauce over the top of the fish and transfer the tin to the oven for 5 minutes. Remove the tin from the oven and allow the fish to rest for 5 minutes. Scatter with the remaining marjoram leaves and serve with the lemon cheeks.

MEDICINAL
BRAIN, HEART
BENEFIT

Nutritionally speaking, you shouldn't underestimate the potency of herbs. Marjoram contains a compound called thymol, which has antifungal and other powerful healing properties. Sage contains rosmarinic acid, which is good for the memory. Parsley contains eugenol, a strong anti-inflammatory and antibacterial compound. Capers are rich in rutin, which helps thin the blood and improve circulation, and contain vitamin B3, which can help lower 'bad' cholesterol. Lemons are a rich source of vitamin C, one of the strongest natural antioxidants there is. Vitamin C plays a health-giving role in so many areas – it promotes collagen synthesis, helps with healing, is antiviral and anticarcinogenic and helps prevent neurodegenerative diseases. It can also help with arthritis, colds and fevers.

218

Yabbies poached in chicken stock with broad beans and basil

SERVES 4

1 litre (34 fl oz/4 cups) chicken
  stock
1 kg (2 lb 3 oz) yabbies
250 g (9 oz) baby (Dutch)
  carrots, peeled
250 g (9 oz) baby turnips,
  peeled
150 g (5½ oz) fresh peas,
  blanched
150 g (5½ oz) broad (fava)
  beans, shelled
1 quantity Yabby butter
  (page 236)
½ bunch basil, leaves picked

**Yabbies are freshwater crayfish found in many dams in Australia and are
often thought of as pests. However, once you taste them you realise they
are the most luxurious pest on the planet! They taste like a very sweet
prawn (shrimp) and have the texture of lobster. You can choose any
vegetable combination you like, but as we are in spring I've chosen my
favourite spring vegetables.**

In a large saucepan, bring the chicken stock to the boil, then poach the
yabbies for 2 minutes and remove with tongs or a spoon. Peel the the yabbies,
reserving the shells to make the yabby butter.

Bring the chicken stock back up to a slow simmer and poach the vegetables
for 3 minutes or until just tender. Taste the stock and season with salt and
freshly ground black pepper. Add half the yabby butter to enrich the stock.
Simmer for 2 minutes then add the yabby and basil leaves and remove from
the heat immediately. Spoon into bowls and serve with the remaining yabby
butter on the side to add more if you wish.

Yabbies are brain food, literally. They boost the intake of choline and
vitamin B12; choline supports the production of neurotransmitters,
while vitamin B12 helps maintain myelin, a substance that supports
nerve integrity. Choline also maintains the health of your cell
membranes and B12 promotes red blood cell function. Peas are rich
in folic acid, which assists cell creation during the early stages of
pregnancy. Peas contain vitamin A for good vision, B for converting
food into energy, C to boost the immune system and K to help with
blood clotting.

220 Strawberry shortcake

SERVES 4

500 g (1 lb 2 oz) strawberries, hulled, halved if large

100 g (3½ oz) caster (superfine) sugar

1 tablespoon strawberry liqueur, or framboise or brandy

Chantilly cream (page 245)

icing (confectioners') sugar for dusting

SHORTCAKE

300 g (10½ oz/2 cups) plain (all-purpose) flour

1 tablespoon baking powder

2 tablespoons caster (superfine) sugar

125 g (4½ oz) butter

125–190 ml (4–6½ fl oz/ ½–¾ cup) pouring (single/ light) cream, plus extra for brushing

A shortcake is a cross between shortbread and a scone (biscuit). It's crucial not to be tempted to overbake these shortcakes as you want them a little cakey inside. Don't serve them hot either, as they need to firm up a little and if they are warm they will melt your cream filling. The shortcakes are also delicious with other fillings, such as lemon curd, or crème fraîche and honey, or you can try different berries or fruit.

Cover the strawberries with the sugar and leave them to purge overnight.

The next day, drain the berries. In a small saucepan over medium heat, reduce the liquid to form a light syrup. Add a splash of strawberry liqueur. Put the strawberries in the pan and, using the back of a fork, squash them a little so they are slightly bruised – this will help thicken the syrup. Cook until the syrup is thick and the strawberries are tender.

For the shortcake, preheat the oven to 200°C (400°F). Grease and line a baking tray with baking paper.

Sift the flour, 1½ teaspoons salt, the baking powder and sugar into a bowl. Rub the butter into the mixture with your fingertips, as you would for scone (biscuit) dough. Add the cream and mix until you have a sticky dough, then allow to rest for 30 minutes in the refrigerator.

On a lightly floured work surface, roll out the dough to a 1 cm (½ in) thickness and cut into discs 7–10 cm (2¾–4 in) in diameter. Place the discs on the prepared baking tray and brush them with the extra cream. Bake for 10–12 minutes until golden. Remove the shortcakes from the oven and place them on a wire rack to cool. To serve, split the shortcakes crossways, fill them with the chantilly cream and strawberries, and dust with icing sugar.

Fresh berries are an excellent source of vitamin C, a powerful natural antioxidant, and of B complex vitamins. These aid in converting food into energy, keeping the body running like a well-oiled machine. Strawberries also contain vitamin A, vitamin E and beta-carotene in small amounts. All of these compounds protect the cells against free radicals, which play a role in premature ageing and in various disease processes.

222 Lavender sable biscuits

MAKES 700 G (1 LB 9 OZ)

125 g (4½ oz) Lavender sugar
(see below), plus 1 tablespoon
for sprinkling

235 g (8½ oz) plain (all-
purpose) flour

40 g (1½ oz) cornflour
(cornstarch)

½ teaspoon salt

230 g (8 oz) cold butter

organic, unsprayed, dried
lavender to sprinkle

LAVENDER SUGAR
(MAKES 250 G/9 OZ)

250 g (9 oz) caster (superfine)
sugar, plus 50 g (1¾ oz) to
decorate

10 g (¼ oz) organic, unsprayed,
dried lavender

Lavender sugar is a great weapon to have in your larder. The longer the lavender sits in the sugar, the stronger the infusion becomes. Always choose organic lavender that has no additives, such as perfumes or pesticides. When making shortbread, always handle the dough gently and never overwork it as this will make the biscuits tough. Try serving these with the Mandarin and rosemary syllabub (opposite).

For the lavender sugar, combine the sugar and lavender in a jar, seal and allow to sit for 1 week in a cool dry place to infuse the sugar with a lavender flavour. You'll need half for the recipe, so store the other half in your larder.

Preheat the oven to 160°C (320°F). Line a baking tray with baking paper.

For the biscuits, sift the dry ingredients, except the dried lavender, together into a large bowl and rub in the butter with your fingertips. Bring the mixture together to form a dough by squashing it between your hands to form a ball.

On a floured work surface, or between two sheets of baking paper, roll the dough out to a 1 cm (½ in) thickness. Rest the rolled dough in the refrigerator for 1 hour, covered with plastic wrap.

Remove the dough from the refrigerator and cut it into 5 cm (2 in) squares using a knife, or into circles using a 5 cm (2 in) pastry cutter. Place the dough on the baking tray and top with a piece of dried lavender and a sprinkling of lavender sugar. Bake for 12–15 minutes until golden brown. Sprinkle with extra lavender sugar as the biscuits come out of the oven.

MEDICINAL BRAIN, SKIN BENEFIT

Lavender contains an essential oil that is rich in substances called linalool and limonene. Commonly used in cosmetics and scented products, they have anti-inflammatory, antimicrobial and anti-stress properties. They also promote weight loss. The smell of lavender is soothing and can help alleviate some headaches.

Mandarin and rosemary syllabub

SERVES 4

1 lemon, zested and juiced

2 mandarins, zested and juiced

100 ml (3½ fl oz) white wine

1 tablespoon brandy

1 rosemary sprig

50 g (1¾ oz) caster (superfine) sugar

2 titanium-strength gelatine leaves, softened in water, then excess water squeezed out

200 ml (7 fl oz) thickened (whipping) cream

Most people would look at this recipe and think it should be called a fool, but it is a syllabub because it has the addition of alcohol. That's the only difference. Make sure to look for the smaller mandarins with a thin skin, as imperials can often be too tough and dry.

In a bowl, combine the citrus zests and juices, wine, brandy and rosemary and leave to macerate overnight.

The next day, strain the mixture into a saucepan and add the sugar and the softened gelatine. Heat gently to dissolve the sugar, making sure not to let the mixture boil. Leave to cool to room temperature.

Transfer the mixture to the bowl of an electric mixer and add the cream. Whisk on high speed to medium peaks then pour into four glasses. Refrigerate for 1 hour to set before serving.

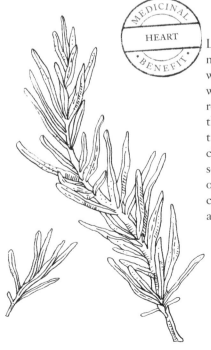

MEDICINAL
HEART
BENEFIT

Like all citrus fruits, mandarins are a rich source of vitamin C, one of nature's most powerful antioxidants. Mandarins also contain pectin, which prevents cholesterol absorption in the gut. Then there's rosemary, which is not only a good source of vitamins A and C, but also of rosmarinic acid. The antioxidant power of this is stronger than even that of vitamin E in helping prevent cell damage. White wine contains trace substances that can actually lower artery-clogging LDL ('bad') cholesterol. It also contributes caffeic acid, a feature of the healthy, so-called 'Mediterranean diet' and associated with a reduced incidence of heart disease. Brandy, a distillation of red wine, contains a high concentration of antioxidants; 30 ml (1 fl oz) of brandy provides the same antioxidant potential as the daily recommended intake of vitamin C.

224 Parsnip and ginger cake

SERVES 8

270 g (9½ oz) plain (all-purpose) flour

½ teaspoon bicarbonate of soda (baking soda)

½ teaspoon baking powder

1 teaspoon ground ginger

2 eggs

155 ml (5 fl oz) vegetable oil

150 g (5½ oz) caster (superfine) sugar

115 g (4 oz) glacé ginger in syrup, drained and finely chopped

285 g (10 oz) coarsely grated parsnip

115 g (4 oz) activated walnuts (see page 237), toasted and chopped

1 quantity Buttercream (page 245)

Every good boy and girl deserves cake. So why not offer cake with some sort of nutrition? Carrot cake is the most famous for this, but I have included a couple of cake recipes in this book that incorporate different vegetables. Glacé ginger in syrup can be found in most good food stores, usually in the cake or gourmet section. If you can't find it, you can use candied ginger, which is slightly sweeter but still packs a ginger punch.

Preheat the oven to 175°C (350°F). Grease and line a 21 × 11 cm (8¼ × 4¼ in) loaf (bar) tin with baking paper on the bottom and long sides.

In a large bowl, sift together the flour, bicarbonate of soda, baking powder and ground ginger.

In a separate large bowl, beat together the eggs, oil, sugar and three-quarters of the chopped ginger to combine. Add the parsnip and ½ teaspoon salt and beat to combine. Add the flour mixture and beat until just combined, then fold through the nuts. Pour the batter into the prepared tin and smooth the surface. Bake for 60–70 minutes or until a skewer inserted in the centre of the cake comes out clean. Cool for 20 minutes in the tin, then turn out onto a wire rack to cool completely.

When cool, spread the top of the cake with the buttercream and scatter with the remaining strained and chopped glacé ginger.

Humble parsnips have a lot going for them, health-wise. They're high in dietary fibre (good for digestion and lowering cholesterol) and contain certain antioxidants that have anti-inflammatory, antifungal and anticancer functions. They can help relieve respiratory conditions, such as bronchitis and asthma and helps prevent blood vessels from swelling, thus helping prevent stroke and heart attack. Parsnips also contain large amounts of potassium, for regulating blood pressure and for the proper functioning of muscles and nerves. Then there's the immune-boosting quantities of vitamin C and vitamin B3, aiding digestion and the nervous system and vitamin K, which assists in blood clotting and protecting the liver from disease. Walnuts are high in omega- fatty acids (heart-healthy fats) and vitamin E antioxidants.

226 Pineapple tarts

SERVES 8

1 large pineapple, peeled and cut
into 5 mm (¼ in) discs, core
removed

30 g (1 oz/¼ cup) icing
(confectioners') sugar, plus
extra for dusting

2 sheets frozen puff pastry (the
best quality you can find)

FRANGIPANE

100 g (3½ oz) butter

100 g (3½ oz) caster (superfine)
sugar

25 g (1 oz) plain (all-purpose)
flour

1 egg

1 teaspoon vanilla bean paste

This pineapple tart recipe can go in many directions. The individual
tarts here are the simplest version and, to my mind, the most effective.
However, another twist would be to make a pineapple *tarte fine*. For
this you would roll out a sheet of puff pastry, cover it entirely with the
frangipane and then cover the tart with very thin, overlapping slices of
pineapple. You bake it the same way, but you can cut it into squares or
rectangles for a different effect. In any guise, these tarts are delicious
with a scoop of vanilla ice cream.

For the frangipane, stir the ingredients together in a bowl until smooth.

Preheat the oven to 220°C (430°F). Line a baking tray with baking paper.

Dust the pineapple pieces with icing sugar.

Cut the puff pastry into discs 1 cm (½ in) larger than the pineapple discs and
place them on the prepared baking tray.

Spread the frangipane 5 mm (¼ in) thick across the top of the pastry discs,
leaving a small border around the edge. Top the discs with the pineapple and
dust with icing sugar. Bake for 10 minutes. Reduce the oven temperature to
180°C (350°F) and cook for a further 10 minutes or until the frangipane is
brown in the centre and the fruit is golden. You can also lift one of the tarts
up to check that the pastry underneath is crisp. If not, give the tarts more
time in the oven until golden and firm.

Pineapple contains an enzyme called bromelain, which helps digest food by breaking down
proteins. Bromelain also has anti-inflammatory, anti-clotting and anticancer properties;
regular consumption of it helps fight against arthritis, indigestion and even worm infestation.
Pineapple is also an excellent source of vitamin C, required for collagen synthesis in the body.
Collagen is the main structural protein in the body and is crucial for maintaining the integrity
of blood vessels, skin, organs and bones. Pineapple also provides vitamin A for healthy skin and
vision, folates for cell reproduction, and potassium for balancing body fluids. Almonds are full
of cholesterol-friendly monounsaturated fatty acids, vitamin E for the skin and vitamin B for
muscle growth.

228

Pink grapefruit bicicletta

MAKES 4

60 ml (2 fl oz/¼ cup) pink
grapefruit juice
60 ml (2 fl oz/¼ cup) Campari
60 ml (2 fl oz/¼ cup) gin
ice
soda water (club soda) to top up

There are lots of different recipes out there for a bicicletta, but with this one you'll still be able to ride your bike home afterwards.

Mix the grapefruit juice, Campari and gin together and divide between long glasses. Top up the glasses up with ice, fill with soda water, stir and serve.

MEDICINAL

GUT, SKIN

BENEFIT

Grapefruit shares much with other citrus fruits; namely, it's rich in both dietary fibre and vitamin C (ascorbic acid) and it contains many other vitamins, minerals and essential oils. Pink grapefruit is high in pectin, which prevents cholesterol absorption in the gut. It's also rich in the anti-inflammatory, antioxidant nutrient called lycopene, which gives the juicy flesh its pink colour; this is the same substance that makes tomatoes red. It's believed that lycopene has anti-ageing and anticancer properties. Some sources claim it even offers weak protection from sunburn by acting like a sort of internal sunscreen.

Whey lemonade

**MAKES 750 ML
(25½ FL OZ/3 CUPS)**

6 lemons, zested and juiced (you
    need 250 ml/8½ fl oz/1 cup
    lemon juice)
225 g (8 oz) sugar (caster/
    superfine or raw/demerara)
375 g (13 oz) pot-set yoghurt

We make a lot of yoghurt in our house and therefore always have lots of whey floating around. This is a quick recipe, which is probiotic and uses few ingredients. Whey is easily collected by straining yoghurt. Some yoghurts, particularly pot-set ones, always have some whey floating on the surface that you can use. A good way to check if your lemonade has produced enough fizz is to turn the bottle upside down and see if there are any bubbles rising up through the bottle. If you notice little bubbles, then it's time to stop the fermentation by placing the broth in the refrigerator.

Mix the lemon zest with the sugar and 1.5 litres (51 fl oz/6 cups) water. Cover and leave at room temperature overnight.

Meanwhile, line a strainer or fine colander with two layers of muslin (cheesecloth) and spoon in the yoghurt. Place the lined strainer suspended over a large bowl in the refrigerator overnight to strain the whey. (See Note.)

The next day, strain the lemon water from the zest and combine with 125 ml (4 fl oz/¼ cup) of the whey. Place in flip-top bottles and leave out at room temperature until you see bubbles, after about 1 week. It's now ready to drink so place it in the refrigerator until needed as it's best icy cold. It will keep for a minimum of 2 weeks, chilled.

Note: *You can use the whey left over from making the labne in the Blueberry, celery and pecan salad with lemon myrtle and labne (page 181).*

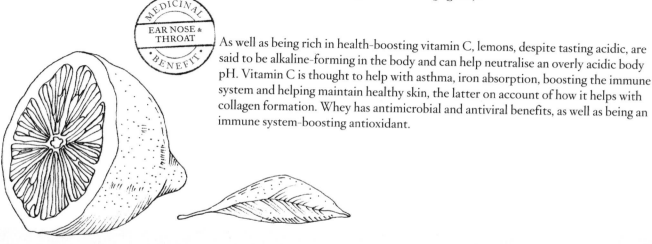

MEDICINAL · EAR NOSE & THROAT · BENEFIT

As well as being rich in health-boosting vitamin C, lemons, despite tasting acidic, are said to be alkaline-forming in the body and can help neutralise an overly acidic body pH. Vitamin C is thought to help with asthma, iron absorption, boosting the immune system and helping maintain healthy skin, the latter on account of how it helps with collagen formation. Whey has antimicrobial and antiviral benefits, as well as being an immune system-boosting antioxidant.

NUT MILKS *page 238*

Chilli salt
Indian spice mix
— MINT OIL —
Basil oil
CURRY OIL
RASPBERRY VINEGAR
— PONZU —
Walnut vinaigrette
Maple vinaigrette
CLARIFIED BUTTER
Garlic butter
Garlic and ginger butter
SORREL BUTTER
OREGANO LIME BUTTER
— YABBY BUTTER —
Blackberry butter
Café de Paris butter
Activated nuts

LARDER
230-245

Nut milks
GREEN TAHINI
CHIMICHURRI
— ROMESCO SAUCE —
ROSEMARY TARATOR
Dill pickles
BREAD AND BUTTER CUCUMBERS
VEGETABLE KRAUT
Sprouted buckwheat sourdough
Shortcrust suet pastry dough
— GLUTEN-FREE PASTRY
DOUGH —
ROSE SYRUP
Chantilly cream
BUTTERCREAM
Raw chocolate–hazelnut spread

Chilli salt **MAKES 75 G (2¾ OZ)**

6 dried long red chillies	75 g (2¾ oz) sea salt flakes

Preheat a grill (broiler) to low. Toast the chillies under the grill for about 2 minutes until dark red. Allow to cool for 5 minutes until crispy.

Pulse the chillies in a spice grinder, or pound using a mortar and pestle, to form flakes. Add the sea salt flakes and pulse or pound once or twice to combine. You can make the chilli salt as coarse or as fine as you wish – just blend longer for a finer finish.

Indian spice mix **MAKES 35 G (1¼ OZ)**

1 teaspoon coriander seeds	1 cinnamon stick
1 teaspoon cumin seeds	5 cloves
2 teaspoons fennel seeds	1 teaspoon mild chilli flakes
seeds from 5 cardamom pods	1 teaspoon ground turmeric

Warm a small frying pan over medium heat and add all the ingredients except the turmeric. Swirl the pan to keep the spices constantly moving and toast them for about 2 minutes, until they are aromatic and a light golden brown. Grind the whole spices in a spice grinder or using a mortar and pestle. Once ground, stir in the turmeric.

Mint oil **MAKES 125 ML (4 FL OZ/½ CUP)**

125 ml (4 fl oz/½ cup) grapeseed oil	½ small handful baby English spinach leaves
10 g (¼ oz/½ cup) firmly packed mint leaves	

Warm the grapeseed oil in a small saucepan over low heat to 80°C (176°F), using a thermometer to check the temperature. Transfer the oil to a high-speed blender with the remaining ingredients and blitz until very finely puréed, about 3–4 minutes. Pass the mixture through a sieve lined with three layers of muslin (cheesecloth) into a bowl and set aside to strain. Don't press on the solids as even a tiny speck of leaf in the oil will turn it brown. Once strained, season to taste with salt and freshly ground black pepper.

Basil oil   MAKES 250 ML (8½ FL OZ/1 CUP)

1 bunch basil, leaves picked

250 ml (8½ fl oz/1 cup) grapeseed oil

Warm the basil and oil in a small saucepan over low heat to 80°C (176°F), using a thermometer to check the temperature. Transfer the mixture to a high-speed blender and blitz for 3 minutes. Pass the mixture through a sieve lined with three layers of muslin (cheesecloth) into a bowl. Don't press on the solids as even a tiny speck of leaf in the oil will turn it brown. Once strained, season to taste with salt and freshly ground black pepper.

Curry oil   MAKES 500 ML (17 FL OZ/2 CUPS)

500 ml (17 fl oz/2 cups) neutral oil, such as grapeseed, rice bran or a good-quality vegetable oil

3 teaspoons mild curry powder
2 curry leaves

Warm all the ingredients in a saucepan over medium heat for about 2 minutes, until they reach 80°C (176°F), using a thermometer to check the temperature. Remove from the heat and allow the oil to infuse overnight. The next day, strain through muslin (cheesecloth) into a bowl and you'll be left with a very aromatic, brightly coloured oil.

Raspberry vinegar   MAKES 500 ML (17 FL OZ/2 CUPS)

An interesting way to preserve and use up blemished fruit is by making home-made vinegar or flavoured vinegar. The former takes a minimum of 1 month to ferment and you also need a 'mother' to help the vinegar form. As most of us are time-poor, here's a recipe for raspberry vinegar, which looks great in a glass bottle and only takes a few days to make. Blackberries, blackcurrants and any other delicate fruit that blemishes easily also works well. It will keep for up to 4 months. This is a secret weapon for adding to dressings.

500 g (1 lb 2 oz/4 cups) raspberries
100 g (3½ oz) caster (superfine) sugar

500 ml (17 fl oz/2 cups) organic unfiltered apple-cider vinegar

Place the berries in a non-reactive bowl and toss with the sugar. Crush the berries with a fork, then stir to dissolve the sugar. Add the vinegar and stir to combine. Cover and set aside at room temperature for 1 week to steep.

Transfer the berries to a colander lined with muslin (cheesecloth) or a clean open-weave kitchen cloth, set over a bowl. Strain for 1 hour – don't press the pulp or the vinegar will become cloudy. Pour the liquid into a sterilised 700 ml (23½ fl oz) bottle and seal. Store in a cool, dark place.

Ponzu   MAKES 100 ML (3½ FL OZ)

1½ tablespoons soy sauce

60 ml (2 fl oz/¼ cup) Japanese
   rice vinegar

1 lemon, juiced

Combine all the ingredients in a glass jar and shake to combine.

Walnut vinaigrette   MAKES 100 ML (3½ FL OZ)

2 teaspoons white-wine vinegar

squeeze of lemon juice

1 pinch salt

1 teaspoon dijon mustard

1 pinch white pepper

2 tablespoons walnut oil

2 tablespoons olive oil

Whisk all the ingredients, except the oils, together until smooth. Slowly whisk
in the oils to emulsify and adjust the seasoning if necessary.

Maple vinaigrette   MAKES 250 ML (8½ FL OZ/1 CUP)

60 ml (2 fl oz/¼ cup) aged balsamic
   vinegar

1 tablespoon maple syrup

190 ml (6½ fl oz/¾ cup) extra-virgin
   olive oil

Whisk the vinegar and maple syrup together until smooth. Whisk in the oil to
emulsify and season with salt and freshly ground black pepper.

Clarified butter   MAKES 500 G (1 LB 2 OZ)

Clarified butter is also known as ghee.

750 g (1 lb 11 oz) unsalted butter

Place the butter in a heavy-based pan over medium heat. Bring to the boil and whisk the
butter as it melts. Once it has simmered for 1 minute, remove the pan from the heat and leave
to settle in a warm place for 2 hours so the fat solids separate from the milk solids. It can't be
left at room temperature as the butter will set. An ideal place would be in an airing cupboard, or
in an oven set on the lowest temperature (50°C/120°F). Strain the melted butter through muslin
(cheesecloth), leaving the white milk solids behind. Store the clear yellow liquid in the
refrigerator until needed. Discard the milk solids.

Garlic butter MAKES 250 G (9 OZ)

5 garlic cloves

squeeze of lemon juice

200 g (7 oz) butter, softened

40 g (1½ oz/1⅓ cups) flat-leaf (Italian) parsley, leaves picked and finely chopped

In a small food processor, or mortar and pestle, blend the garlic with a pinch of salt to a paste. Add the lemon juice and butter and process to combine. Fold through the parsley and season with salt and freshly ground black pepper. Roll into a cylinder in plastic wrap and store in the freezer.

Garlic and ginger butter MAKES 250 G (9 OZ)

5 garlic cloves

2 cm (¾ in) piece fresh ginger

¼ lemon, juiced

200 g (7 oz) butter, softened

20 g (¾ oz/⅔ cup) flat-leaf (italian) parsley, leaves picked and finely chopped

In a small food processor, or mortar and pestle, blend the garlic and ginger with a pinch of salt to a paste. Add the lemon juice and butter and process to combine. Fold through the parsley and season with salt and some freshly ground black pepper. Roll into a cylinder in plastic wrap and store in the freezer.

Sorrel butter MAKES 175 G (6 OZ)

1 bunch sorrel

130 g (4½ oz) butter, softened

1 lemon, juiced

½ garlic clove, finely chopped

Sorrel goes black in its raw state, so first sauté the leaves in 5 g (¼ oz) of the butter in a frying pan over medium heat for 1 minute until wilted. Remove from the heat and allow to cool.

In a blender, process the sorrel with the remaining butter, lemon juice, garlic and a pinch of salt, until the mixture is bright green. Roll into a cylinder shape in plastic wrap and store in the freezer.

Oregano lime butter MAKES 250 G (9 OZ)

250 g (9 oz) butter
¼ bunch oregano, leaves picked
   and roughly chopped

1 lime
1 garlic clove

There are two ways you can make this butter:

Method 1: Put the butter, oregano, a squeeze of lime juice, half the garlic clove (crushed) and a pinch of salt in a mortar and grind with a pestle or press with a wooden spoon.

Method 2: Using a slow juicer, juice half the oregano, the the flesh of half the lime and the garlic clove. Fold this mixture through the butter and add a pinch of salt. Then I like to chop the remaining oregano leaves and fold them through the butter.

Roll into a cylinder in plastic wrap, label well and store in the freezer.

Yabby butter MAKES 300 G (10½ OZ)

If you're making Yabbies poached in chicken stock with broad beans and basil (page 218), you can use the reserved shells to make this butter.

shells from 1 kg (2 lb 3 oz) yabbies
60 ml (2 fl oz/¼ cup) olive oil
½ lemon, juiced

250 g (9 oz) unsalted butter
sea salt

Sauté the yabby shells in the olive oil in a large saucepan over high heat. Remove the pan from the heat, add the lemon juice and allow to cool thoroughly.

Pour into a blender and process to a paste. Once the shells are broken down, pulse the butter through and season with sea salt. Pass the butter mixture through a fine-mesh sieve. Roll the butter into a cylinder in plastic wrap, label well and store in the freezer.

Blackberry butter MAKES 250 G (9 OZ)

125 g (4½ oz) blackberries
1 tablespoon raw panela sugar (see Note, page 16)

125 g (4½ oz) butter

Combine the berries and sugar in a bowl and leave for an hour or two (or preferably overnight) to bleed. The next day, strain the syrup and set aside. Beat the butter until light and creamy using a wooden spoon, then gradually beat in the syrup until it's absorbed and you have a purple butter. Beat in the whole fruit to combine. It can be as rough or as refined as you like – I rather like the ripples of syrup and chunks of berry, rather than a smooth purple butter. It's entirely up to you as it will still taste the same. Use it straight away while it's soft, or roll the butter into a cylinder in plastic wrap, label well and store in the freezer.

Café de Paris butter   MAKES 300 G (10½ OZ)

1 brown onion, finely diced

1 pinch sea salt

2 tablespoons vegetable oil

1 teaspoon curry powder

1 pinch white pepper

¼ teaspoon ground ginger

250 g (9 oz) unsalted butter

2 thyme sprigs

30 g (1 oz) anchovies, finely chopped

30 g (1 oz) salted capers, rinsed and drained well

1 garlic clove, crushed

1 tablespoon lemon juice

15 g (½ oz/½ cup) loosely packed basil leaves, finely shredded

20 g (¾ oz/⅔ cup) flat-leaf (Italian) parsley leaves, finely shredded

10 g (¼ oz/½ cup) tarragon leaves, finely shredded

In a frying pan over medium heat, sweat the onion and salt for 3 minutes in the oil until soft and translucent. Add the curry powder, white pepper and ground ginger and cook for 1 minute. Remove from the heat. Allow to cool.

Transfer the cool spice mixture to a blender, along with the remaining ingredients, and blitz until smooth. Roll the butter into a cylinder in plastic wrap, label well and store in the freezer.

Activated nuts   MAKES 2 CUPS

'Activated' has become a buzz word whenever we use nuts. The main reason people activate nuts is that raw nuts contain phytates and enzyme inhibitors, which can reduce the body's ability to absorb certain nutrients properly. It's best to activate all nuts and pulses, and even seeds, to purge them, although some seeds are very small and difficult to handle. There have also been arguments on the other side of the fence, however, saying that phytates are anti-inflammatory and have antioxidant properties. The choice is yours.

I activate nuts because I like the texture of them. The crunch is deep and far more satisfying than just toasting them in the oven. Once they've been soaked and rinsed, they're ready to be made into nut milks (see page 238) or dehydrated until crisp. Try using tamari instead of salt for a different toasted flavour, but you will need to use double the amount of tamari.

2 cups raw nuts, shelled

2 teaspoons salt

500 ml (17 fl oz/2 cups) water

Combine all the ingredients in a non-reactive container, then cover and soak overnight.

Preheat the oven to the lowest setting (about 50°C/120°F) or turn on your dehydrator, if you have one.

Drain the nuts and rinse them well, patting them dry with a clean tea towel (dish towel). Lay them on a baking tray and roast them for 24–48 hours.

Nut milks   MAKES 750 ML (25½ FL OZ/3 CUPS)

Nut milks are full of vitamins and minerals and, although not packed with calcium, are a great substitute to give your body a rest from digesting dairy milk. The important thing about making nut milk is to use high-quality organic nuts and first soak them in filtered water, changing the water a number of times throughout their activation. Before blending be sure to strain and rinse the nuts and use fresh filtered water to blend them. The meal left over from the milk can be dried out in a 60°C (140°F) oven for 3 hours, to use in cakes – or, if you have chickens they will absolutely love the soft nut meal straight from the muslin (cheesecloth).

240 g (8½ oz/1½ cups) brazil nuts, macadamia nuts or almonds

750 ml (25½ fl oz/3 cups) filtered water, plus extra for soaking

Rinse the nuts under cold water, then drain them. Place them in clean bowl, cover with extra filtered water and a pinch of salt, and leave to soak overnight.

The next day, rinse the nuts again, cover with the filtered water and blitz in a high-speed blender for 2 minutes. Strain the mixture through fine gauze or muslin (cheesecloth) into a bowl, and squeeze the nut meal in the gauze tightly to extract all the nut milk.

Green tahini   MAKES 250 G (9 OZ)

225 g (8 oz) tahini
1 tablespoon crushed garlic
½ teaspoon sea salt
2 lemons, juiced

10 g (¼ oz) baby English spinach leaves, chopped
100 ml (3½ fl oz) extra-virgin olive oil
½ bunch flat-leaf (Italian) parsley leaves, chopped
½ bunch coriander (cilantro) leaves, chopped

In a food processor, blend the tahini, 125 ml (4 fl oz/½ cup) water, the garlic, sea salt, lemon juice and spinach leaves until green and smooth. Blend in the olive oil to emulsify, then fold through the parsley and coriander and pulse to combine. Adjust the salt and lemon juice to taste.

Note: *As you can see, this is a dairy-free green tahini. You can omit half the water and add 60 g (2 oz) yoghurt instead, for a thicker, richer tahini.*

Chimichurri MAKES 250 G (9 OZ)

½ bunch flat-leaf (Italian) parsley, leaves picked and finely chopped

¼ bunch oregano, leaves picked and finely chopped

¼ bunch thyme, leaves picked and finely chopped

¼ bunch sage, leaves picked and finely chopped

1 long red chilli

1 teaspoon sea salt

1 pinch white pepper

60 ml (2 fl oz/¼ cup) red-wine vinegar

100 ml (3½ fl oz) olive oil

75 g (2¾ oz) garlic, finely chopped

Put all the ingredients in a blender and pulse gently to form a rustic sauce. The longer you pulse, the thicker and smoother the sauce becomes. It's up to you to choose the finish, but I like mine quite coarse with an almost chopped appearance. Store in a sealed jar in the refrigerator, with a puddle of oil on top so the chimichurri keeps its colour.

Romesco sauce MAKES 225 G (8 OZ)

1 tomato

60 ml (2 fl oz/¼ cup) extra-virgin olive oil

2 garlic cloves, peeled and chopped

2 dried chillies, seeded and refreshed in warm water for 15 minutes to rehydrate

60 g (2 oz) whole tinned piquillo peppers

15 g (½ oz) crustless sourdough bread, cut into 2 cm (¾ in) slices, fried in a little extra-virgin olive oil

30 g (1 oz) almonds, toasted

60 g (2 oz) hazelnuts, toasted

1 teaspoon red-wine vinegar

½ bunch flat-leaf (Italian) parsley, leaves picked and chopped

Preheat the oven to 200°C (400°F).

Put the tomato in a roasting tin and drizzle over a quarter of the olive oil. Roast for 10 minutes or until the skin blisters and the tomato is soft. Remove the tomato from the oven and allow it to cool so you can handle it with your fingers. Peel the skin from the tomato and discard. Cut the tomato in half and squeeze out the seeds so all you have left is the flesh. Reserve the oil.

In a blender, blitz the garlic, soaked chillies and piquillo peppers to form a smooth paste. Add the tomato, followed by the bread, then the nuts, pulsing after the addition of each ingredient into a smooth texture. Use the vinegar to loosen the mixture. Slowly trickle in the reserved olive oil from the tomato and the remaining olive oil to form a smooth sauce – you're looking for the consistency of mayonnaise. Pulse through the chopped parsley and season with salt and freshly ground black pepper.

Rosemary tarator   MAKES 400 G (14 OZ)

50 g (1¾ oz) sourdough bread, crusts removed, roughly torn

20 g (¾ oz) activated walnuts (see page 237)

50 ml (1¾ fl oz) full-cream (whole) milk

1 hard-boiled egg, coarsely crumbled

20 g (¼ oz/½ cup) firmly packed rosemary leaves

10 g (¼ oz/½ cup) firmly packed mint leaves

10 g (¼ oz/½ cup) firmly packed flat-leaf (Italian) parsley leaves

10 g (¼ oz/½ cup) coarsely chopped chives

5 g (¼ oz/¼ cup) firmly packed tarragon leaves

2 teaspoons baby salted capers, rinsed and drained well

4 anchovy fillets

200 ml (7 fl oz) extra-virgin olive oil

1 lemon, juiced

Soak the bread and walnuts in the milk to soften, about 4–5 minutes. Squeeze the excess milk from the bread and transfer it to a blender with the walnuts. Add the egg, herbs, capers and anchovies and process to a rough paste. Add the oil in a thin stream and blitz until you have a rustic sauce. Add the lemon juice and season to taste with salt and freshly ground black pepper. The tarator will keep refrigerated in an airtight container for up to 1 week

Dill pickles   MAKES 1 KG (2 LB 3 OZ)

100 g (3½ oz) sea salt

2 litres (68 fl oz/8 cups) filtered water

4 fresh vine leaves or horseradish leaves

10 garlic cloves, peeled

2 bunches dill, chopped

2 teaspoons black peppercorns

½ teaspoon chilli flakes

1 tablespoon yellow mustard seeds

1 tablespoon fennel seeds

1 kg (2 lb 3 oz) pickling cucumbers (or enough to fill a 2 litre/68 fl oz/8 cup jar)

In a bowl, dissolve the sea salt in the filtered water and set aside.

To a sterilised 3.5 litre (118 fl oz/14 cup) jar, add two vine leaves, a few garlic cloves, half the dill and all the spices. Pack the cucumbers tightly into the jar with the remainder of the ingredients on top, making sure two vine leaves are right at the top to act as a lid over the cucumbers. Pour the salt water over the pickles, leaving a 2 cm (¾ in) gap at the top of the jar so the mixture can expand when it releases carbon dioxide. Use something small, such as a ceramic ramekin, to act as a weight to place on top and hold the cucumbers under the water and pack them in tightly. Now place the lid on the jar tightly. Place the jar in the larder or somewhere at a stable room temperature between 15 and 20°C (59 and 68°F).

Every day for 1 week, undo the lid to release the carbon dioxide. (You can remove the ramekin after about a week.) Don't be alarmed by the liquid turning cloudy and bubbly. Try a pickle after a week – if you prefer it sourer, just leave the jar fermenting. Once you're happy with the taste, store the pickles in the refrigerator to slow the fermentation down.

Bread and butter cucumbers MAKES 1 KG (2 LB 3 OZ)

5 Lebanese (short) cucumbers

5 French shallots, peeled

iced water

3 tablespoons sea salt

400 ml (13½ fl oz) apple-cider vinegar

200 g (7 oz) caster (superfine) sugar

2 teaspoons brown mustard seeds

3 teaspoons mustard powder

½ teaspoon freshly ground black pepper

1 teaspoon coriander seeds

2 bay leaves

Slice the cucumbers and shallots thinly and place them in a bowl of iced water with the sea salt for 1 hour. Remove from the water and drain well.

Combine the remaining ingredients in a saucepan over medium heat and bring to the boil. Cook for 3 minutes, then remove the pan from the heat and leave to cool.

Combine the liquid and cucumbers in a bowl and mix well. Spoon the contents into sterilised jars and leave overnight before using. The cucumbers are best kept in the refrigerator and will last around 3 months.

Vegetable kraut MAKES 1 KG (2 LB 3 OZ)

½ white cabbage, shredded

1 carrot, grated

1 radish, grated

1 fennel bulb, grated

two 4 cm (1½ in) pieces fresh turmeric, grated

1 teaspoon caraway seeds

45 g (1½ oz) salt

Combine all the ingredients in a bowl and knead together with your hands for 5 minutes until plenty of water has been released. Stuff the vegetables into a sterilised 2 litre (68 fl oz/8 cup) jar, pressing down and forcing the vegetables underneath the liquid. If necessary, add a very small amount of water to completely cover the cabbage, leaving a 2 cm (¾ in) gap at the top.

Cover the jar tightly with a lid and place it in a cool, dark place (15–20°C/59–68°F) for 2 weeks. During this time you will have to open the jar once a day to release the carbon dioxide. Once the kraut is ready, place it in the refrigerator, with the lid on, to slow the fermentation down. It should be a little sour but the vegetables should still be crispy.

Note: *This recipe works well with regular cabbage, or you could use red cabbage and beetroot (beets) if you'd prefer a purple kraut.*

242

Sprouted buckwheat sourdough

MAKES 1 x 1.5 KG (3 LB 5 OZ) LOAF

This sprouted buckwheat bread, made by using a sourdough starter, is the perfect gluten-free substitute for regular sourdough bread. You can buy sprouted buckwheat from the freezer section of most health food stores or, if you have the capacity and inclination, you could sprout your own. Once you've made the starter, you use this to make a sponge. This sponge is then used to make the final bread. The starter recipe for this bread will make enough to bake one loaf, so give the other half to a friend or store the remainder in a sealed jar in the refrigerator. Once you get into the rhythm, you'll find that you take half your starter out and feed it back with equal quantities of water and buckwheat flour, so you will maintain the same amount of starter in your refrigerator. If you're not making your bread regularly, I suggest removing half your starter once a week and adding fresh water and buckwheat flour to it, to keep your starter active and fed. Give your starter a name and, if you look after it, it will be with you for the rest of your baking life.

STARTER (MAKES 500 G/1 LB 2 OZ)

35 g (¼ cup) organic raisins

455 ml (15½ fl oz) lukewarm filtered water

385 g (13½ oz) buckwheat flour

SPONGE

2 teaspoons salt

100 g (3½ oz) starter (see above)

225 ml (7½ fl oz) lukewarm water

225 g (8 oz) cracked sprouted buckwheat (blended lightly just to crack)

DOUGH

all of the sponge (see left)

210 g (7½ oz) sprouted buckwheat

500 g (1 lb 2 oz) cracked sprouted buckwheat (blended lightly just to crack)

30 g (1 oz/¼ cup) pepitas (pumpkin seeds)

30 g (1 oz) buckwheat flour

210 ml (7 fl oz) lukewarm water

For the starter, soak the raisins in the lukewarm filtered water for 15 minutes, then strain the raisin-infused water and use it immediately. Discard the raisins.

Place 40 g (1½ oz/⅓ cup) of the buckwheat flour in a non-reactive bowl. Add 80 ml (2½ fl oz/⅓ cup) of the raisin water to the flour and mix well to form a paste. Cover the bowl with plastic wrap and leave to ferment for 24 hours in a warm spot (around 20°C/68°F is ideal).

The next day, add another 40 g (1½ oz/⅓ cup) buckwheat flour and 55 ml (1¾ fl oz) filtered water to the bowl and mix well to make a slightly thicker paste, ensuring there are no lumps. Cover again and leave to ferment for another 24 hours.

By the following day (day three), the paste may have separated and look curdled, but don't worry – just whisk in another 75 g (2¾ oz) buckwheat flour and 115 ml (4 fl oz) filtered water to bring it back to a smooth texture. Cover again and leave to ferment for another 24 hours.

By day four, the starter should have a vinegar-like smell and surface bubbles should be evident. Discard half the mixture, then whisk in 75 g (2¾ oz) buckwheat flour and 115 ml (4 fl oz) filtered water. Cover again and leave to ferment for 24 hours in the same spot.

On day five, your starter should be quite lively with active bubbles. Whisk in the remaining 155 g (5½ oz) buckwheat flour and 225 ml (7½ fl oz) filtered water. Cover loosely to allow the gases that are released during fermentation to escape, then set aside to ferment for 4 hours or until very bubbly. Place in the refrigerator and leave for 12 hours before using.

For the sponge, mix the ingredients together in a bowl, cover, and leave for 8–12 hours at room temperature to ferment (see Note).

For the dough, preheat the oven to 200°C (400°F) and oil a 23 × 12.5 cm (9 × 5 in) loaf (bar) tin.

Mix all the ingredients in an electric mixer on low speed for 1 minute. Turn off the mixer and let the mixture rest for 30 minutes, for all the ingredients to hydrate.

Turn the mixer back on low speed and mix until everything is completely combined, about 2 minutes. Pour the batter into the prepared tin, cover with plastic wrap and leave to prove for 1½ hours at room temperature.

When the dough has proved, using a water atomiser, spray the top of the loaf with water so it's nice and moist. Place the tin in the oven, reduce the heat to 165°C (330°F) and bake the bread for 1½ hours or until the temperature inside the loaf reaches 98°C (208°F).

Turn the oven off and leave the bread to rest in the oven for 2 hours. Turn the bread out onto a wire rack to cool completely. Wrap tightly in greaseproof (wax) paper or plastic wrap and refrigerate overnight as it's best the next day. Store it in the refrigerator to keep it moist so it doesn't crack.

Note: *If you can't make a sourdough starter, mix 1 teaspoon dried yeast with 50 g (1¾ oz) cracked buckwheat and 50 ml (1¾ fl oz) tepid water and allow to slowly rise in the refrigerator for 8–12 hours.*

Shortcrust suet pastry dough

MAKES 250 G (9 OZ)

70 g (2½ oz) suet
140 g (5 oz) self-raising flour
2 teaspoons baking powder

10 g (¼ oz) thyme leaves, chopped
1 tablespoon iced water
2 eggs, lightly whisked

Blitz the suet, flour, baking powder, thyme and 2 pinches of salt together in a food processor. Add the iced water and blitz to bring the ingredients together. Transfer the dough to a floured work surface and knead quickly to form a ball (the less handling the better). Cover the pastry with plastic wrap and store it in the refrigerator for at least 30 minutes until ready to use.

Gluten-free pastry dough   MAKES 500 G (1 LB 2 OZ)

120 g (4½ oz) rice flour
120 g (4½ oz) ground almonds
100 g (3½ oz/¾ cup) buckwheat flour
¼ teaspoon salt

1 tablespoon gluten-free cornflour (cornstarch)
120 g (4½ oz) unsalted butter, cold and diced
2 eggs

Blitz all the ingredients, except the eggs, in a food processor until the mixture resembles breadcrumbs. Blitz in the eggs and 2 tablespoons water. Turn the dough out onto some plastic wrap and bring the mixture together with your hands. Shape the dough into a disc, wrap it in the plastic wrap and refrigerate for at least 30 minutes until ready to use.

Rose syrup   MAKES 250 ML (8½ FL OZ/1 CUP)

100 g (3½ oz/2 cups) fresh rose petals
   (scrupulously sourced and guaranteed
   unsprayed and organic)
500 ml (17 fl oz/2 cups) boiling water

230 g (8 oz/1 cup) caster (superfine) sugar
1 star anise
1 clove

Brush the rose petals gently to remove any dirt, then place them on a tray lined with paper towel. Put the tray in a safe, draught-free place for 2 days to allow the petals to dry.

Once the rose petals are brittle, place them in a sterilised 500 ml (17 fl oz) clip-lock jar and pour the boiling water over them. Allow the petals to cool, then steep for 24 hours in the water.

Strain the water into a saucepan and add the sugar and spices. Boil for 10 minutes until the syrup lightly coats the back of a spoon, then remove from the heat. Allow to cool then strain back into the clip-lock jar. The rose syrup will keep for several months in the refrigerator.

Chantilly cream MAKES 400 G (14 OZ)

400 ml (13½ fl oz) pouring (single/ light) cream, very cold

60 g (2 oz) caster (superfine) sugar

½ vanilla bean, seeds scraped (pod discarded)

Put all the ingredients in a large mixing bowl and whip to soft peaks using an electric mixer.

Buttercream MAKES 375 G (13 OZ)

250 g (9 oz) unsalted butter, softened

1 vanilla bean, split lengthways and seeds scraped

1 tablespoon tepid water

125 g (4½ oz) icing (confectioners') sugar, sifted

Using an electric mixer, whip the butter on low speed for 3 minutes until pale. Add the vanilla seeds and the tepid water (as cold will make the butter set and hot will make the butter split – you can use milk instead if you like). Turn the speed to high and add the sugar. Whip for 5 minutes or until the mixture is white, glossy and silky smooth.

Raw chocolate–hazelnut spread MAKES 400 G (14 OZ)

Some commercial chocolate and hazelnut spreads are laden with processed sugar, so I created this heathy version, not only to reduce my family's sugar intake, but to derive the health benefits that cacao, extra-virgin coconut oil and maple syrup deliver in their purest forms.

100 g (3½ oz/⅔ cup) hazelnuts

filtered water

100 g (3½ oz) cacao powder

100 ml (3½ fl oz) extra-virgin coconut oil

100 ml (3½ fl oz) maple syrup

Soak the hazelnuts in filtered water to cover overnight. The next day, drain and rinse the nuts well. Transfer the hazelnuts to a blender, add ¼ teaspoon salt and pulse to combine. Add 25 g (1 oz/¼ cup) of the cacao powder and pulse to combine. Add 25 ml (¾ fl oz) of the coconut oil and pulse to combine. Repeat, alternating between the cacao and coconut oil, scraping down the side of bowl, until combined.

Add the maple syrup in a thin stream and blitz to form a paste. If the mixture splits, add some warm water, 1–2 tablespoons at a time, with the motor running, to bring the mixture back together. Transfer to an airtight container and store at room temperature for up to 1 week.

A

Activated nuts 237
adrenal activity 125, 128
Alastair's caramelised oranges with toasted almonds 169
allergy prevention 124
almond milk
  Chia and almond milk pudding with coconut yoghurt and stewed rhubarb 76
  Maple-toasted buckwheat, nuts and seeds with smashed banana and almond milk 182
almonds 226
  Alastair's caramelised oranges with toasted almonds 169
  Green beans, tangelo and nduja 193
  Maple-toasted buckwheat, nuts and seeds with smashed banana and almond milk 182
  Romesco sauce 239
  White gazpacho 25
Alzheimer's disease 190
amino acids 71, 126, 134, 137, 156, 182, 187
anaesthetics 84
anchovies, Peas and mint on toast with a poached egg 190
anti-ageing 228
anti-arthritis 67, 124, 156, 162, 165, 189, 193, 216, 226
antibacterials/antimicrobials
  fruit 71, 124, 165
  herbs and spices 18, 62, 67–8, 84, 92, 94, 104, 128, 142, 144, 161, 175, 180, 215–16
  vegetables 37, 96
anticancer properties
  fruit 21, 28, 30, 124, 138, 166, 181, 193, 216, 226
  grains 125
  herbs 189
  meat 210
  vegetables 38, 133, 142, 144, 197–8, 224
anti-clotting (anti-coagulants) 50, 137, 181, 226
antifungals 37, 58, 96, 124, 133, 161, 181, 216, 224
anti-inflammatories
  fish 162
  fruit 21, 28, 116, 165, 226, 228
  herbs and spices 22, 62, 67, 84, 94, 99, 104, 128, 142, 144, 161, 175, 180, 189, 190
  seeds and grains 76
  vegetables 38, 79, 92, 133, 190, 224
  see also vitamin C; vitamin A; B complex vitamins; vitamin E
antioxidants
  dairy 108
  drinks 68
  fish and seafood 52, 110
  fruit 18, 21, 26, 28, 30, 58, 71, 116, 118, 124, 165–6, 181, 220, 223, 228
  herbs and spices 22, 50, 62, 84, 95–6, 99, 104, 144, 158, 181, 189, 197, 223
  meat 103, 206

nuts 26, 81, 84, 116, 142
vegetables 25, 38, 83, 114, 132–3, 138, 141, 147, 184, 194, 197, 200, 205, 224
wines and spirits 223
see also selenium; vitamin A vitamin C; vitamin E
antiseptics 18, 38, 58
anti-stress 128, 137, 144, 180, 215, 220
antivirals 37, 96, 124, 165, 193, 215
Aperol spritz 118
apple-cider vinegar 61
apples
  Celeriac and apple soup with walnuts and cloves 84
  Mussels in cider with apples and sorrel 107
  Rhubarb and strawberry fizz 119
apricots, Poached apricots with lemon thyme junket 58
artichokes
  Artichoke vinaigrette 200
  see also globe artichokes; Jerusalem artichokes
arugula see rocket
Asian greens slaw with lime and sesame dressing 88
Asian ratatouille 99
asparagus
  Asparagus, peas and chamomile with ricotta 190
  Poached asparagus 198
  Spring tabouleh 197
asthma 224, 229
atherosclerosis prevention 19, 21, 22, 37, 46, 64, 132
aubergines see eggplants
avocados
  Chilled avocado, turmeric and cashew nut soup 189
  Mango, avocado, lime and lentil salad 33
  Smashed avocado, tomato and Persian feta on toast 19

B

bacon
  Borscht with horseradish cream 131–2
  Coq au vin blanc 106
Baked eggs with piperade and sorrel 184
Baked mushrooms 'Saint-Jacques' style 150
Baked okra with tomato, ginger and mustard seeds 34
Baked scallops with watermelon and hazelnut curry 54
Baked whole cauliflower with Indian spices, mint and yoghurt 143–4
Baked whole leather jackets, marjoram, capers and lemon 216
bananas, Maple-toasted buckwheat, nuts and seeds with smashed banana and almond milk 182
Basil oil 233
basmati rice, Kedgeree 126
B complex vitamins see Vitamin B
bean sprouts
  Asian ratatouille 99
  Mushroom omelette with nori and sesame 78–9
beef
  Borscht with horseradish cream 131–2
  Daube of beef oyster blade 156
  Mike's steak bordelaise in a hurry 103
beetroot (beets)
  Beetroot kvass 172
  Beetroot, quinoa, rhubarb and ponzu 134
  Borscht with horseradish cream 131–2
bell peppers see capsicums
beta-carotene 22, 33, 133, 194, 197, 205, 220
bile excretion 200
birth defects prevention 200
biscuits, Lavender sable biscuits 222
Blackberry butter 21, 236

bladder cancers 197
blood clotting
  fish 128
  fruit 21, 169
  grains 125
  vegetables 25, 37, 88, 100, 126, 133–4, 141, 180, 224
blood oranges, Grilled mackerel with blood oranges and dill 162
blood pressure regulation
  fish and seafood 52, 54, 128
  fruit 26, 166, 169–70
  herbs 92
  nuts 168
  seeds and grains 57, 76, 125–6, 182
  vegetables 41, 83, 100, 132, 184, 210, 224
blood sugar regulation 18, 28, 34, 46, 52, 54, 61, 162
blood thinning 81, 126
blueberries 14
  Blueberry, celery and pecan salad with lemon myrtle and labne 181
body fluid balance
  dairy 19
  fruit 67, 86, 170, 226
  seeds and grains 126
  vegetables 19, 41, 88, 100, 132, 141, 147, 184, 187, 202
bok choy, Asian greens slaw with lime and sesame dressing 88
bone formation/growth 16, 64, 86, 96, 110
bone health 16, 19, 34, 42, 64, 133, 134, 141, 210, 215
  see also muscles, bones & joint health
bone marrow 103
Borscht with horseradish cream 131–2
bottarga, Red mullet, café de Paris butter and cured roe 108
Bottled pears 166
brain health 14, 15, 16, 122, 123
  afters 58, 61, 62, 113, 114, 165, 168, 220, 222, 223, 224
  breakfast 16, 79, 125, 128, 180
  drinks 119
  fish 52, 54, 57, 108, 110, 158, 162, 215, 216, 218
  meat 42, 46, 103, 104, 210, 213
  salads 28, 137, 194
  soups 83
  vegetables 96, 142
Braised quince and witlof 148
Braised red cabbage 100
brandy 223
brazil nuts, Melon salad with fregola, gorgonzola, olives and brazil nuts 26
bread
  Bread and butter cucumbers 42, 241
  Cabbage, bread and cheese soup 186–7
  Chopped salad of iceberg, corn and jalapeño 194
  Coconut bread with blackberry butter 21
  French toast with nectarines and cinnamon sugar 16
  Parsnip, kale and white bean soup with 133
  Peas and mint on toast with a poached egg 180
  Smashed avocado, tomato and Persian feta on toast 19
  Sprouted buckwheat bread with vegetable kraut and goat's curd 126
  Sprouted buckwheat sourdough 242–3
  White gazpacho 25
breast cancer 197
brine, saltwater brine 143
broad beans, Paella on the barbecue 56–7
broccoli, Spring tabouleh 197
Broccolini with walnut and rosemary tarator 142
bronchitis 224

brussels sprouts, Shredded brussels sprouts, lentils, speck and parsley 141
buckwheat
    Buckwheat crêpes with raw chocolate–hazelnut spread and crème fraîche 81
    Maple-toasted buckwheat, nuts and seeds with smashed banana and almond milk 182
    Sprouted buckwheat sourdough 126, 242–3
burghul (bulgur wheat), Spring tabouleh 197
Buttercream 224, 245
butters
    Blackberry butter 21, 236
    Café de Paris butter 108, 237
    Clarified butter (ghee) 234
    Garlic and ginger butter 83, 235
    Garlic butter 245
    Oregano lime butter 38, 236
    Sorrel butter 202, 235
    Yabby butter 218, 236

C

cabbage 88, 126
    Borscht with horseradish cream 131–2
    Cabbage, bread and cheese soup 186–7
    Slow-cooked pork shoulder with chimichurri 104
    Stuffed spring cabbage with pork and chestnuts 212–13
    Sweet potato and red cabbage gratin 100
    Vegetable kraut 241
cacao 81
Café de Paris butter 108, 237
calasparra rice, Paella on the barbecue 56–7
calcium 19, 50, 108, 125, 155, 162, 169, 187, 206, 215
cannellini beans, Parsnip, kale and white bean soup 133
capers 216, 237
capsicums
    Asian ratatouille 99
    Baked eggs with piperade and sorrel 184
    Chopped salad of iceberg, corn and jalapeño 194
    Grilled haloumi, grapes and red rice 30
    Soffritto 147
carbohydrates 57
carminatives 38, 144, 175
carotenoids 58, 142, 158, 197
    see also beta-carotene
carrots
    Borscht with horseradish cream 131–2
    Cumin-scented carrots 205
    Daube of beef oyster blade 156
    Octopus braised in red wine with lemon and oregano 161
    Parsnip, kale and white bean soup 133
    Stuffed spring cabbage with pork and chestnuts 212–13
    Vegetable kraut 241
    Yabbies poached in chicken stock with broad beans and basil 218
cashew nut milk, Chilled avocado, turmeric and cashew nut soup 189
cataract protection 158, 194
cauliflower, Baked whole cauliflower with Indian spices, mint and yoghurt 143–4
Celeriac and apple soup with walnuts and cloves 84
celery
    Blueberry, celery and pecan salad with lemon myrtle and labne 181
    Borscht with horseradish cream 131
    Daube of beef oyster blade 156
    Octopus braised in red wine with lemon and oregano 161
cell division/production 34, 37, 67, 91, 114, 125, 128, 132, 134, 148, 168, 180, 200, 202

Chamomile dressing 190
Champagne, Lilly pilly Champagne cocktail 70–1
Chantilly cream 220, 245
Chargrilled sardines, nasturtiums, oregano and chilli 215
chayotes *see* chokos
cheese *see* feta; goat's curd; gorgonzola; gruyère; haloumi; ricotta
chestnuts
    Chestnut purée 168
    Mont Blanc 168
    Stuffed spring cabbage with pork and chestnuts 212–13
Chia and almond milk pudding with coconut yoghurt and stewed rhubarb 76
chicken
    Coq au vin blanc 106
    Grilled spatchcock marinated in crème fraîche 206
    Paella on the barbecue 56–7
    Roast chicken with verjuice, white grapes and tarragon 49–50
chickpeas, Salted kale with chickpeas and green tahini 137
chicory *see* witlof
Chilled avocado, turmeric and cashew nut soup 189
chillies
    Broccolini with walnut and rosemary tarator 142
    Chargrilled sardines, nasturtiums, oregano and chilli 215
    Chilli salt 124, 232
    Chopped salad of iceberg, corn and jalapeño 194
    Malaysian spiced pumpkin and coconut soup 22
    Soffritto 147
Chimichurri 239
    Slow-cooked pork shoulder with chimichurri 104
Chinese cabbage, Asian greens slaw with lime and sesame dressing 88
chloride 19
chokos, Steamed choko with sorrel butter 202
cholesterol
    'bad', lowering 46, 52, 54, 61, 88, 137, 158, 162, 168, 189, 190, 215, 216, 223
    'good', increasing 21, 22, 88, 137, 189
    regulation 18, 57, 76, 91, 103, 125, 148, 168, 169, 193, 200, 228
Chopped salad of iceberg, corn and jalapeño 194
chromium 198
chutneys, Prickly pear chutney 45
cilantro *see* coriander
cinnamon 94
cinnamon sugar 16
circulation improvement 81, 126, 182, 216
Clarified butter (ghee) 234
cloves 84
Coconut bread with blackberry butter 21
coconut milk, Malaysian spiced pumpkin and coconut soup 22
coconut oil 81
coconut yoghurt, Chia and almond milk pudding with coconut yoghurt and stewed rhubarb 76
colds 38, 124, 161, 170, 190, 216
collagen/collagen synthesis 16, 67, 106, 114, 124, 148, 165, 170, 216, 226, 229
colon cancers 125, 141, 197
cookies *see* biscuits
copper 33, 91, 110, 125, 148, 156, 161, 166, 189
Coq au vin blanc 106
coriander
    Asian greens slaw with lime and sesame dressing 88
    Asian ratatouille 99
    Baked okra with tomato, ginger and mustard seeds 34

Malaysian spiced pumpkin and coconut soup 22
corn
    Chopped salad of iceberg, corn and jalapeño 194
    Sweetcorn soup with garlic and ginger butter 83
Cornish pasties 152
courgettes *see* zucchini
Crab cakes with red mayonnaise 110
crème fraîche
    Buckwheat crêpes with raw chocolate–hazelnut spread and crème fraîche 81
    Grilled spatchcock marinated in crème fraîche 206
    Potato, leek and thyme galette 96
cucumbers
    Bread and butter cucumbers 42, 241
    Chopped salad of iceberg, corn and jalapeño 194
    White gazpacho 25
Cumin-scented carrots 205
Cumquat Sussex pond 165
curries
    Curry oil 233
    Watermelon curry 54

D

dandelion leaves, Plum, radish, lemon thyme and green pistachio nuts 92
Daube of beef oyster blade 156
depression 58, 125
diabetes 52, 147, 162, 165, 202, 228
dietary fibre 169, 190, 193
    fruit 46, 58, 62, 92, 166, 169, 226
    nuts 150, 168
    seeds and grains 125, 137, 155
    vegetables 83, 150, 190, 193, 224
dill pickles 240
    Lamb burek, dill pickles and yoghurt 82
diverticulitis 30, 148
DNA synthesis 37, 42
dressings 94, 194
    Chamomile dressing 190
    Green pistachio nut dressing 92
    Lemon dressing 215
    Sesame dressing 88
    Yoghurt dressing 144
    Yuzu ponzu dressing 134
    see also mayonnaise
duck
    Borscht with horseradish cream 131–2
    Freekeh-stuffed duck with saffron, olives and preserved lemon 155

E

E. coli-induced diarrhoea 175
ear, nose & throat health 15, 74, 75, 178
    afters 170
    breakfast 124
    drinks 118, 229
    fish 161
    salads 92, 190, 197
    soups 22, 84
    vegetables 38, 41, 99, 142, 202
eczema 82
eggplants, Asian ratatouille 99
eggs 123
    Baked eggs with piperade and sorrel 184
    Kedgeree 128
    Mushroom omelette with nori and sesame 78–9
    Poached eggs 180
essential fatty acids 125
essential oils 18, 38, 58, 67, 92, 144, 161, 165, 180, 181, 205, 220, 228
eye health *see* vision

F

fava beans *see* broad beans
fennel
  Beetroot, quinoa, rhubarb and ponzu 134
  Borscht with horseradish cream 131–2
  Mussels in cider with apples and sorrel 107
  Nashi pear, shaved fennel, parmesan, raisins and
    pine nuts 91
  Octopus braised in red wine with lemon and
    oregano 161
  Spring tabouleh 197
  Vegetable kraut 241
feta, Smashed avocado, tomato and Persian feta
  on toast 19
fevers 38, 190, 216
Figs, roast onions, walnuts and radicchio 28
fish 122
  Baked whole leather jackets, marjoram, capers
    and lemon 216
  Chargrilled sardines, nasturtiums, oregano and
    chilli 215
  Grilled mackerel with blood oranges and dill 162
  Kedgeree 128
  Picnic ocean trout, wild black pepper and
    verjuice mayonnaise 51–2
  Red mullet, café de Paris butter and cured
    roe 108
  Roasted whole John Dory with vanilla and
    saffron 157–8
  see also seafood
flavonoids 41, 46, 64, 81, 126, 133, 141, 182,
flax seeds *see* linseeds
fluoride 64
folic acid/folates
  fish 162
  fruit 61, 67, 86, 91, 226
  herbs and spices 132, 197
  nuts 168
  vegetables 34, 37–8, 114, 134, 138, 148, 180, 193,
    200, 202
Frangipane 226
free radicals 22, 41, 108, 141, 144, 165, 200, 205,
  220
Freekeh-stuffed duck with saffron, olives and
  preserved lemon 155
fregola, Melon salad with fregola, gorgonzola,
  olives and brazil nuts 26
French toast with nectarines and cinnamon
  sugar 16

G

gall bladder function 38
garbanzo beans *see* chickpeas
garlic 74
  Garlic butter 235
  Garlic and ginger butter 83, 235
  White gazpacho 25
gelatine 116, 156, 187
ghee *see* Clarified butter
ginger 75, 99
  Ginger beer 175
  ginger beer bug liquid 175
  ginger beer plant 175
  ginger plant food 175
Glazed ham with prickly pear chutney 45–6
globe artichokes
  Artichoke vinaigrette 200
  Stuffed baby artichokes with olive, citrus and
    herb salad 138
gluten-free 21, 76, 81
  Gluten-free pastry dough 96, 244
  Gluten-free plum, rosemary and hazelnut
    cake 62

goat's curd, Sprouted buckwheat bread with
  vegetable kraut and goat's curd 126
'good' cholesterol *see* cholesterol, 'good'
gooseberries, Sheep's kefir with gooseberries and
  lemon verbena 18
gorgonzola, Melon salad with fregola, gorgonzola,
  olives and brazil nuts 26
grapefruit
  Pink grapefruit bicicletta 228
  Pink grapefruit with chilli salt and honey 124
grapes
  Grilled haloumi, grapes and red rice 30
  Roast chicken with verjuice, white grapes and
    tarragon 49–50
  White gazpacho 25
Green beans, tangelo and nduja 193
green pistachio nuts
  Green pistachio jelly 116
  Green pistachio jelly with persimmons in rose
    syrup 116
  Green pistachio nut dressing 92
Green tahini 137, 238
Grilled haloumi, grapes and red rice 30
Grilled mackerel with blood oranges and dill 162
Grilled marinated lamb skirt with bread and
  butter cucumbers 42
Grilled spatchcock marinated in crème fraîche 206
gruyère, Cabbage, bread and cheese soup 186–7
gut health 75, 123, 178, 179
  afters 58, 61, 62, 166, 169, 224
  breakfast 18, 19, 21, 82, 125, 126
  drinks 68, 71, 172, 175, 228
  meat 42, 46, 104
  salads 28, 30, 33, 193
  soups 132
  vegetables 34, 37, 96, 142, 144, 200, 205

H

haloumi, Grilled haloumi, grapes and red rice 30
ham, Glazed ham with prickly pear chutney 45–6
hazelnuts
  Baked scallops with watermelon and hazelnut
    curry 54
  Gluten-free plum, rosemary and hazelnut
    cake 62
  Raw chocolate–hazelnut spread 81, 245
  Roast Jerusalem artichokes, soffritto and
    hazelnuts 147
  Romesco sauce 239
headaches 58, 125, 215, 222
healthy skin *see* skin health
heart attack, reduction 50, 224
heartbeat/heart rate 41, 52, 61, 88, 132, 147, 170,
  187, 202
heart disease, reduction 52, 54, 107, 119, 132,
  134, 189
heart health 14, 15, 74, 122, 123, 178, 179
  afters 61, 62, 64, 113, 116, 166, 168, 169, 223, 224
  breakfast 18, 19, 21, 81, 82, 125, 126, 128, 180,
    181, 184
  drinks 68, 119
  fish 52, 54, 57, 107, 108, 110, 158, 162, 215, 216
  meat 103, 152, 210
  salads 26, 28, 30, 33, 86, 88, 91, 134, 137, 141, 193
  soups 21, 83, 132, 133, 189
  vegetables 34, 37, 41, 94, 100, 144, 147, 148, 198,
    200, 205
homocysteine lowering 107, 119, 132, 134, 210
honey 179
  Gluten-free plum, rosemary and hazelnut
    cake 62
  Pink grapefruit with chilli salt and honey 124

honeydew melon, Melon salad with fregola,
  gorgonzola, olives and brazil nuts 26
Horseradish cream 132

I

immune system function 82, 156, 206
  fruit 16, 21, 33, 62, 86, 91, 118, 124, 148, 170, 229
  herbs and spices 99, 181
  meat 42, 46, 103
  nuts 26
  seeds and grains 126, 155, 182
  vegetables 37, 84, 96, 100, 114, 132–3, 138, 142,
    172, 180, 184, 187, 190, 193, 200, 224
  see also vitamin A; vitamin C
Indian spice mix 143, 232
indigestion 38, 58, 67, 226
inflammatory bowel disease/syndrome 30, 82,
  148, 172
influenza 38, 142, 161, 170
insomnia 58, 125, 205
iodine 79
iron/iron metabolism
  fish and seafood 54, 107, 161
  fruit 33, 148, 229
  herbs and spices 184, 193–4, 205
  meat 42, 210
  nuts 189
  seeds and grains 125, 155
  vegetables 94, 96, 133, 141

J

jams and marmalades
  Chimichurri 104
  Tomato jam 34
  Zucchini and marmalade cake 114
jellies, Green pistachio jelly 116
Jerusalem artichokes, Roast Jerusalem artichokes,
  soffritto and hazelnuts 147
John Dory, Roasted whole John Dory with vanilla
  and saffron 157–8
joints 68, 106
  see also muscles, bones & joint health
junket (rennet), Lemon thyme junket 58

K

kale
  Parsnip, kale and white bean soup 133
  Salted kale with chickpeas and green tahini 137
Kedgeree 128
keratin 156
Kombucha 68
  Pineapple, mint and kombucha iceblocks 67

L

labne 181
  Baked okra with tomato, ginger and mustard
    seeds 34
Lactobacillus bacteria 126
lamb
  Grilled marinated lamb skirt with bread and
    butter cucumbers 42
  Lamb burek, dill pickles and yoghurt 82
  Lamb filling (Cornish pasties) 152
  Pot-roasted shoulder of lamb cooked in
    buttermilk with roast pears and potatoes
    209–10
lavender
  Lavender sable biscuits 222
  Lavender sugar 222
learning 137
leather jackets, Baked whole leather jackets,
  marjoram, capers and lemon 216

leeks
  Borscht with horseradish cream 131–2
  Leeks à la grecque 37
  Octopus braised in red wine with lemon and
    oregano 161
  Parsnip, kale and white bean soup 133
  Potato, leek and thyme galette 96
lemon myrtle, Blueberry, celery and pecan salad
  with lemon myrtle and labne 181
lemon thyme
  Lemon thyme junket 58
  Plum, radish, lemon thyme and green pistachio
    nuts 92
lemon verbena, Sheep's kefir with gooseberries
  and lemon verbena 18
lemons/lemon juice 75, 216
  Ginger beer 175
  Lemon dressing 215
  Lemon drizzle cake 170
  Whey lemonade 229
lentils
  Mango, avocado, lime and lentil salad 33
  Shredded brussels sprouts, lentils, speck and
    parsley 141
lettuce, Chopped salad of iceberg, corn and
  jalapeño 194
lilly pilly
  Lilly pilly Champagne cocktail 70–1
  Lilly pilly cordial 70
lima beans see cannellini beans
limes, Oregano lime butter 38, 236
linseeds, Maple-toasted buckwheat, nuts and seeds
  with smashed banana and almond milk 182
liver detoxification 68, 79, 172, 200

M

Macadamia milk 125
mackerel, Grilled mackerel with blood oranges
  and dill 162
macular disease 41
magnesium 34, 54, 125, 162, 166, 182, 189
Malaysian spiced pumpkin and coconut soup 22
Mandarin and rosemary syllabub 223
manganese 34, 86, 107, 116, 125, 148, 166, 189, 194
mangetout see snow peas
Mango, avocado, lime and lentil salad 33
Maple-toasted buckwheat, nuts and seeds with
  smashed banana and almond milk 182
Maple vinaigrette 234
marjoram, Baked whole leather jackets, marjoram,
  capers and lemon 216
marmalade see jams and marmalade
mayonnaise
  Red mayonnaise 110
  Wild black pepper and verjuice mayonnaise 51–2
Melon salad with fregola, gorgonzola, olives and
  brazil nuts 26
memory 62, 104, 137, 142, 215
menstrual cramps 38, 58
meringue 61
  Mont Blanc 168
  Queen of puddings 113
Mike's steak bordelaise in a hurry 103
milk 123
  full-cream (whole) 58, 113, 168
milk kefir grains, Sheep's kefir with gooseberries
  and lemon verbena 18
mint
  Mint oil 232
  Peas and mint on toast with a poached egg 180
  Pineapple, mint and kombucha iceblocks 67
monounsaturated fatty acids 25, 88, 137, 168, 189,
  213, 226

Mont Blanc 168
mood lifters 46, 92
mucilage 34
mulberries 15
muscle contraction/relaxation 88, 126, 158, 169, 187
muscle cramps 54, 171
muscles, bones & joint health 15, 74, 123, 178
  afters 67, 113, 169, 226
  breakfast 76, 182
  meat 50, 106, 155, 156, 206
  salads 138
  soups 25, 187
  vegetables 96, 150
mushrooms 123
  Asian greens slaw with lime and sesame
    dressing 88
  Baked mushrooms 'Saint-Jacques' style 150
  Coq au vin blanc 106
  Daube of beef oyster blade 156
  Mushroom omelette with nori and sesame 78–9
  Pork stuffing 212
mussels 74
  Mussels in cider with apples and sorrel 107
  Paella on the barbecue 56–7
myoglobin 155, 193

N

Nashi pear, shaved fennel, parmesan, raisins and
  pine nuts 91
nasturtium leaves, Chargrilled sardines,
  nasturtiums, oregano and chilli 215
nduja, Green beans, tangelo and nduja 193
nectarines, French toast with nectarines and
  cinnamon sugar 16
neurodegenerative diseases 124, 165, 190, 193, 216
niacin see vitamin B$_3$
nori, Mushroom omelette with nori and sesame
  78–9
nut milks 182, 238
  see also almond milk; cashew nut milk;
    macadamia milk
nuts
  Activated nuts 237
  see also almonds; brazil nuts; chestnuts;
    hazelnuts; pistachio nuts; walnuts

O

ocean trout
  Kedgeree 128
  Picnic ocean trout, wild black pepper and
    verjuice mayonnaise 51–2
Octopus braised in red wine with lemon and
  oregano 161
oils
  Basil oil 233
  Curry oil 233
  Mint oil 232
okra, Baked okra with tomato, ginger and mustard
  seeds 34
olives
  Freekeh-stuffed duck with saffron, olives and
    preserved lemon 155
  Mango, avocado, lime and lentil salad 33
  Melon salad with fregola, gorgonzola, olives and
    brazil nuts 26
  Nashi pear, shaved fennel, parmesan, raisins and
    pine nuts 91
  Octopus braised in red wine with lemon and
    oregano 161
  Olive, citrus and herb salad 138
omega-3 fatty acids
  dairy 108
  fish and seafood 52, 110, 128, 158, 162, 215

meat 103, 152
  nuts 84, 114, 142, 224
  seeds and grains 76, 126, 182
  vegetables 197
omega-6 fatty acids 155, 189
onions 178
  Asian ratatouille 99
  Baked eggs with piperade and sorrel 184
  Borscht with horseradish cream 131–2
  Daube of beef oyster blade 156
  Figs, roast onions, walnuts and radicchio 28
  Freekeh-stuffed duck with saffron, olives and
    preserved lemon 155
  Octopus braised in red wine with lemon and
    oregano 161
  Parsnip, kale and white bean soup 133
  Pork stuffing 212
  Shredded brussels sprouts, lentils, speck and
    parsley 141
  Soffritto 147
  Sweet potato and red cabbage gratin 100
oranges
  Alastair's caramelised oranges with toasted
    almonds 169
  Braised quince and witlof 148
  Cumin-scented carrots 205
  see also blood oranges
oregano 104
  Chargrilled sardines, nasturtiums, oregano and
    chilli 215
  Octopus braised in red wine with lemon and
    oregano 161
  Oregano lime butter 38, 236
osteoporosis 25, 133, 156, 200

P

Paella on the barbecue 56–7
painkillers 28
pak choy see bok choy
pancetta, Stuffed spring cabbage with pork and
  chestnuts 212–13
pancreatic cancer 197
parsley 104, 197, 216
parsnip
  Parsnip and ginger cake 224
  Parsnip, kale and white bean soup 133
pastry
  Cornish pasties 152
  Gluten-free pastry dough 96, 244
  Lamb burek, dill pickles and yoghurt 82
  Pineapple tarts 226
  Pudding dough 165
  Shortcrust suet pastry dough 244
Pavlova with raspberries in vinegar 61
Peach Melba 64
pears 91
  Bottled pears 166
  Roast pears with vanilla, thyme and verjuice
    209–10
peas
  Asparagus, peas and chamomile with ricotta 190
  Peas and mint on toast with a poached egg 180
  Spring tabouleh 197
  Yabbies poached in chicken stock with broad
    beans and basil 218
pecans, Blueberry, celery and pecan salad with
  lemon myrtle and labne 181
pectin 61, 169, 228
pepitas, Maple-toasted buckwheat, nuts and seeds
  with smashed banana and almond milk 182
peppers see capsicums
persimmons

Green pistachio jelly with persimmons in rose syrup 116

Shaved persimmon, preserved lemon and capers 86

phosphorus 19, 42, 50, 81, 96, 107, 110, 156, 206, 210, 213, 215

phytochemicals 91, 132, 142, 144, 189

Picnic ocean trout, wild black pepper and verjuice mayonnaise 51–2

pine nuts, Nashi pear, shaved fennel, parmesan, raisins and pine nuts 91

pineapple

Pineapple, mint and kombucha iceblocks 67

Pineapple tarts 226

Pink grapefruit bicicletta 228

Pink grapefruit with chilli salt and honey 124

piquillo peppers 147

Romesco sauce 239

pistachio nuts 92, 116

Kedgeree 128

Maple-toasted buckwheat, nuts and seeds with smashed banana and almond milk 182

plaque build-up in the arteries *see* atherosclerosis prevention

plums

Gluten-free plum, rosemary and hazelnut cake 62

Plum, radish, lemon thyme and green pistachio nuts 92

Poached apricots with lemon thyme junket 58

Poached asparagus 198

Poached eggs 180

pomegranates

Pomegranate and Aperol spritz 118

Quinoa porridge with pomegranate and macadamia milk 125

ponzu 234

Yuzu ponzu dressing 134

pork 46

Parsnip, kale and white bean soup 133

Pork stuffing 212

Slow-cooked pork shoulder with chimichurri 104

Pot-roasted shoulder of lamb cooked in buttermilk with roast pears and potatoes 209–10

potassium

fish and seafood 52, 54, 107, 158, 162

fruit 26, 33, 61, 64, 67, 86, 166, 169–70, 189, 226

nuts 168

seeds and grains 125

vegetables 22, 41, 88, 100, 126, 132, 137, 141, 147, 150, 184, 187, 194, 202, 210, 224

potatoes

Pot-roasted shoulder of lamb cooked in buttermilk with roast pears and potatoes 209–10

Potato, leek and thyme galette 96

Sweet potato and red cabbage gratin 100

prawns, Paella on the barbecue 56–7

Prickly pear chutney 45

probiotics 67, 68, 82, 193, 206

prostate cancer 141, 197

protein 82, 110, 132, 155, 162

lean 50, 206

non-meat 19

protein synthesis 42

Pudding dough 165

pumpkins (squash)

Malaysian spiced pumpkin and coconut soup 22

Roast pumpkin with chai spice and buttermilk 94

pumpkin seeds *see* pepitas

pyridoxine *see* vitamin B$_6$

Q

Queen of puddings 113

quince, Braised quince and witlof 148

quinoa

Beetroot, quinoa, rhubarb and ponzu 134

Quinoa porridge with pomegranate and macadamia milk 125

R

radicchio

Figs, roast onions, walnuts and radicchio 28

Grilled haloumi, grapes and red rice 30

Nashi pear, shaved fennel, parmesan, raisins and pine nuts 91

Roast chicken with verjuice, white grapes and tarragon 49–50

radishes

Plum, radish, lemon thyme and green pistachio nuts 92

Vegetable kraut 241

raisins

Nashi pear, shaved fennel, parmesan, raisins and pine nuts 91

Raisins in tea 143

raspberries 15

Pavlova with raspberries in vinegar 61

Raspberry coulis 64

Raspberry vinegar 61, 233

Raw chocolate-hazelnut spread 81, 245

red blood cells

eggs 184

fish and seafood 107, 110

fruit 33, 91, 119, 148

herbs and spices 193

meat 42, 46, 82

seeds and grains 94, 125, 155

vegetables 141, 205

Red mayonnaise 110

Red mullet, café de Paris butter and cured roe 108

red rice, Grilled haloumi, grapes and red rice 30

rheumatism 181

rhubarb

Beetroot, quinoa, rhubarb and ponzu 134

Chia and almond milk pudding with coconut yoghurt and stewed rhubarb 76

Rhubarb and strawberry fizz 119

riberry *see* lilly pilly

riboflavin *see* vitamin B$_2$

rice *see* basmati rice; calasparra rice; red rice

ricotta, Asparagus, peas and chamomile with ricotta 190

Roast baby squash with oregano and lime 38

Roast chicken with verjuice, white grapes and tarragon 49–50

Roast Jerusalem artichokes, soffritto and hazelnuts 147

Roast pears with vanilla, thyme and verjuice 209–10

Roast pumpkin with chai spice and buttermilk 94

Roasted whole John Dory with vanilla and saffron 157–8

rocket, Mango, avocado, lime and lentil salad 33

rockmelon, Melon salad with fregola, gorgonzola, olives and brazil nuts 26

Romesco sauce 110, 239

Rose syrup 114, 244

rosemary 62

Mandarin and rosemary syllabub 223

Rosemary tarator 142, 215, 240

rutabagas *see* swedes

S

saffron 158

sage 104, 216

salivary glands 205

salmon 52

Kedgeree 128

Salted kale with chickpeas and green tahini 137

saltwater brine 143

sardines, Chargrilled sardines, nasturtiums, oregano and chilli 215

sauces 99

Chimichurri 239

Green tahini 137, 238

Romesco sauce 110, 239

Rosemary tarator 142, 215, 240

scallions *see* spring onions

scallops, Baked scallops with watermelon and hazelnut curry 54

seafood

Baked scallops with watermelon and hazelnut curry 54

Crab cakes with red mayonnaise 110

Mussels in cider with apples and sorrel 107

Octopus braised in red wine with lemon and oregano 161

Paella on the barbecue 56–7

Yabbies poached in chicken stock with broad beans and basil 218

see also fish

seaweed, Picnic ocean trout, wild black pepper and verjuice mayonnaise 51–2

sedatives 28

selenium

fish and seafood 52, 107, 110, 161–2

meat 46, 50, 156, 206, 210

nuts 26, 81, 189

vegetables 79, 110, 150

sesame seeds 137

Maple-toasted buckwheat, nuts and seeds with smashed banana and almond milk 182

Sesame dressing 88

shallots

Coq au vin blanc 106

Kedgeree 128

Mussels in cider with apples and sorrel 107

Shaved persimmon, preserved lemon and capers 86

Sheep's kefir with gooseberries and lemon verbena 18

sheep's milk, Sheep's kefir with gooseberries and lemon verbena 18

Shortcake 220

Shortcrust suet pastry dough 244

Shredded brussels sprouts, lentils, speck and parsley 141

shrimp *see* prawns

Sichuan peppercorns 99

skin health 14, 15, 74, 75, 122, 123, 178

afters 58, 64, 114, 165, 166, 168, 220, 222, 223

breakfast 16, 21, 79, 81, 82, 125, 128, 184

drinks 68, 71, 228

fish 52, 54, 57, 108, 110, 158, 162

fruit 16, 67, 226, 229

meat 42, 46, 104, 152, 210, 213

salads 26, 86, 91, 134, 137, 141, 194

soups 25, 83, 132, 133, 189

vegetables 37, 41, 94, 96, 100, 142, 144, 147, 148, 198, 200, 205

sleep regulation 46, 137, 190

see also insomnia

Slow-cooked pork shoulder with chimichurri 104

Smashed avocado, tomato and Persian feta on toast 19

smell sensation 155
snow peas, Asparagus, peas and chamomile with
ricotta 190
Soffritto 147
sore throat 92
sorrel
Baked eggs with piperade and sorrel 184
Mussels in cider with apples and sorrel 107
Sorrel butter 202, 235
speck
Baked mushrooms 'Saint-Jacques' style 150
Shredded brussels sprouts, lentils, speck and
parsley 141
sperm production 205
spinach, Baked okra with tomato, ginger and
mustard seeds 34
spring onions
Asian greens slaw with lime and sesame
dressing 88
Crab cakes with red mayonnaise 110
Spring tabouleh 197
Sprouted buckwheat bread with vegetable kraut
and goat's curd 126
Sprouted buckwheat sourdough 242–3
squash, Roast baby squash with oregano and
lime 38
Steamed choko with sorrel butter 202
stomach upsets 38, 190
strawberries 15
Rhubarb and strawberry fizz 119
Strawberry shortcake 220
stroke reduction 50, 107, 119, 132, 134, 224
Stuffed baby artichokes with olive, citrus and herb
salad 138
Stuffed spring cabbage with pork and
chestnuts 212–13
sugar-free 21
sulphur 187, 213
'super' foods 137
swedes
Lamb filling (Cornish pastry) 152
Parsnip, kale and white bean soup 133
sweet potatoes 74
Sweet potato and red cabbage gratin 100
Sweetcorn soup with garlic and ginger butter 83
syrups, Rose syrup 114, 244

T
tahini, green 137, 238
tangelos, Green beans, tangelo and nduja 193
tarragon, Roast chicken with verjuice, white
grapes and tarragon 49–50
thiamine see vitamin B₁
thyme 58, 92, 104
thyroid hormone activity 46, 50, 52, 79, 81, 110,
125, 128, 206, 210
tomato passata (puréed tomatoes), Paella on the
barbecue 56–7
tomatoes
Asian ratatouille 99
Baked eggs with piperade and sorrel 184
Chopped salad of iceberg, corn and jalapeño 194
Romesco sauce 239
Smashed avocado, tomato and Persian feta on
toast 19
Spring tabouleh 197
Tomato jam 34
Tomatoes provençal 41
tooth decay prevention 25
turmeric 178, 189
Vegetable kraut 241
turnips, Yabbies poached in chicken stock with
broad beans and basil 218

U
urinary tract cancers 197
urinary tract infections 82, 172
UV rays blocking properties 41, 52

V
vanilla 158
Vegetable kraut 126, 241
vinegars/vinaigrettes
apple-cider vinegar 61
Artichoke vinaigrette 200
Maple vinaigrette 234
Ponzu 234
Raspberry vinegar 61, 233
Walnut vinaigrette 200, 234
vision
eggs 184
fruit 16, 21, 33, 46, 58, 62, 67, 169, 170, 226
vegetables 22, 83, 94, 100, 114, 132, 141–2, 147–8,
180, 193–4, 202, 205
vitamin A 197, 202, 210, 220
dairy 113
eggs 184
fish 162
fruit 16, 21, 26, 28, 33, 46, 58, 64, 67, 71, 92, 134,
166, 169–70, 189, 220, 226
herbs and spices 22, 62, 128, 202, 223
seeds and grains 125
vegetables 22, 25, 34, 37–8, 83, 100, 114, 132–3,
141–2, 147–8, 180, 190, 193–4, 197, 205, 210, 218
vitamin B complex 22
eggs 79
fruit 61–2, 64, 92, 134, 169, 170, 189, 220
herbs and spices 128, 158
meat 46, 50, 206, 210
nuts 213, 224
seeds and grains 76, 125
vegetables 37, 84, 96, 100, 114, 132–3, 138, 141–2,
144, 148, 180, 190, 197–8, 200, 210, 218
vitamin B₁ 57, 119
vitamin B₂ 57, 110, 119, 150, 184
vitamin B₃ 42, 57, 82, 119, 137, 150, 162, 168,
216, 224
vitamin B₅ 119
vitamin B₆ 22, 33, 34, 96, 119, 137, 161, 205
vitamin B₇ 119
vitamin B₁₂ 19, 42, 82, 107, 161, 162, 184, 210
vitamin C
fish 158
fruit 16, 21, 26, 33, 46, 62, 64, 67, 71, 86, 91, 92,
118, 124, 148, 165–6, 169–70, 193, 216, 220, 223,
226, 228, 229
herbs and spices 22, 96, 158, 194, 197, 200, 215,
218, 223
nuts 168
seeds and grains 137
vegetables 25, 34, 37–8, 84, 96, 100, 114, 126,
132–3, 138, 141–2, 144, 147, 180, 184, 187, 190,
193, 197–8, 200, 205, 210, 213
vitamin D 57, 81, 113, 150, 162, 215
vitamin E
dairy 108, 113
eggs 184
fish 162
fruit 16, 21, 28, 64, 71, 189, 220
herbs and spices 62, 128, 197
meat 103
nuts 25–6, 84, 114, 142, 182, 224, 226
seeds and grains 125
vegetables 37, 133, 141, 147, 190, 198
vitamin K
fish 162
fruit 21, 28, 76, 134, 189

herbs and spices 22, 197
vegetables 25, 34, 37, 88, 100, 126, 133, 138, 141–2,
144, 180, 187, 190, 200, 213, 224

W
walnuts 215
Broccolini with walnut and rosemary tarator 142
Celeriac and apple soup with walnuts and
cloves 84
Figs, roast onions, walnuts and radicchio 28
Mango, avocado, lime and lentil salad 33
Parsnip and ginger cake 224
Roast chicken with verjuice, white grapes and
tarragon 49–50
Salted kale with chickpeas and green tahini 137
Walnut vinaigrette 200, 234
Zucchini and marmalade cake 114
watercress 178
Watermelon curry 54
weight loss 67, 181, 222
Whey lemonade 229
White gazpacho 25
Wild black pepper and verjuice mayonnaise 51–2
witlof, Braised quince and witlof 148
worm infestation 226
wound healing 46, 124, 165

Y
yabbies
Yabby butter 218, 236
Yabbies poached in chicken stock with broad
beans and basil 218
yoghurt 75
Chia and almond milk pudding with coconut
yoghurt and stewed rhubarb 76
labne 181
Lamb burek, dill pickles and yoghurt 82
Yoghurt dressing 144
Yuzu ponzu dressing 134

Z
zinc 42, 46, 107, 126, 155, 182, 189, 210
zucchini
Asian ratatouille 99
Zucchini and marmalade cake 114

252 Acknowledgements

Where to start? So many people influence, inspire and support me daily.

My wonderful wife Joss: you are my best friend, and have been the biggest influence in my life. To my boys George, Alfie and William: you are my heroes and will always be my most revered critics.

To kitchen staff, past and present: Jeffrey De Rome, business partner and left hand (thank you for your honesty), Julian Nikiel, Sam Parsons, Felicia Chan, Chukin Park, Scott Flannery, Marta Zuccon, Ziaul Haque, Edwina Reid, Francsico Ardiles-Martines and Takahiko Hakamata.

To floor staff, past and present: Greg Frazer, Christian Denier, Gemma Frapwell, Chee Khiang Mok, Charlotte White, Colin Nelson, Tom Harrison, Mary Penzikis, Rory Brown, Abigail Scott, Ronald Augustine, Arnaud Grospeillet, Bronte Currie, Tania Campos Linares, George Kerr and Sopitta Prasertpol, and a special mention to Tanya Pont who keeps me organised every day.

Petrina Baker, thanks always for your guidance and experience and for introducing me to the fabulous Jane Willson at Hardie Grant. Thanks also to Loran McDougall, Mark Campbell, Emily O'Neill (for a second time as designer), Ariana Klepac and the rest of the team at Hardie Grant – thank you for believing in me and producing such a wonderful book. It was a pleasure to write, and I look forward to the next. Alan Benson and Vanessa Austin, you shot and styled my first cookbook and became part of the family. When I was asked who was doing this cookbook, you were the only guys I wanted to work with.

To Lisa Havilah and the staff of Carriageworks, thank you for asking me to be the creative director of the Carriageworks Farmers Market, and allowing me to be part of your incredible vision. To Stephanie Andrews, your knowhow and 'can do' approach has taken the Carriageworks Farmers Market into the stratosphere. To all of the wonderful stall holders, your passion and integrity have inspired me no end and have made Carriageworks the most authentic urban farmers' market in Australia, or maybe even the world.

Finally, thank you to anyone who has bought this book. Enjoy it and make it your own.

Mike x

254 About the author

Mike McEnearney is executive chef and owner of No. 1 Bent Street by Mike and Kitchen by Mike, both in Sydney.

Mike began his career in 1990 at Sydney's internationally renowned Rockpool, before moving to London, where he worked at the Michelin-starred Pied à Terre, and ran the kitchens of Mezzo, Bluebird, The Pharmacy and Scott's. He returned to Australia in 2006 to lead the kitchen at Rockpool. In 2011 he launched Mike's Table, an acclaimed underground dining experience that gained cult status. Kitchen by Mike opened in 2012 and was swiftly awarded Best Cafe in the Time Out Sydney Food Awards. The ingenious Kitchen by Mike canteen-style eatery champions egalitarian dining and the use of the best local and seasonal produce.

In 2014 Mike pioneered the creation of Australia's first urban physic garden, putting a new spin on the kitchen garden and underpinning his long-held belief that food is medicine.

A natural evolution of Kitchen by Mike has been the 2016 launch of No. 1 Bent Street by Mike, in Sydney's CBD, which offers a slightly more refined dining experience, while still maintaining Mike's generous-spirited and approachable attitude to food and eating out.

A strong belief and trust in simplicity, generosity and sustainable wholefoods form the foundation of everything Mike does. The joy of eating real food, in its purest form, is at the helm of all his endeavours. Mike's business covers more than just restaurants. He has a number of publishing projects, a product range, and is the creative director of the Carriageworks Farmers Market.

In 2015 Mike's first book, *Kitchen by Mike*, was named 'Best Cookbook written by a Chef' at the Gourmand World Cookbook Awards.

Mike lives in Sydney with his wife and their three boys.

First published in 2016 by the Royal Opera House
in association with Oberon Books Ltd
Oberon Books Ltd
521 Caledonian Road, London N7 9RH
Tel +44 (0)20 7607 3637
info@oberonbooks.com
www.oberonbooks.com

Cover and book design: James Illman

For the Royal Opera House:

Commissioning Editor: John Snelson

Project Manager: Will Richmond

Content Production Assistant: Nicholas Manderson

Every effort has been made to trace the
copyright holders of all images reprinted in this
book. Acknowledgement is made in all cases
where the image source is available, but we
would be grateful for information about any
images where sources could not be traced.

A catalogue record for this book is available
from the British Library.

PB ISBN 978-1-78319-743-9

Printed and bound by
CPI Group (UK) Ltd, Croydon, CR0 4YY

Royal Opera House
Covent Garden
London WC2E 9DD
Box Office +44 (0)20 7304 4000
www.roh.org.uk

ROYAL
BALLET

2016/17

THE 2016/17 ROYAL BALLET YEARBOOK AND ROYAL BALLET SEASON GENEROUSLY SUPPORTED BY
AUD JEBSEN

THE 2016/17 SEASON

WELCOME TO THE 2016/17 SEASON, FROM KEVIN O'HARE

The Royal Ballet is a unique company both in the variety of its day-to-day activity and in the breadth of work it draws on and performs. In one typical day during the 2015/16 Season the Company may have been making new work, such as Liam Scarlett's *Frankenstein*, before a rehearsal of the first revival of a recent creation, such as Christopher Wheeldon's *The Winter's Tale*, followed by an evening performance of *Giselle*, broadcast live to cinemas.

From the 19th-century classics and heritage works by Frederick Ashton and Kenneth MacMillan, to revivals of recent works made on the Company or elsewhere and the commissioning and creating of new work, our Seasons offer an exciting range of performances for audiences all over the world.

The 2016/17 Season will be one of celebration: Wayne McGregor has been The Royal Ballet's Resident Choreographer for ten years. We celebrate the brilliant and original works he has made on the Company and his unique collaborations with artists from other creative spheres. We also celebrate his valuable work nurturing and developing young choreographers, with our 'Draft Works' projects in The Royal Ballet Studio Programme and the continuation of the Young Choreographer programme through which Charlotte Edmonds enters her second Season as a choreographer with the Company. Charlotte has developed her choreography and secured international commissions during her first Season, and with the Clore Studio Upstairs becoming a more formal performance space, we present some of her work in a mixed programme with work by Robert Binet. In 2012 Wayne introduced Robert to the Company and, having since worked in New York, Robert is returning as part of our support for emerging choreographers.

Wayne's first work for the main stage at Covent Garden was *Qualia* in 2003, and it was after the premiere of his era-defining ballet *Chroma* in 2006, that he was made Resident Choreographer. *Chroma*, a very special, once-in-a-decade work that has been performed in 13 countries in the last ten years, will be revived this Season. The cast will be split between Royal Ballet dancers and dancers from Alvin Ailey American Dance Theater, who performed the ballet in 2013. Alongside *Chroma*, we revive Wayne's 2012 ballet *Carbon Life*, and Mark Ronson will return to perform the music along with many of the original collaborators and some exciting new artists.

The centrepiece of the McGregor mixed programme is a new work that will be set to a brand-new score by Steve Reich, one of today's greatest composers, who celebrates his 80th birthday in October 2016. The internationally acclaimed Pakistani artist Rashid Rana is creating the designs.

In the 2016/17 Season we also revive Wayne's 2015 *Woolf Works*, which won an Olivier Award in 2016. The ballet was created on former Royal Ballet Principal Alessandra Ferri, who also won an Olivier Award for her performances. Alessandra was such an inspiration to the Company and dancers and we are thrilled to invite her back for the revival performances this Season. She will share the role with former Royal Ballet Principal Mara Galeazzi,

who left the Company in 2013. It will be a pleasure to have Alessandra and Mara back with the Company for these performances.

Finally, Wayne is also creating a work for the 'Chance to Dance' programme this Season – a very important opportunity for young people to find their way into dance – working with the Royal Opera House Learning and Participation department.

This Season we also celebrate 70 years since the Company became resident at the Royal Opera House. In 1946, to reopen the building after World War II, Ninette de Valois mounted performances of a new production of *The Sleeping Beauty*, with designs by Oliver Messel. The ballet occupies a special place in the Company's heritage, and this Season we revive the current production, which remains faithful to the designs and choreography of the De Valois production, and which was created by Monica Mason and Christopher Newton in 2006. The first post-war Season also included the world premiere of Ashton's *Symphonic Variations*. In honour of Ashton we are reviving *The Dream* and *Marguerite and Armand*; his perennially popular *La Fille mal gardée* will open the Season, and *Symphonic Variations* will be a fitting finale.

We're also looking forward to two revivals of works from our Kenneth MacMillan repertory: *Anastasia* and *Mayerling*. These ballets contain some of MacMillan's most powerful roles with great dramatic opportunities for the Company dancers.

Each Season we are fortunate to be able to draw on the tremendous knowledge and experience of our répétiteurs, ballet masters and ballet mistresses. This Season we also welcome former Royal Ballet Principals Viviana Durante and Leanne Benjamin as coaches for *Anastasia* and *Mayerling* respectively. The contribution of all this experience in the fostering of a new

This page:
Artists of The Royal Ballet in *The Sleeping Beauty*
©2014 ROH. Photograph by Tristram Kenton
Opposite page:
Top: Olivia Cowley and Edward Watson in *Chroma*
©2013 ROH. Photograph by Bill Cooper
Bottom: Eric Underwood in *Carbon Life*
©2012 ROH. Photograph by Bill Cooper

generation of coaches and dancers is indispensable for us to sustain the works of The Royal Ballet's repertory.

We are thrilled at the success of the Aud Jebsen Young Dancers programme, which started two years ago, allowing young talent to work and train with The Royal Ballet in preparation for joining the Company, or other leading ballet companies, should a position become available. All five of last Season's group are joining the Company this Season as Artists and a new group of seven join from The Royal Ballet School (see below).

This Season we also bring back George Balanchine's *Jewels* as well as another of his works, *Tarantella*, never before performed by The Royal Ballet, which will be performed in a mixed programme with William Forsythe's *The Vertiginous Thrill of Exactitude*.

We welcome the first revivals of two ballets recently created on the Company: David Dawson's 2013 *The Human Seasons* and Christopher Wheeldon's *Strapless*, which received its premiere in 2016. The pas de deux from Wheeldon's *After the Rain* was first performed by The Royal Ballet as part of a gala in 2012 and the full ballet was staged as part of last Season's Wheeldon mixed programme. *After the Rain* will also return this Season in a mixed programme with a new work by Crystal Pite. Crystal is creating new work on the Company dancers for the first time in her first UK ballet commission.

Royal Ballet Artist in Residence Liam Scarlett will create a new abstract ballet in May. Following last Season's premiere of his first full-length narrative

ballet, inspired by Mary Shelley's *Frankenstein*, the previous Season's premiere of his semi-narrative ballet based on W.H. Auden's poem *The Age of Anxiety* and the 2013 premiere of his *Hansel and Gretel*, Liam returns to a non-narrative style. His other abstract works include *Asphodel Meadows*, given its premier in 2010, and *Viscera*, which he created on Miami City Ballet in 2012.

Off the main stage, new productions will include a new collaboration between The Royal Ballet, The Royal Opera's Jette Parker Young Artists programme and Javier de Frutos. De Frutos will direct a new production of Philip Glass's 2005 dance opera, *Les Enfants terribles*, based on Jean Cocteau's 1929 novel and Jean-Pierre Melville's 1950 film. The work will feature a mixture of Royal Ballet dancers, contemporary dancers and opera singers. This major project, commissioned by The Royal Ballet Studio Programme, will be performed at the Barbican.

After the success of our 2014/15 collaboration with ZooNation Dance Company, we are reviving *The Mad Hatter's Tea Party*, which will be performed at the Roundhouse from December. This collaboration between the Royal Opera House, ZooNation and the Roundhouse is another great opportunity for the Company to get outside the Royal Opera House and reach new audiences.

Alongside our valuable Chance to Dance programme, The Royal Ballet is collaborating with the Royal Opera House Learning and Participation department on our 'National Nutcracker' project, which was piloted last year. National Nutcracker presents opportunities for schools around the country to engage with our celebrated production of *The Nutcracker*, through workshops and creative exchanges, culminating in a visit to see this festive ballet at the Royal Opera House or in cinemas across the UK.

No fewer than six of our performances this Season will be relayed live to audiences all over the world as part of the Royal Opera House Live Cinema Season. Audiences in more than 35 countries will be able to watch live performances of *Anastasia*, *The Nutcracker*, *Woolf Works*, *The Sleeping Beauty*, *Jewels* and the Ashton mixed programme.

World Ballet Day Live returns too, with exclusive coverage of international ballet companies in rehearsal, a chance to see how the different companies warm up for the day, and interviews with choreographers and leading figures in the dance world. This year collaborating companies include The Royal Ballet, The Australian Ballet, Bolshoi Ballet, The National Ballet of Canada and San Francisco Ballet, offering audiences rare insights into the busy lives of professional dancers.

Ballet is both historical and contemporary, rooted in rich local heritage and international at the same time. We are proud to be presenting another Season of work that reflects all these aspects of our art form.

Kevin O'Hare
Director, The Royal Ballet

THE 2016/17 SEASON AT A GLANCE

This page:
(*top left*)
Natalia Osipova as Lise and Philip Mosley as Widow Simone in Frederick Ashton's *La FIlle mal gardée* ©2015 ROH. Photograph by Tristram Kenton
(*bottom right*)
Alessandra Ferri in 'Tuesday' from Wayne McGregor's *Woolf Works* ©2015 ROH. Photograph by Tristram Kenton

2016

SEPTEMBER–OCTOBER

LA FILLE MAL GARDÉE
Choreography Frederick Ashton
Music Ferdinand Hérold
Arranged and orchestrated by John Lanchbery
Scenario Jean Dauberval
Designer Osbert Lancaster
Lighting designer John B. Read
Conductor Barry Wordsworth
Premiere
28 January 1960
(The Royal Ballet)

OCTOBER–NOVEMBER

ANASTASIA
Choreography Kenneth MacMillan
Music Pyotr Il'yich Tchaikovsky, Bohuslav Martinů
Electronic music Fritz Winckel, Rüdiger Rüfer
Production realized by Deborah MacMillan
Designer Bob Crowley
Lighting designer John B. Read
Conductor Simon Hewitt
Premiere
22 July 1971
(The Royal Ballet)

NOVEMBER

CHROMA
Choreography Wayne McGregor
Music Joby Talbot, Jack White III
Arranged by Joby Talbot
Orchestrated by Christopher Austin
(by arrangement with Chester Music Ltd)
Set designer John Pawson
Costume designer Moritz Junge
Lighting designer Lucy Carter
Conductor Koen Kessels
Premiere
17 November 2006
(The Royal Ballet)

NEW WAYNE MCGREGOR
Choreography Wayne McGregor
Music Steve Reich
Artist Rashid Rana
Lighting designer Lucy Carter
Conductor Koen Kessels
Premiere
10 November 2016
(The Royal Ballet)

CARBON LIFE
Choreography Wayne McGregor
Music Mark Ronson, Andrew Wyatt
Orchestrated by Rufus Wainwright
Designer Gareth Pugh
Lighting designer Lucy Carter
Conductor Koen Kessels
Premiere
5 April 2012
(The Royal Ballet)

NOVEMBER

NEW CHARLOTTE EDMONDS AND NEW ROBERT BINET
Choreography Charlotte Edmonds
Music TBC
Choreography Robert Binet
Music TBC
Premieres
10 November 2016
(The Royal Ballet)

NOVEMBER 2016–JANUARY 2017

THE NUTCRACKER
Choreography Peter Wright
after Lev Ivanov
Music Pytor Il'yich Tchaikovsky
Original scenario Marius Petipa *after* E.T.A Hoffmann's Nussknacker und Mausekönig
Production and scenario Peter Wright
Designer Julia Trevelyan Oman
Lighting designer Mark Henderson
Production consultant Roland John Wiley
Conductors Boris Gruzin, Dominic Grier
Premiere
16 December 1882
(Mariinsky Theatre, St. Petersburg)
20 December 1984
(The Royal Ballet, this production)

DECEMBER 2016–JANUARY 2017

THE MAD HATTER'S TEA PARTY
Direction and writer Kate Prince
Choreography Members of ZooNation Dance Company
Music DJ Walde, Josh Cohen
Set and costume designer Ben Stones
Premiere
6 December 2014
(The Royal Ballet/ZooNation Dance Company)

2017

JANUARY

LES ENFANTS TERRIBLES
Direction and choreography Javier De Frutos
Music Philip Glass
Designer Jean-Marc Puissant
Lighting designer Bruno Poet
Video artist Tal Rosner
Conductor TBC
Premiere
27 January 2017
(The Royal Ballet)

DECEMBER–MARCH

THE SLEEPING BEAUTY
Choreography Marius Petipa
Additional choreography Frederick Ashton, Anthony Dowell, Christopher Wheeldon
Production Monica Mason and Christopher Newton *after* Ninette de Valois and Nicholas Sergeyev
Music Pyotr Il'yich Tchaikovsky
Original designer Oliver Messel
Additional designs Peter Farmer
Lighting designer Mark Jonathan
Conductors Koen Kessels, Valeriy Ovsyanikov
Premieres
20 February 1946
(Sadler's Wells Ballet)
15 May 2006
(The Royal Ballet, this production)

JANUARY–FEBRUARY

WOOLF WORKS
Concept and direction Wayne McGregor
Choreography Wayne McGregor
Music Max Richter
Designers Ciguë, We Not I, Wayne McGregor
Costume designer Moritz Junge
Lighting designer Lucy Carter
Film designer Ravi Deepres
Sound designer Chris Ekers
Make-up designer Kabuki
Dramaturg Uzma Hameed
Conductor Koen Kessels
Premiere
11 May 2015
(The Royal Ballet)

MARCH

THE HUMAN SEASONS
Choreography David Dawson
Music Greg Haines
Set and projection designer
Eno Henze
Costume designer
Yumiko Takeshima
Lighting designer Bert Dalhuysen
Assistant to the choreographer
Tim Couchman
Conductor Koen Kessels

Premiere
9 November 2013
(The Royal Ballet)

AFTER THE RAIN
Choreography
Christopher Wheeldon
Music Arvo Pärt
Costume designer Holly Hynes
Lighting designer 59 Productions
Conductor Koen Kessels

Premieres
22 January 2005
(New York City Ballet)

30 October 2012
(The Royal Ballet)

NEW CRYSTAL PITE
Choreography Crystal Pite
Music Henryk Mikolaj Górecki
Set designer Jay Gowler Taylor
Costume designer Nancy Bryant
Lighting designer Tom Visser
Conductor Koen Kessels

Premiere
16 March 2017
(The Royal Ballet)

JEWELS
Choreography George Balanchine
Music Gabriel Fauré ('Emeralds'), Igor
Stravinsky ('Rubies'), Pyotr Il'yich
Tchaikovsky ('Diamonds')
Set designer Jean-Marc Puissant
Costume designer Barbara Karinska
Costume design consultant
Holly Hynes
Lighting designer Jennifer Tipton
Conductor Pavel Sorokin

Premieres
13 April 1967
(New York City Ballet)

23 November 2007
(The Royal Ballet, this production)

APRIL–MAY

MAYERLING
Choreography Kenneth MacMillan
Music Franz Liszt
Arranged and orchestrated by
John Lanchbery
Scenario Gillian Freeman
Designer Nicholas Georgiadis
Lighting designer John B. Read
Conductor Martin Yates

Premiere
14 February 1978
(The Royal Ballet)

MAY

THE VERTIGINOUS THRILL
OF EXACTITUDE
Choreography William Forsythe
Music Franz Schubert
Set designer William Forsythe
Costume designer
Stephen Galloway
Original lighting designer
William Forsythe
Revival lighting designer
John B. Read
Conductor Koen Kessels

Premieres
20 January 1996
(Frankfurt Ballet)

23 November 1999
(The Royal Ballet)

TARANTELLA
Choreography George Balanchine
Music Louis Moreau Gottschalk
Reconstructed and orchestrated by
Hershy Kay
Designers TBC
Conductor Koen Kessels

Premieres
7 January 1964
(New York City Ballet)

18 May 2017
(The Royal Ballet)

STRAPLESS
Choreography
Christopher Wheeldon
Scenario Christopher Wheeldon
and Charlotte Westenra *after*
Deborah Davis
Music Mark-Anthony Turnage
Designer Bob Crowley
Lighting designer Natasha Chivers
Conductor Koen Kessels

Premiere
12 February 2016
(The Royal Ballet)

NEW LIAM SCARLETT
Choreography Liam Scarlett
Conductor Koen Kessels

Premiere
18 May 2017
(The Royal Ballet)

JUNE

THE DREAM
Choreography Frederick Ashton
Music Felix Mendelssohn
Arranged by John Lanchbery
Designer David Walker
Lighting designer John B. Read
Conductor Emmanual Plasson

Premiere
2 April 1964
(The Royal Ballet)

SYMPHONIC VARIATIONS
Choreography Frederick Ashton
Music César Franck
Set and costume designer
Sophie Fedorovitch
Lighting designer John B. Read
Conductor Emmanual Plasson

Premiere
24 April 1946
(Sadler's Wells Ballet)

MARGUERITE AND ARMAND
Choreography Frederick Ashton
Music Franz Liszt
Orchestration Dudley Simpson
Designer Cecil Beaton
Lighting designer John B. Read
Conductor Emmanual Plasson

Premiere
12 March 1963
(The Royal Ballet)

This page:
(*top left*)
Marianela
Nuñez and
Federico
Bonelli
in David
Dawson's
*The Human
Seasons*
©2013 ROH.
Photograph
by Bill
Cooper
(*top right*)
Laura Morera
and Ryoichi
Hirano in
'Emeralds'
part of
Jewels
©2013 ROH.
Photograph
by Bill
Cooper
(*bottom*)
Edward
Watson
as Crown
Prince Rudolf
©2009 ROH.
Photograph
by Bill
Cooper

Carlos Acosta
on stage
after his last
performance
as Principal
Guest Artist
with The Royal
Ballet
©2015 ROH.
Photograph
by Andrej
Uspenski

COMPANY NEWS AND PROMOTIONS

CARLOS ACOSTA BY LYNDSEY WINSHIP

Carlos Acosta, a dancer who has made a huge impact on ballet worldwide, is retiring from The Royal Ballet after 17 years with the Company. Although it will not be the end of his dance career, he is saying farewell to classical ballet.

The famously charismatic Cuban makes sparks fly when he takes to the stage, with soaring leaps and seemingly infinite turns spinning with smooth revolutions. He has been a dream romantic lead, and had a particularly fruitful partnership with ballerina Tamara Rojo, with whom he opened the Royal Ballet's O_2 Arena season in 2011, dancing *Romeo and Juliet* for an audience of 13,500.

Carlos's own story is as much a fairytale as those of the ballets he has starred in. As an unruly child from a large family in Havana who liked Michael Jackson and breakdancing, he was sent to Cuba's National Ballet School by his father, hoping it would channel his energy and instil some discipline. Despite a lack of commitment in the early years, his pure talent saw him through until he finally decided his future lay in ballet.

At the Prix de Lausanne in 1990, aged 16, Carlos took the Gold Medal with an exuberant variation from *Don Quixote* – a ballet he was later to dance many times. He first came to Britain when he was invited to join English National Ballet for their 1991/92 season. He then returned to the National Ballet of Cuba for a year, before joining Houston Ballet as a principal in 1993.

In 1998, Carlos arrived at The Royal Ballet, then under the direction of Anthony Dowell. 'A lot of people said I was crazy when I came to London,' Carlos has said, '[but] I really wanted to see how big I could be.' A huge hit with London audiences, Carlos made his mark in such firecracker roles as Basilio in *Don Quixote* (and as a guest with the Bolshoi Ballet in *Spartacus*), and in classic romantic leads such as Siegfried in *Swan Lake*, Albrecht in *Giselle*, Prince Florimund in *The Sleeping Beauty* and, of course, Romeo. He danced a fine Apollo, bringing inner life to the young god as well as elegant nobility, and perhaps unexpectedly, the Cuban also made a very English role his own, showing off his comic timing (and winning grin) as Colas in Ashton's *La Fille mal gardée*.

In 2003, Carlos became a Principal Guest Artist, the same year he choreographed his first ballet, *Tocororo – A Cuban Tale*, which broke box office records at Sadler's Wells. For The Royal Ballet he staged his own, buoyant version of *Don Quixote* in 2013, and choreographed a new *Carmen* in 2015. Outside the Company, Carlos has produced a series of his own shows, choreographed a musical, *Guys and Dolls*, and is now launching a new company, based in Cuba. He has plans to restore Havana's abandoned School of Ballet as a new dance centre.

Away from the ballet stage, Carlos has also written a best-selling autobiography, *No Way Home*, a novel, *Pig's Foot* (which was chosen for the Waterstones 11), and appeared in the films *Day of the Flowers*, *New York, I Love You* and *Our Kind of Traitor*. A man of enormous talent and industry, he has inspired many of those around him. 'He was one of my idols growing up and he still is,' says Royal Ballet Principal Matthew Golding. 'What he's accomplished is incredible. I asked him, "What's the secret, Carlos?" And he said, "Just hard work, my friend, hard work"'.

Royal Ballet Director Kevin O'Hare and members of the cast of Acosta's *Carmen* congratulate him on his final performance ©2015 ROH. Photograph by Andrej Uspenski

ROBERTA MARQUEZ BY LYNDSEY WINSHIP

Roberta Marquez is leaving The Royal Ballet after 11 years as a Principal. The Brazilian dancer is known for her bright personality, dancing that's full of spark, speed and vivacity, and the brilliant partnership she forged with fellow Principal Steven McRae. The pair thrived in each other's company on stage, performing together in *The Nutcracker*, *The Sleeping Beauty*, *Romeo and Juliet*, *Symphony in C* and *Cinderella*, among many other ballets. McRae much admired her work ethic and her enthusiasm and told *The Ballet Bag* in 2010: 'I step on stage and I know I can trust Roberta a million per cent. I know she will go up there and make it a performance to remember.'

Born in Rio de Janeiro to a Peruvian mother and Portuguese father, Roberta began dancing at the age of four, and at six, after watching a performance of *Swan Lake*, decided to become a ballerina. She trained at the Maria Olenewa State Dance School in Rio, with the former Ballets Russes de Monte Carlo dancer Tatiana Leskova as one of her teachers. In 1994 Roberta joined Brazil's Municipal Theatre Ballet and was promoted to principal in 2002.

She first danced at Covent Garden as a guest artist in Natalia Makarova's *The Sleeping Beauty* in 2003 on Makarova's invitation, after working with her in Brazil. Roberta was offered a contract with American Ballet Theatre, but when she was invited to join The Royal Ballet by Director Monica Mason in 2004, she knew London was where she wanted to be. Since then she has become a firm favourite with audiences for performances that show her dramatic versatility as well as luminous stage presence, including Swanilda in *Coppélia*, Titania in *The Dream*, Manon, Odette/Odile and Giselle. One of Roberta's favourite roles is temple dancer Nikiya in *La Bayadère*, the ballet that made her career back in Brazil. She told the Ballet Association in 2008: 'When I put the costume on I feel like Nikiya. She is very sensual, there's drama, the music is beautiful, the steps magical, I can close my eyes and feel the steps in my body.'

Roberta favours theatrical works, and credits The Royal Ballet with teaching her a graceful approach to acting, but she combines that with her own instincts and passionate Latin nature, she revealed in an interview with the *Japan Times*. 'Every time [I perform] my dancing becomes different because I'm always changing, through my experience as a dancer, and as a human being, and finding new things in my roles on stage.'

Along with her elegant feet and impeccable technique, the petite ballerina has a particular gift for comedy, and was chosen to dance Lise in the live cinema relay of *La Fille mal gardée* in 2012, a role to which she brought great wit and warmth, 'The whole ballet [was] lit by her charm' according to Clement Crisp in the *Financial Times*. And it is the role of Lise that Roberta will return to dance as a guest in the 2016/17 Season in a farewell performance to celebrate her career.

Roberta is already passing on her wealth of experience as a talented teacher, in much-sought-after masterclasses.

Roberta
Marquez
as Nikiya in
La Bayadère
©2013 ROH.
Photograph
by Tristram
Kenton

13

GENESIA ROSATO BY LYNDSEY WINSHIP

A 40-year career with The Royal Ballet comes to a close as Principal Character Artist Genesia Rosato retires this Season. Most recently she has been known for brilliant character performances, from Juliet's kind and doting nurse (and her less-than-doting mother, Lady Capulet) to the obsequious servant Aya in *La Bayadère*, those small but essential roles that bring richness and detail to any performance. But in four decades, working under six different Company directors, Genesia has danced a huge variety of roles. In fact, she's one of the few dancers to have performed different characters and generations within the same ballets – in *The Sleeping Beauty*, for example, she has played the Lilac Fairy, the Queen, the Countess and Carabosse – an experience Genesia says she has treasured.

Genesia began her dance training as a child at a local school in Surrey before joining The Royal Ballet Upper School at 16. Her talent was spotted by the Royal Ballet's then director Kenneth MacMillan, and she joined the Company in 1976. In her first year MacMillan created the role of Princess Louise in *Mayerling* on her, and she has called working with the choreographer 'wonderful and scary'. Genesia also worked with the Company's other great choreographer, Frederick Ashton, who created roles for her in the ballets *Rhapsody* and *Varii Capricci*. She also worked with The Royal Ballet's Founder, Ninette de Valois, on *The Sleeping Beauty*.

Genesia was promoted to Soloist in 1982 and to Principal Character Artist in 1993. Favourite roles have included the Summer Fairy in Ashton's *Cinderella*, and Profane Love in the company's first performance of *Illuminations*, by the same choreographer. A dancer with strong acting talents, who always relished character parts over pure classical roles, her long list of credits includes dancing both Katya and Natalia in *A Month in the Country*, Myrtha, Bathilde and Berthe in *Giselle*, Lykanion in *Daphnis and Chlo*, Terpsichore in *Apollo*, the Siren in *The Prodigal Son*, the Wife in *The Invitation* and the title role in MacMillan's one-act version of *Anastasia*. And in *Mayerling*, as well as Princess Stephanie, she went on to perform the roles of Marie Larisch, Mitzi Caspar, the Empress Elizabeth and Helene Vetsera.

'It is time, after spending my whole career with this wonderful Company, to retire from dancing,' says Genesia. 'I have loved my life as a dancer, and I know I will miss working with the many talented and dedicated individuals who make up The Royal Ballet.'

One such talented individual whom Genesia has worked with often is Gary Avis, a fellow Principle Character Artist, who spoke to ballet blogger Gramilano about Genesia's commitment and dedication, and the legacy she leaves behind her: 'She is one of the finest artistes The Royal Ballet has ever had. She leaves us all a lasting impression of what was expected of you from those monumental choreographers she worked with. The pure talent and versatility she brought to every role since 1976 will be forever etched in our memories.'

Genesia
Rosato as
Carabosse in
*The Sleeping
Beauty*
©2011 ROH/
Johan Persson

Right: Aud Jebsen with this Season's Young Dancers – from left Charlotte Tonkinson, Giacomo Rovero, Arianna Maldini, Francisco Serrano, Maria Castillo Yoshida and Estelle Bovay – photographed at The Royal Ballet School ©2016 ROH. Photograph by Andrej Uspenski

Opposite page: all of the 2015/16 Aud Jebsen Young Dancers joined the Company, including (*top*): Julia Roscoe, here rehearsing *The Nutcracker* with the Company, and (*bottom*) Lukas Bjørneboe Brændsrød and Isabel Lubach, here performing in Sander Blommaert's *She Remembers,* part of last Season's *Draft Works* ©2015 ROH. Photographs by Andrej Uspenski

AUD JEBSEN YOUNG DANCERS PROGRAMME

Since its inauguration at the start of the 2014/15 Season the Aud Jebsen Young Dancers Programme has offered a handful of outstanding young dancers the opportunity of a year's contract to rehearse and perform with The Royal Ballet.

Each year the Programme invites six recent graduates of The Royal Ballet School to gain a unique experience in their transition from students to professional dancers. During the Season year the Young Dancers work and perform alongside the corps de ballet of The Royal Ballet and receive mentoring and coaching by the Company's resident and guest teachers. Guest teachers this Season will include Darcey Bussell, Olga Evreinoff and Roland Price.

The programme has brought several young and talented dancers into the ranks of The Royal Ballet and others to contracts with other leading ballet companies. Artists Grace Blundell and Ashley Dean both joined the Company at the beginning of the 2015/16 Season after their year as Aud Jebsen Young Dancers and their fellow dancers were offered contracts at other professional ballet companies: Maria Barroso joined National Ballet of Portugal, Grace Holder joined Scottish Ballet and Ashleigh McKimmie joined Estonian National Ballet.

For the 2016/17 Season all five of the 2015/16 Young Dancers – Lukas Bjørneboe Brændsrød, Harry Churches, Leo Dixon, Isabel Lubach and Julia Roscoe – were offered contracts at The Royal Ballet.

For the 2016/17 Season The Royal Ballet welcomes Estelle Bovay, Maria Castillo Yoshida, Arianna Maldini, Giacomo Rovero, Francisco Serrano and Charlotte Tonkinson into the programme. They will spend their year with the Company taking class, rehearsing the Season's repertory, including classics, heritage works and new works by resident, associate and visiting choreographers, and participating in performances on stage.

PROMOTIONS AND NEW MEMBERS

For the 2016/17 Season First Soloists **Alexander Campbell**, **Francesca Hayward**, **Ryoichi Hirano** and **Akane Takada** are promoted to Principal.

Soloists **Claire Calvert**, **Yasmine Naghdi** and **Beatriz Stix-Brunell** are promoted to First Soloist. First Artists **Matthew Ball** and **Mayara Magri** are promoted to Soloist. Artist **Tierney Heap** was promoted to First Artist mid-Season and for the new Season is also promoted to Soloist. Artists **Reece Clarke**, **David Donnelly**, **Benjamin Ella**, **Isabella Gasparini**, **Anna Rose O'Sullivan** and **Demelza Parish** are promoted to First Artist.

Mica Bradbury from Ballet Vlaanderen joined the Company as Artist.

For the 2016/17 Season all five of the 2015/16 Aud Jebsen Young Dancers – **Lukas Bjørneboe Brændsrød**, **Harry Churches**, **Leo Dixon**, **Isabel Lubach** and **Julia Roscoe** – all of whom trained at The Royal Ballet School, join the Company on permanent contracts as Artists, along with **Joseph Sissens** from The Royal Ballet School and **Leticia Dias** from Birmingham Royal Ballet.

Vincenzo Di Primo joins the Company as Prix de Lausanne dancer for the 2016/17 Season.

Principal Guest Artist **Carlos Acosta**, who joined The Royal Ballet in 1998, retired from the Company mid-Season with final performances in his production of *Carmen* on the main stage in November 2015 and in the Linbury Studio Theatre in **Will Tuckett**'s *Elizabeth* in January 2016.

Principal **Roberta Marquez** also left mid-Season, after 11 years with The Royal Ballet, but returns in October 2016 for two farewell performances in **Frederick Ashton**'s *La Fille mal gardée*.

Principal Character Artist **Genesia Rosato** retired from the Company mid-Season after a career spanning 40 years with The Royal Ballet.

First Soloist **Ricardo Cervera** made his last appearance as a dancer in *The Nutcracker* in December 2015 after 22 years with the Company. He continues in his role as Assistant Ballet Master.

First Artist **Leanne Cope**, formerly on sabbatical from the Company, left mid-Season to focus on her Tony-nominated role as Lise Dassin in Christopher Wheeldon's Tony award-winning production of *An American in Paris*. First Artists **Donald Thom** and **James Wilkie** also left mid-Season. First Artists **Sian Murphy** and **Sander Blommaert** retired from The Royal Ballet at the end of the 2015/16 Season.

First Soloist **Melissa Hamilton** continues her sabbatical from The Royal Ballet during the 2016/17 Season while she performs as a principal dancer with the Semperoper Ballett in Dresden.

Ricardo Cervera and **Jonathan Howells** have been appointed Ballet Masters and **Sian Murphy** Assistant Ballet Mistress for the 2016/17 Season.

ROMEO AND JULIET

Choreography Kenneth MacMillan

Opposite page: Yasmine Naghdi and Matthew Ball as Juliet and Romeo

This page: (*top*) Vadim Muntagirov as Romeo; (*bottom*) Sarah Lamb as Juliet

©2015 ROH. Photographs by Alice Pennefather

19

RAVEN GIRL

Choreography
Wayne
McGregor

This page:
Beatriz Stix-
Brunell as the
Raven Girl and
Ryoichi Hirano
as the Raven
Prince

Opposite page:
Artists of The
Royal Ballet

©2015 ROH.
Photographs
by Bill Cooper

CONNECTOME

Choreography
Alastair Marriott

This page:
Lauren Cuthbertson

Opposite page:
Sarah Lamb

©2015 ROH.
Photographs
by Bill Cooper

This page:
Solomon Golding
©2015 ROH. Photograph by Bill Cooper

VISCERA

Choreography
Liam Scarlett

Opposite page:
Meghan Grace
Hinkis and
artists of The
Royal Ballet

This page:
Leticia Stock
and Nehemiah
Kish

©2015 ROH.
Photographs
by Tristram
Kenton

AFTERNOON OF A FAUN

Choreography
Jerome
Robbins

Opposite page: Eric
Underwood

This page:
Lauren
Cuthbertson

©2015 ROH.
Photographs
by Tristram
Kenton

**TCHAIKOVSKY
PAS DE DEUX**

Choreography
George
Balanchine

*Opposite
page:* Lauren
Cuthbertson
and Matthew
Golding

This page: Iana
Salenko and
Steven McRae

CARMEN

Choreography
Carlos Acosta

Opposite page:
Marianela
Nuñez as
Carmen and
Carlos Acosta
as Don José

This page:
Marianela
Nuñez as
Carmen and
Federico
Bonelli as
Escamillo

©2015 ROH.
Photographs
by Tristram
Kenton

This page: (top) Tierney Heap as Carmen with artists of The Royal Ballet (bottom) Tierney Heap as Carmen and Vadim Muntagirov as Don José Opposite page: Artists of The Royal Ballet ©2015 ROH. Photographs by Tristram Kenton

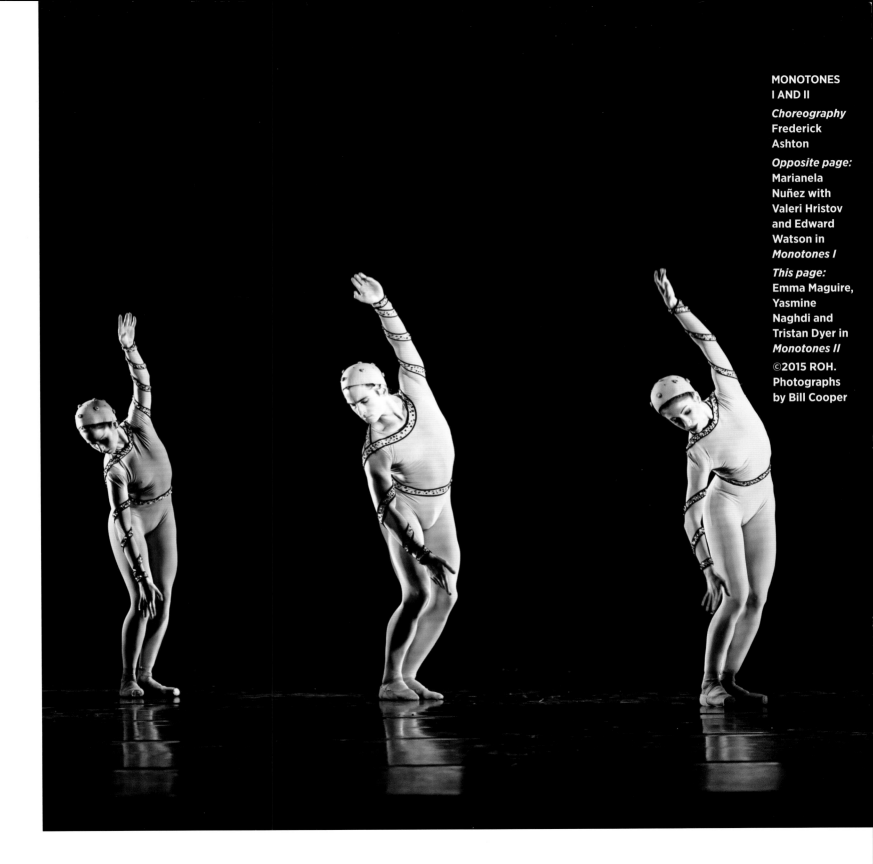

MONOTONES
I AND II

Choreography
**Frederick
Ashton**

Opposite page:
**Marianela
Nuñez with
Valeri Hristov
and Edward
Watson in**
Monotones I

This page:
**Emma Maguire,
Yasmine
Naghdi and
Tristan Dyer in**
Monotones II

©**2015 ROH.
Photographs
by Bill Cooper**

THE TWO
PIGEONS

Choreography
Frederick
Ashton

This page:
Lauren
Cuthbertson
as the Young
Girl and Vadim
Muntagirov as
the Young Man

*Opposite
page:* Laura
Morera as the
Gypsy Girl

©2015 ROH.
Photographs
by Bill Cooper

This page:
Mayara Magri
as the Gypsy
Girl and James
Hay as the
Young Man

Opposite
page: Yuhui
Choe as the
Young Girl
and Alexander
Campbell as
the Young Man
©2015 ROH.
Photographs
by Bill Cooper

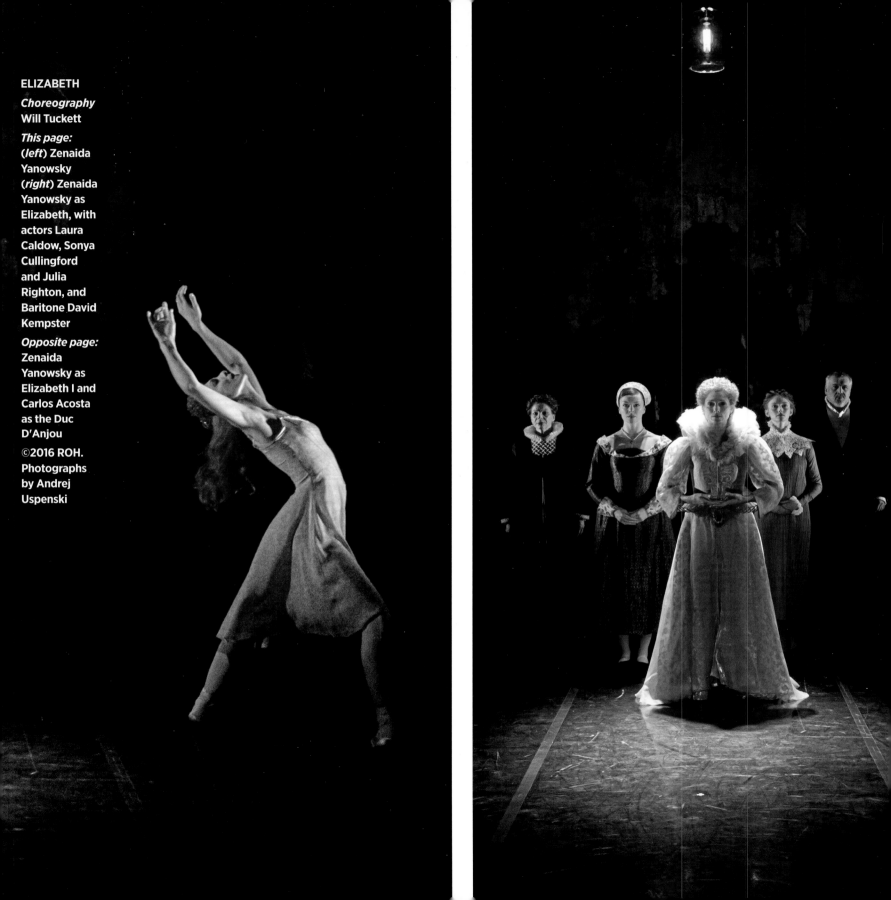

ELIZABETH

Choreography
Will Tuckett

This page:
(*left*) Zenaida Yanowsky (*right*) Zenaida Yanowsky as Elizabeth, with actors Laura Caldow, Sonya Cullingford and Julia Righton, and Baritone David Kempster

Opposite page:
Zenaida Yanowsky as Elizabeth I and Carlos Acosta as the Duc D'Anjou

©2016 ROH. Photographs by Andrej Uspenski

RHAPSODY

Choreography
Frederick
Ashton

This page:
Natalia Osipova
and Steven
McRae

Opposite page:
Francesca
Hayward and
James Hay

©2016 ROH.
Photographs
by Helen
Maybanks

AFTER THE RAIN

Choreography Christopher Wheeldon

This page: Marianela Nuñez and Thiago Soares

Opposite page: Zenaida Yanowsky, Tierney Heap, Olivia Cowley, Reece Clarke, Nicol Edmonds and Tomas Mock

©2016 ROH. Photographs by Bill Cooper

STRAPLESS

Choreography
**Christopher
Wheeldon**

This page:
**Natalia Osipova
as Amélie
Gautreau
and Federico
Bonelli as Dr
Samuel-John
Pozzi**

*Opposite
page:* **Edward
Watson as
John Singer
Sargent and
Matthew Ball
as Albert de
Belleroche**

© 2016 ROH.
Photographs
by Bill Cooper

This page: Lauren Cuthbertson as Amélie Gautreau

Opposite page: Reece Clarke as Dr Samuel-John Pozzi

WITHIN THE GOLDEN HOUR

Choreography
Christopher Wheeldon

This page:
Francesca Hayward and Valentino Zucchetti

Opposite page:
Romany Pajdak and Matthew Golding

© 2016 ROH. Photographs by Bill Cooper

This page:
Tomas Mock as Hilarion

Opposite page:
Marianela Nuñez as Giselle and Vadim Muntagirov as Prince Albrecht

©2016 ROH. Photographs by Tristram Kenton

FRANKENSTEIN

Choreography
Liam Scarlett

This page:
Laura Morera
as Elizabeth
Lavenza and
Federico Bonelli
as Victor
Frankenstein

Opposite page:
Steven McRae
as the Creature

©2016 ROH.
Photographs by
Bill Cooper

his page:

(*eft*) Elizabeth
cGorian
s Madame
oritz (*right*)
arah Lamb
s Elizabeth
avenza

opposite page:
ederico
onelli
s Victor
rankenstein
2016 ROH.
hotographs
 Bill Cooper

This page:
(top) Nehemiah
Kish as the
Creature and
Ethan Bailey
as William
Frankenstein
(bottom)
Nehemiah Kish
as the Creature

Opposite page:
Tristan Dyer
as Victor
Frankenstein
and Ryoichi
Hirano as the
Creature
©2016 ROH.
Photographs by
Bill Cooper

THE INVITATION

Choreography
Kenneth MacMillan

This page:
Francesca Hayward as the Girl and Gary Avis as the Husband

©2016 ROH. Photograph by Andrej Uspenski

Opposite page:
(*left*) **Zenaida Yanowsky as the Wife and Gary Avis as the Husband**

©2016 ROH. Photograph by Bill Cooper

(*top right*) **Yasmine Naghdi as the Girl and David Donnelly as the Cousin**

(*bottom right*) **Olivia Cowley as the Wife**

©2016 ROH. Photographs by Bill Cooper

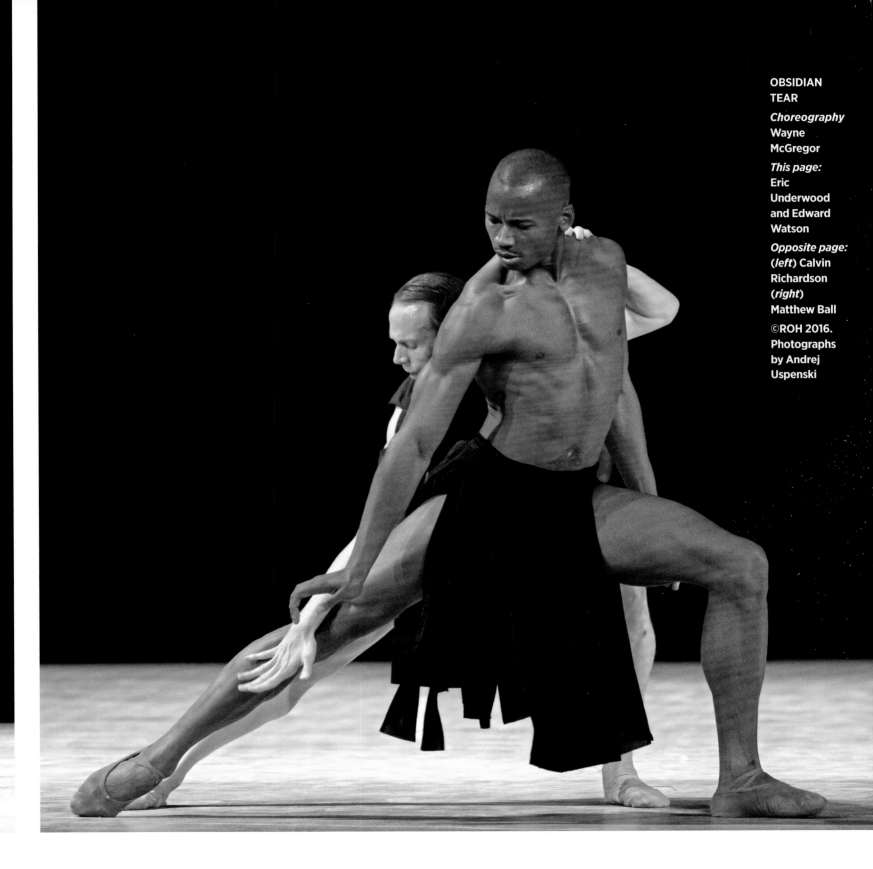

**OBSIDIAN
TEAR**

Choreography
**Wayne
McGregor**

This page:
**Eric
Underwood
and Edward
Watson**

Opposite page:
(*left*) **Calvin
Richardson**
(*right*)
Matthew Ball

©ROH 2016.
**Photographs
by Andrej
Uspenski**

This page:
(*top, left to right*) Paul Kay, Edward Watson, Eric Underwood, Tristan Dyer, Matthew Ball, Alexander Campbell, Luca Acri, Ryoichi Hirano and Calvin Richardson

(*bottom*) Reece Clarke, Lukas Bjørneboe Brændsrød, Fernando Montaño and David Donnelly, with Marcelino Sambé, Sander Blommaert, Nicol Edmonds, Benjamin Ella and Alexander Campbell

Opposite page:
(*top, left to right*) Tristan Dyer, Edward Watson, Luca Acri, Paul Kay, Ryoichi Hirano, Matthew Ball, Eric Underwood, Alexander Campbell and Calvin Richardson

(*bottom*) Matthew Ball

©2016 ROH. Photographs by Andrej Uspenski

Répétiteur Jonathan Cope coaches Yasmine Naghdi and Matthew Ball for the title roles in MacMillan's *Romeo and Juliet*

Opposite page: (top) Carlos Acosta and Marianela Nuñez rehearse for their roles as Don José and Carmen in Acosta's new production of *Carmen* (bottom) Artists of The Royal Ballet rehearse Acosta's *Carmen* ©2015 ROH. Photograph by Andrej Uspenski

This page:
(*top*) Royal Ballet Soloist Kristen McNally presenting World Ballet Day 2015 (on 1 October), in which The Royal Ballet, The Australian Ballet, Bolshoi Ballet, The National Ballet of Canada and San Francisco Ballet all live-streamed rehearsals, interviews and insight events via YouTube
(*bottom*) The Company's morning class was streamed live
©2015 ROH. Photographs by Andrej Uspenski

(*top*) Senior Ballet Master Christopher Carr rehearses Yuhui Choe as the Young Girl and Alexander Campbell as the Young Man, one of several casts in Frederick Ashton's *The Two Pigeons*, revived and staged by Carr after an absence of 30 years from the Company repertory (*bottom left*) Yuhui Choe and Itziar Mendizabal rehearsing their roles as the Young Girl and the Gypsy Girl (*bottom right*) Laura Morera and Ryoichi Hirano rehearsing their roles as the Gypsy Girl and her Lover ©2016 ROH. Photographs by Andrej Uspenski

This page: Christopher Wheeldon's rehearses Lauren Cuthbertson for the role of Amélie Gautreau in his new ballet *Strapless*
Opposite page: (*left*) Itziar Mendizabal and Eric Underwood rehearse Wheeldon's *After the Rain* (*right*) Sarah Lamb and Steven McRae rehearse Wheeldon's *Within the Golden Hour* ©2016 ROH. Photographs by Andrej Uspenski

This page:
Former
Director of The
Royal Ballet
Monica Mason
rehearses
Tierney Heap
for the role
of Myrthe in
Peter Wright's
Giselle
Opposite page:
Peter Wright
rehearses
Akane Takada
for the role of
Giselle
©2016 ROH.
Photographs
by Andrej
Uspenski

This page: (*left*) Liam Scarlett rehearses Sarah Lamb in the role of Elizabeth Lavenza for his new ballet *Frankenstein* (*right*) Federico Bonelli as Victor Frankenstein and Steven McRae as the Creature in rehearsal

Opposite page: Wayne McGregor rehearses Calvin Richardson, Edward Watson and Matthew Ball for his new ballet *Obsidian Tear*

©2016 ROH. Photographs by Andrej Uspenski

THE 2015/16 SEASON AT A GLANCE

P. 18 ROMEO AND JULIET
Choreography Kenneth MacMillan
Music Sergey Prokofiev

Conductor Koen Kessels
Designer Nicholas Georgiadis
Lighting designer John B. Read
Staging Julie Lincoln,
Christopher Saunders
Ballet Master Christopher Saunders
Ballet Mistress Samantha Raine
Principal coaching Alexander
Agadzhanov, Gary Avis, Lesley Collier,
Jonathan Cope, Julie Lincoln

Premiere
9 February 1965
(The Royal Ballet)

P. 22 RAVEN GIRL
A new fairytale by
Audrey Niffenegger
*Adapted, directed and
choreographed for the stage by*
Wayne McGregor
Music Gabriel Yared

Conductor Koen Kessels
Designer Vicki Mortimer
Lighting designer Lucy Carter
Film designer Ravi Deepres
Associate lighting designer
Simon Bennison
Ballet Master Gary Avis
Benesh notator Amanda Eyles

Premiere
24 May 2013
(The Royal Ballet)

P. 24 CONNECTOME
Choreography Alastair Marriott
Music Arvo Pärt

Conductor Koen Kessels
Set designer Es Devlin
Costume designer
Jonathan Howells
Lighting designer Bruno Poet
Video designer Luke Halls
Assistant to the choreographer
Jonathan Howells
Assistant Ballet Master
Jonathan Howells

Premiere
31 May 2014
(The Royal Ballet)

P. 27 DRAFT WORKS
Choreography
Joshua Beamish (*Study of Giselle*)
Sander Blommaert
(*She Remembers*)
Travis Clausen-Knight and James
Pett (Company Wayne McGregor)
(*Splinter the Noise*)
Charlotte Edmonds
(*Forgotten Frontline*)
Arianna Maldini (The Royal Ballet
School) (*Lancia il Cuore*)
Kristen McNally (*Checkpoint 19*)
Fernando Montaño (*Michelangelo*)
Erico Montes and Daniela Cardim
Fonteyne (*Similarities Between
Diverse Things*)
Sian Murphy
(*Clarence and Alabama*)
Calvin Richardson (Untitled)
Marcelino Sambé
(*The Chosen Victim*)
Fukiko Takase
(from *Cultivate a Quiet Joy*)
Kenneth Tindall ('Scents group
number', from *Perfume*)
Valentino Zucchetti (*Alpha*)

P. 28 VISCERA
Choreography Liam Scarlett
Music Lowell Liebermann

Conductor Emmanuel Plasson
Solo piano Robert Clark
Costume designer Liam Scarlett
Lighting designer John Hall
Assistant Ballet Master
Ricardo Cervera
Benesh notator Amanda Eyles

Premieres
6 January 2012
(Miami City Ballet)

3 November 2012
(The Royal Ballet)

P. 30 AFTERNOON OF A FAUN
Choreography Jerome Robbins
Music Claude Debussy

Conductor Emmanuel Plasson
Costume designer Irene Sharaff
*Set designer and original lighting
designer* Jean Rosenthal
Lighting design re-created by
Les Dickert

Staging Jean-Pierre Frohlich,
Jonathan Cope
Ballet Master Jonathan Cope
Benesh notator Gregory Mislin

Premieres
14 May 1953
(New York City Ballet)

14 December 1971
(The Royal Ballet)

**P. 32 TCHAIKOVSKY
PAS DE DEUX**
Choreography George Balanchine
Music Pyotr Il'yich Tchaikovsky

Conductor Emmanuel Plasson
Costume designer Anthony Dowell
Lighting designer John B. Read
Staging Patricia Neary
Ballet Master Christopher Saunders

Premieres
29 March 1960
(New York City Ballet)

16 March 1964
(The Royal Ballet)

P. 34 CARMEN
Choreography Carlos Acosta
Music Georges Bizet
Arranged and orchestrated by
Martin Yates

Conductor Martin Yates
Designer Tim Hatley
Lighting designer Peter Mumford
Ballet Master Christopher Saunders
Assistant to the choreographer
Ivan Gil-Ortega
Benesh notator Anna Trevien

Premiere
26 October 2015
(The Royal Ballet)

P. 38 MONOTONES I AND II
Choreography Frederick Ashton
Music Erik Satie
Orchestration Claude Debussy,
Roland-Manuel and John Lanchbery

Conductor Barry Wordsworth
Designer Frederick Ashton
Lighting designer John B. Read
Staging Lynn Wallis
Assistant Ballet Master
Ricardo Cervera

Premiere
25 April 1965
(The Royal Ballet)

P. 40 THE TWO PIGEONS
Choreography Frederick Ashton
Music André Messager
Adapted and arranged by
John Lanchbery

Conductor Barry Wordsworth
Set and costume designer
Jacques Dupont
Lighting designer Peter Teigen
Revived and staged by
Christopher Carr
Ballet Mistress Samantha Raine
Principal coaching Gary Avis,
Christopher Carr, Lesley Collier
Benesh notator Gregory Mislin

Premiere
14 February 1961
(The Royal Ballet)

P. 46 THE NUTCRACKER
Choreography
Peter Wright *after* Lev Ivanov
Production and scenario
Peter Wright
Music Pyotr Il'yich Tchaikovsky

Conductor Boris Gruzin
Designer Julia Trevelyan Oman
Lighting designer Mark Henderson
Production consultant
Roland John Wiley
Staging Christopher Carr
Ballet Master Gary Avis
Ballet Mistress Samantha Raine
Principal coaching Alexander
Agadzhanov, Gary Avis, Christopher
Carr, Lesley Collier, Jonathan Cope,
Christopher Saunders
Benesh notators Mayumi Hotta,
Anna Trevien

Premieres
16 December 1882
(Mariinsky Theatre, St. Petersburg)

20 December 1984
(The Royal Ballet, this production)

P. 48 ELIZABETH

(Linbury Studio Theatre)
Director and choreography
Will Tuckett
Co-director and text
Alasdair Middleton
Music Martin Yates
Solo cello Raphael Wallfisch
Costume designer Fay Fullerton
Lighting designer Paule Constable
Sound designer Emma Laxton
Assistant choreographer
Emma Brunton

Premieres
27 November 2013 (Painted Hall,
Old Naval College, Greenwich)
8 January 2016 (The Royal Ballet)

P. 50 RHAPSODY

Choreography Frederick Ashton
Music Sergey Rachmaninoff

Conductor Barry Wordsworth
Set designer Frederick Ashton
Original costume designer
William Chappell
Costume designs re-created by
Natalia Stewart
Lighting designer Peter Teigen
Staging Christopher Carr
Principal coaching Alexander
Agadzhanov, Lesley Collier
Benesh notator Grant Coyle

Premiere
4 August 1980
(The Royal Ballet)

P. 52 AFTER THE RAIN

Choreography
Christopher Wheeldon
Music Arvo Pärt

Conductor Koen Kessels
Costume designer Holly Hynes
Lighting designers 59 Productions
Staging Christopher Saunders
Ballet Master Christopher Saunders

Premieres
22 January 2005
(New York City Ballet)
30 October 2012
(The Royal Ballet)

P. 54 STRAPLESS

Choreography
Christopher Wheeldon
Scenario Christopher Wheeldon
and Charlotte Westenra inspired
by the book by Deborah Davis
Music Mark-Anthony Turnage

Conductor Koen Kessels
Designer Bob Crowley
Lighting designer Natasha Chivers
Staging Jacquelin Barrett
Assistant Ballet Master
Jonathan Howells
Benesh notator Anna Trevien

Premiere
12 February 2016
(The Royal Ballet)

P. 58 WITHIN THE GOLDEN HOUR

Choreography
Christopher Wheeldon
Music Ezio Bosso

Conductor Koen Kessels
Original costume designer
Martin Pakledinaz
Costume designs recreated by
Lynette Mauro
Lighting and projection designers
59 Productions
Staging Damian Smith
Ballet Mistress Samantha Raine
Principal coaching Jonathan Cope
Benesh notator Lorraine Gregory

Premieres
22 April 2008
(San Francisco Ballet)
12 February 2016
(The Royal Ballet)

P. 60 GISELLE

Choreography Marius Petipa *after*
Jean Coralli and Jules Perrot
Scenario Théophle Gautier
after Heinrich Heine
*Production and additional
choreography* Peter Wright
Music Adolphe Adam
revised by Joseph Horovitz

Conductor Barry Wordsworth
Designer John Macfarlane
Original lighting Jennifer Tipton
recreated by David Finn

Staging Christopher Carr
Ballet Mistress Samantha Raine
Assistant Ballet Master
Ricardo Cervera
Principal coaching Alexander
Agadzhanov, Lesley Collier, Jonathan
Cope, Olga Evreinoff, Monica Mason,
Peter Wright

Premieres
28 June 1841
(Paris: Original choreography by Jean
Coralli and Jules Perrot; later versions
by Petipa, notably 1884)
1 January 1934
(Vic-Wells Ballet)
28 November 1985
(The Royal Ballet, this production)

P. 64 THE WINTER'S TALE

Choreography
Christopher Wheeldon
Music Joby Talbot

Conductor David Briskin
Designer Bob Crowley
Lighting designer Natasha Katz
Projection designer Daniel Brodie
Silk effects designer Basil Twist
Staging Jacquelin Barrett,
Christopher Saunders
Ballet Masters Christopher Saunders,
Gary Avis
Assistant to the Ballet Mistress
Nathalie Harrison
Principal coaching Jacquelin Barrett,
Jonathan Cope, Jonathan Howells
Benesh notator Anna Trevien

Premiere
10 April 2014
(The Royal Ballet)

P. 66 FRANKENSTEIN

Choreography Liam Scarlett
Music Lowell Liebermann

Conductors Koen Kessels,
Tom Seligman
Designer John Macfarlane
Lighting designer David Finn
Projection designer Finn Ross
Ballet Mistress Samantha Raine
Assistant Ballet Master
Ricardo Cervera
Benesh notator Gregory Mislin

Premiere
4 May 2016
(The Royal Ballet)

P. 72 THE INVITATION

Choreography and scenario
Kenneth MacMillan
Music Mátyás Seiber

Conductor Tim Murray
Designer Nicholas Georgiadis
Lighting designer John B. Read
Staging Gary Harris
Assistant Ballet Master Jonathan
Howells
Principal coaching Jonathan Cope,
Anya Sainsbury

Premiere
10 November 1960
(The Royal Ballet)

P. 74 OBSIDIAN TEAR

Choreography Wayne McGregor
Music Esa-Pekka Salonen

Conductor Esa-Pekka Salonen
Set designer Wayne McGregor
Fashion director Katie Shillingford
Lighting designer Lucy Carter
Dramaturg Uzma Hameed
Assistant to the choreographer
Amanda Eyles
Benesh notator Amanda Eyles

Premiere
28 May 2016
(The Royal Ballet)

Orchestra of the Royal Opera House

THE ROYAL BALLET 2016 TOUR TO JAPAN

Bunka Kaikan Theatre, Tokyo
ROMEO AND JULIET
GISELLE

Sun Palace Hall, Fukuoka
GISELLE

Hyogo Performing Arts Centre, Osaka
GISELLE

Aichi Arts Center, Nagoya
ROMEO AND JULIET

Reed and Rose, Fukuyama
GISELLE

Tokyo City Philharmonic Orchestra
Osaka Symphony Orchestra

THE ROYAL BALLET AT HOME AND ABROAD BY ZOË ANDERSON

'Everybody knew everything,' explains Principal Marianela Nuñez, remembering the warm welcome that greeted her at The Royal Ballet's first American tour in six years. 'I hadn't performed in America since 2007. When I got there, they knew me. They had followed my performances, with all the DVDs, and on YouTube, and all the rehearsals we do online. It's just fantastic, because you can follow people's careers from all over the world.' The Royal Ballet is based at the Royal Opera House, but its reach is far beyond it.

This year, the Company's home theatre is opening up and out, undergoing a transformation that will allow it to welcome new shows and new audiences with the development of a new Linbury Theatre. In the meantime, the building work means more performances beyond the walls of the Royal Opera House, as shows that might have been created or revived in the non-main stage performance spaces go elsewhere. This is a new project but the Company has always taken its work abroad and out of its home theatre.

One of the quirks of Royal Ballet history is that, across several name changes, it's spent a surprising amount of time being named after venues it had mostly stopped dancing in. For its first decade at Covent Garden, until the Royal Charter was granted in 1956, it was still known as the Sadler's Wells Ballet, after its former home theatre in Islington. Whatever the name, and whatever the base, this was a company that always performed elsewhere, and in a range of media.

Its ambitious founder, Ninette de Valois, was always looking to the next step, the next stage. In 1932, after its very first full Season, her fledgling troupe provided the repertory and most of the dancers for a visit to Copenhagen. A British journalist's reaction at the time underlines the value of overseas touring: 'It is a remarkable thing that we have to come all the way to Copenhagen to have brought home to us that we have such good dancers in England.' Performing elsewhere means new audiences, new perspectives and a different chance to build a reputation, both abroad and at home.

The early years were filled with touring, from building audiences in the 1930s to the morale-boosting wartime tours of the 1940s. The dancers were so used to travelling that they developed their own ways of catching up on rest. Ballerina Beryl Grey, who joined the Company in 1941, remembers sleeping in the luggage racks of trains – one of the few places where she could find room to stretch out her long limbs. The next decades would be dominated by international tours, building the Company's status across the world.

In recent years, there has been a huge expansion in the ways The Royal Ballet can appear away from its home stage. The touring landscape has changed: across the ballet world, changes in transport costs and logistics have made it less common. Filmed performance has been a breakthrough, now being used in increasingly sophisticated ways. Just look at Nuñez's list of ways audiences can connect with the Company: not just performances, but behind-the-scenes filming, up-close glimpses of the dancers at work – and many different ways for audiences to get hold of this material.

Again, the Company was a pioneer. It took part in the earliest days of British television, making its BBC debut in 1936. Those first recordings took place under blazing television lights, in cramped studios, for broadcast on equally cramped early televisions. Lilian Baylis, the manager of Sadler's Wells, was not impressed: '*That's* no good,' she complained. '*Much* too small. Those girls will never get married like that.' It's a jump from the tiny, foggy screens of the 1930s to the High Definition digital films of the 21st century, but the sense of experimentation continues.

The very widest screens are now a long-established part of the Company's work. The Big Screen programme, started in 1989, relays live performances to outdoor locations across the UK. The free performances reach out from the opera house – almost literally: one of the first locations was in Covent Garden piazza, right on the theatre's doorstep, allowing artists to step out and give final curtain calls to the outdoor as well as the indoor audiences. Other locations have ranged from Trafalgar Square (just down the road) to Aberdeen, more than 500 miles away. It's a way of reaching both a dedicated audience and passers-by; people who arrive early with picnics, and casual viewers drawn in by the dancing.

Over time, this kind of broadcast has become much more ambitious. Cinema relays are increasingly part of the cultural landscape, with ballet, opera and theatre performances now available around the world. In live relays, the same show can be seen by audiences on multiple continents. There are repeats and encores, more chances to catch the same theatrical moment; many of the filmed recordings are also released on DVD.

For the dancers, it's brought new challenges. They're dancing for two different audiences – for the theatre audience, as far away as the back row of the amphitheatre, and for the camera zooming in for a close-up. Just as lighting and make-up may be adjusted for film, without losing the original concept, dancers have learned to pitch their performances even more precisely, to make each step and gesture register on both a grand and an intimate scale.

In some respects, the live relay attempts to bring the theatrical experience to an audience outside the theatre: you're still going out for a show, whether to a cinema or a park. It also adds its own insights, with interviews, commentary and delightful extras. One much-loved moment recorded the time when Peregrine, the Shetland pony who appears in *La Fille mal gardée*, received his own edible bouquet, arranged by a group of his ardent admirers. Necessarily, the presentation happened behind the scenes – ponies don't usually take curtain calls, and might not enjoy loud applause. This was a backstage moment seen by thousands.

Where cinema and DVDs tend to focus on the final performance, online content has proved to be particularly good at capturing the build-up to shows, and the day-to-day work of the Company. One of the most high-profile endeavours is World Ballet Day, in which ballet companies around the world unite for a 24-hour broadcast, moving from country to country as the sun moves around the earth. Showing dancers at daily class and in rehearsal, it's also a nice glimpse of how companies have influenced each other. In the 2014 edition, The Royal Ballet's own segment included rehearsals of new works and established classics such as Kenneth MacMillan's *Manon*. When the stream moved on to the National Ballet of Canada, there was Anthony Dowell, former Principal and also former Director of The Royal Ballet, coaching the same ballet. International connections were visible on screen.

For all the demands of the digital age, the dancers have come to love it. 'It takes a lot of skills to find the right balance,' Nuñez says. 'But it gives me such a buzz – and also I know how much people appreciate it. I feel I can connect with people all over the world.'

Wayne McGregor rehearsing *Raven Girl* with Beatriz Stix-Brunell and Ryoichi Hirano during World Ballet Day Live in 2015 ©2015 ROH. Photograph by Sim Canetty-Clarke

THE ROYAL BALLET AND ITS HERITAGE: STYLE AND TRADITION BY SARAH CROMPTON

Ninette de Valois rehearsing her ballet *Job* in 1948 © ROH/ Roger Wood, 1948

Many twisting strands make up the story of a ballet company. Looking at a chronology, it's possible to imagine a direct ascent towards a goal, a sunny, upward progress, an unbroken span of success. But unpicking the threads of the narrative, different patterns forged of people, places and things begin to emerge.

The Royal Ballet's relatively short lifespan – at 85 it is a stripling compared with the centuries-long traditions of the Paris Opera Ballet (founded in 1669) and the Mariinsky (formed in 1740) – means that its history looks simple to read. Its redoubtable founder Ninette de Valois was fond of making it look as straightforward as possible. When the critic Clement Crisp suggested that she must have had great vision to transform a troupe of six dancers working on a pittance into a world-class company in the space of less than 20 years, she was dismissive: 'Women are housekeepers,' she told him, 'And I learnt to take every opportunity that was presented.'

Company Chronology

1931 **20 January** Bizet's opera *Carmen* is staged at the newly reopened Sadler's Wells Theatre with dancers from a fledgling ballet company, the Vic-Wells Opera Ballet, under the creative direction of their founder Ninette de Valois. The product of many developments of this company is today's Royal Ballet. **5 May** The Company gives a performance of short works by De Valois at Lilian Baylis's Old Vic theatre. Baylis's use of dancers in operas and plays enables De Valois to bring her emerging Company together. **July** The Camargo Society presents the Company in a programme that includes De Valois's *Job* and two works by Frederick Ashton, a young dancer also beginning to choreograph.

1932 **January** Alicia Markova becomes a regular Guest Artist with the Company, alongside Anton Dolin. **March** Revival of *Les Sylphides* with Markova and Dolin. **September** The Company tours for the first time, to Denmark. **October** The Company first performs classical repertory with Act II of *Le Lac des cygnes*.

1933 **March** Nicholas Sergeyev stages a full-length *Coppélia*, with Lydia Lopokova as Swanilda. Sergeyev, former *régisseur général* of the Mariinsky Theatre, brought written notation of classic Russian ballets to the West after fleeing Russia in the wake of the October Revolution.

1934 **January** Sergeyev stages *Giselle*, with Markova and Dolin. **April** Sergeyev stages *Casse-Noisette*. **20 November** The Company performs *Le Lac des cygnes* in full, with Markova and new Company Principal Robert Helpmann.

1935 Ashton becomes Resident Choreographer. **20 May** Premiere of De Valois's *The Rake's Progress*, with Markova as the Betrayed Girl. **26 November** Premiere of Ashton's *Le Baiser de la fée*. The cast includes the young Margot Fonteyn.

1937 The Company represents British culture at the International Exhibition in Paris. Their performances include the premiere of De Valois's *Checkmate*. **16 February** Premiere of Ashton's *Les Patineurs*. **27 April** Premiere of Ashton's *A Wedding Bouquet*. **5 October** London premiere of *Checkmate*.

1939 **2 February** Sergeyev stages *The Sleeping Princess*, with Fonteyn and Helpmann.

1940 **23 January** Premiere of Ashton's *Dante Sonata*. **May** The Company tours to the Netherlands. **November** The Company begins wartime tours throughout Britain.

1941 The New Theatre, St Martin's Lane, becomes the Company's home for much of the war. *The Sleeping Princess* is revived.

1942 **19 May** Premiere of Helpmann's ballet *Hamlet*, with Helpmann in the title role.

1944 **26 October** Premiere of Helpmann's *Miracle in the Gorbals*.

1945 The Company tours the Continent with the Entertainments National Service Association (ENSA).

1946 **20 February** The Company becomes resident at Covent Garden, and after the War reopens the Royal Opera House with *The Sleeping Beauty*. **24 April** Premiere of Ashton's *Symphonic Variations*.

1947 **February** *The Three-Cornered Hat* and *La Boutique fantasque* are revived by Léonide Massine, one of the biggest stars of Diaghilev's Ballets Russes, at De Valois's invitation.

1948 **23 December** Premiere of Ashton's *Cinderella*, the Company's first home-grown full-length ballet.

1949 **9 October** The Company performs *The Sleeping Beauty* in New York at the start of a hugely successful tour to many cities in the USA and Canada.

1950 **20 February** Premiere of De Valois's production of *Don Quixote*. **5 April** George Balanchine and his New York City Ballet make their first European visit. Balanchine revives his *Ballet Imperial* for the Company. **5 May** Premiere of Roland Petit's *Ballabile*. **September** The Company embarks on a five-month, 32-city tour of the USA.

1951 **21 August** Music Director Constant Lambert dies, aged 45. With De Valois and Ashton, Lambert was one of the chief architects of the Company.

1952 **3 September** Premiere of Ashton's *Sylvia*.

1953 **2 June** Premiere of Ashton's *Homage to the Queen*, as part of a coronation gala for HM The Queen.

1954 **23 August** The Company performs *The Firebird* at the Edinburgh Festival on the 25th anniversary of Diaghilev's death. Margot Fonteyn takes the title role.

1956 1 March Premiere of Kenneth MacMillan's *Noctambules*, his first ballet for the Company. **31 October** Sadler's Wells Ballet, Sadler's Wells Theatre Ballet and the School are granted a Royal Charter. The main Company becomes The Royal Ballet.

1957 1 January Premiere of John Cranko's *The Prince of the Pagodas*, with a new score by Benjamin Britten. This is the Company's first full-length work to a commissioned score.

1958 27 October Premiere of Ashton's *Ondine*, with a new score by Hans Werner Henze and Fonteyn in the title role.

1959 13 March Company premiere of MacMillan's *Danses concertantes*, created for Sadler's Wells Theatre Ballet in 1955.

1960 28 January Premiere of Ashton's *La Fille mal gardée*, with Nadia Nerina and David Blair.

1961 15 June The Company performs *Ondine* in Leningrad at the start of a tour to the USSR. The Kirov Ballet perform at Covent Garden as part of an exchange agreement. **14 February** The Royal Ballet Touring Company gives the premiere of Ashton's *Les Deux Pigeons* (later *The Two Pigeons*) with Lynn Seymour as Gourouli (later The Young Girl), Christopher Gable as Pepino (later The Young Man) and Elizabeth Anderton as the Gypsy Girl.

1962 21 February Rudolf Nureyev makes his Company debut in *Giselle* with Fonteyn, after his controversial defection from the Kirov in 1961. **3 May** Premiere of MacMillan's *The Rite of Spring*, with Monica Mason. **16 October** The Royal Ballet first performs Ashton's *The Two Pigeons*, with Lynn Seymour, Alexander Grant and Georgina Parkinson in the main roles.

1963 12 March Premiere of Ashton's *Marguerite and Armand*, with Fonteyn and Nureyev. **7 May** De Valois retires as Director of the Company, succeeded by Ashton. De Valois becomes Supervisor of The Royal Ballet School. **28 November** Nureyev stages the 'Kingdom of the Shades' scene from *La Bayadère*.

Rudolf Nureyev and Margot Fonteyn in *Romeo and Juliet*, The Royal Ballet © ROH/Roger Wood, 1965

This rather ignores the fact that as early as 1921, she wanted to found her own company and set about learning how to do that with considerable resolve. Her greatest inspiration was the two and a half years she spent dancing for Diaghilev's Ballets Russes, from which she emerged in 1927 impressed by the model of 'a repertory company running classical and modern ballet side by side – and what is more important – in many cases blended.'

That is what she set out to create, and in a radio interview at the end of her life, she expressed her gratitude for the way Diaghilev had shaped her ideas. 'You came up against everything there,' she said, talking about the sense of creative ferment. '...What could I do but stand and sort it out like a jigsaw puzzle, and realize that we had absolutely *nothing* in England and all I wanted to do was to get back and start *something*.'

Her determination from that point on was something to behold, as by sheer force of will she dragged that something into being. Julia Farron, who was the first pupil to win a scholarship to the Vic Wells School that De Valois founded, and subsequently joined the company in 1936 at the age of 14, remembers: 'She was that sort of woman. If she wanted to do something, she was going to do it.'

De Valois gathered around her, and cemented to her side, the best of talent she could find to bolster her fledgling company, including Constant

Lambert as conductor and Musical Director, and Frederick Ashton, whom she enticed away from Marie Rambert and appointed as Resident Choreographer as early as 1935. Later, she gave up her own choreographic time to nurture the abilities of Kenneth MacMillan. She was lucky their talents existed; but she did everything she could to make sure their creativity served her vision. She made her own luck. Beryl Grey, another of her young protégés remembers her as 'living on a wonderful star which reflected on all of us.'

The most major opportunity she seized was the apparent disaster of World War II, the event that for all its hardship forged the Vic Wells ballet into a company that was ready to take on all comers. The relentless touring, the nine shows a week in the West End, built an audience for dance that had not existed in Britain before. 'We went to all sorts of places,' says Grey. 'We danced in every city. People needed to be taken out of the horrors of war, and I think ballet perhaps, more than anything else because it wasn't using words, was somehow inspiring and refreshing and enjoyable.'

The constant dancing might have been exhausting but it also honed the dancers into performers capable of rising to the most arduous physical challenge. When the fighting ended and the Company was invited into the Royal Opera House, they were ready. Ashton was there to stamp onto the Company a style that is now regarded as English, with its quick feet and a contrapuntal flow of movement that made dancers look as if they were really dancing. Peter Wright, whose own versions of the classics have done so much to build on that style, remembers: 'He was always poking you in the back, and saying, "Use your back, use your back." It made everything look effortless – defying gravity, no strain, all flow.'

The exemplar of that style was Margot Fonteyn, the home-grown ballerina who burnished the reputation of what came to be called The Royal Ballet. On the legendary 1949 tour to the United States, when the Company opened a four-week season at the Metropolitan Opera House with its hallmark production of *The Sleeping Beauty*, it was Moira Shearer – famous from *The Red Shoes* – that people wanted to see. But it was Fonteyn who triumphed – 'a vision of potential' according to Maria Tallchief, ballerina of New York City Ballet.

Fonteyn's dominance was fading by 1961 when a comet arrived from the East in the form of Rudolf Nureyev. De Valois made the most of the opportunity once more, offering him a home at The Royal Ballet and in the process revitalizing her star ballerina and making British ballet in the 1960s almost as sexy and compelling as The Beatles and The Rolling Stones. In this context, another generation of dancers began to emerge – Antoinette Sibley, Anthony Dowell, Lynn Seymour, Christopher Gable, Svetlana Beriosova, Donald MacLeary, Merle Park, David Wall – different from their predecessors, but just as dazzling.

Nothing, however, is ever simple. Nureyev and Fonteyn's box office appeal led to one of the greatest rows in Royal Ballet history, when they replaced Seymour and Gable as the opening night cast of *Romeo and Juliet* in 1964 –

1964 **29 February** Antoinette Sibley dances Princess Aurora in the Company's 400th performance of *The Sleeping Beauty*. **2 April** Premiere of Ashton's *The Dream*, with Sibley and Anthony Dowell, as part of celebrations of the 400th anniversary of Shakespeare's birth. **2 December** Bronislava Nijinska revives her *Les Biches*, with Svetlana Beriosova as the Hostess.

1965 **9 February** Premiere of MacMillan's first full-length work, *Romeo and Juliet*, created on Lynn Seymour and Christopher Gable but danced on opening night by Fonteyn and Nureyev.

1966 **23 March** Nijinska revives her *Les Noces* in a mixed programme with *Les Biches*. **May** MacMillan becomes Director of Deutsche Oper Ballet, Berlin. **19 May** Company premiere of MacMillan's *Song of the Earth*, created for Cranko's Stuttgart Ballet in 1965.

1967 **25 January** Premiere of Antony Tudor's *Shadowplay* with Anthony Dowell as the boy with the matted hair.

1968 **29 February** Premiere of Nureyev's staging of *The Nutcracker*. **26 April** Announcement of Ashton's retirement as Director in 1970 and his succession by MacMillan. **25 October** Premiere of Ashton's *Enigma Variations*.

1971 **22 July** Premiere of MacMillan's long-awaited *Anastasia*, with Seymour. **4 August** Premiere of Glen Tetley's contemporary ballet *Field Figures*.

1972 **20 June** Natalia Makarova makes her Company debut as a Guest Artist in *Giselle*, with Dowell.

1973 **8 June** Nureyev and Makarova dance *The Sleeping Beauty* together for the first time.

1974 **7 March** Premiere of MacMillan's *Manon*, with Sibley, Dowell and David Wall. **7 October** Premiere of MacMillan's *Elite Syncopations*, with Wayne Sleep in the Principal Character role.

1975 **April** The Royal Ballet makes its first tour of the Far East.

1976 **12 February** Premiere of Ashton's *A Month in the Country*, with Dowell and Seymour.

1977 **13 June** Norman Morrice succeeds MacMillan as Director of The Royal Ballet.

1978 **14 February** Premiere of MacMillan's *Mayerling*, with Wall and Seymour.

1980 13 March Premiere of MacMillan's *Gloria*. **4 August** Premiere of Ashton's *Rhapsody*, with Lesley Collier and Mikhail Baryshnikov, in celebration of the 80th birthday of HM Queen Elizabeth The Queen Mother.

1981 30 April Premiere of MacMillan's *Isadora* with Merle Park, in celebration of the Company's golden jubilee.

1982 2 December Premiere of Nureyev's *The Tempest*.

1984 24 February Premiere of MacMillan's *Different Drummer*. **20 December** Premiere of Peter Wright's production of *The Nutcracker*, with Collier and Dowell.

1986 Dowell succeeds Morrice as Director of The Royal Ballet.

1987 12 March Premiere of Dowell's production of *Swan Lake*, with Cynthia Harvey and Jonathan Cope. **16 December** Ashton revives his *Cinderella*, in his final production for the Company.

1988 9 March Premiere of David Bintley's *'Still Life' at the Penguin Café*. **10 May** Revival of Ashton's *Ondine*, after a 22-year absence from the repertory. **19 August** Ashton dies.

1989 18 May Company premiere of the full-length *La Bayadère*, in a staging by Makarova. **8 December** Premiere of MacMillan's final, full-length ballet, *The Prince of the Pagodas*, with Darcey Bussell and Cope.

1990 19 July Bussell and Irek Mukhamedov perform MacMillan's 'Farewell' pas de deux at a London Palladium gala.

1991 7 February Premiere of MacMillan's *Winter Dreams* (developed from the 'Farewell' pas de deux). **2 May** Premiere of Bintley's *Cyrano*, in celebration of the Company's 60th anniversary.

1992 13 February Company premiere of William Forsythe's *In the middle, somewhat elevated*. **19 March** Premiere of MacMillan's last work, *The Judas Tree*, with Viviana Durante and Mukhamedov. **29 October** MacMillan dies backstage at the Royal Opera House during a revival of *Mayerling*. **6 December** Stage premiere of Ashton's *Tales of Beatrix Potter*.

1993 7 April Company premiere of Baryshnikov's *Don Quixote*.

Frederick Ashton watches Rosemary Lindsay, Michael Somes, Anya Linden and Margot Fonteyn in rehearsal for *Symphonic Variations*, 1948

Roger Wood Photographic Collection/ ©ROH Collections

opening wounds that took time to heal. Yet the triumph of MacMillan's first three-act ballet confirmed him as the new dominant choreographic voice in British ballet. 'His contribution is huge,' says Peter Wright. 'He broke down the barriers more than anyone, bringing in different and more contemporary movement.'

His influence is also responsible for the other quality that would be regarded as part of the Royal Ballet style – an extremely naturalistic sense of drama and complete involvement in every role, however minor. Senior Ballet Master Christopher Saunders remembers rehearsing under MacMillan's watchful eye. 'It was all about naturalism,' he says. 'He wouldn't say much, but he would tell Paris, for example, to look in Juliet's eyes when he kisses her hand. Little details like that, rather than explaining how people were thinking. And he loved people to walk naturally. He didn't want them to walk like ballet princes, and it is very hard not to.'

The combination of the Ashtonian elegance and MacMillan's sense of drama has always been the root of the Royal Ballet style, the template into which dancers and choreographers alike have adapted their personalities. It sustained them through the tricky decades of the 1970s and 80s, attracting international stars even when times were tough. Sylvie Guillem, one of those who was invited as a guest artist by Director Anthony Dowell, noticed the courage and commitment of the British dancers. 'In Paris, it was more athletic, more technique, more performance,' she says. 'Here it was more about the soul and what theatre represents. That is a huge tradition here.'

The drawing power of that tradition remains a lodestone for dancers from outside the Company to this day, meaning that international talents perform alongside those trained and moulded by The Royal Ballet School. This occasionally has given rise to mutterings about the preservation of style, just as the varying success of different directorial regimes and different new ballets has prompted concerns about the future of the Company. Yet history is written by the victors: it is the triumphs that are remembered not the disappointments and defeats. Ashton's *Tiresias* is all but forgotten, but *Symphonic Variations* will be danced for ever. MacMillan's *Isadora* will always be less performed than his masterly *Mayerling*.

Without the benefit of hindsight, it is sometimes difficult to judge whether the new works of today will join the credit or the debit column, though the betting has to be that contributions such as Wayne McGregor's *Chroma* and Christopher Wheeldon's *The Winter's Tale* are likely to be the classics of tomorrow.

What is certain, however, is that the instinct to keep moving forward, to try different things, is in keeping with the pioneering spirit with which De Valois started her company 85 years ago. 'Her motto was respect the past, herald the future and concentrate on the present,' remembers Peter Wright. It makes a fine motto for The Royal Ballet today.

1994 **6 April** Premiere of Dowell's new production of *The Sleeping Beauty* on tour in Washington D.C.. **18 June** Premiere of Ashley Page's *Fearful Symmetries*. **3 November** UK Premiere of Dowell's production of *The Sleeping Beauty*.

1996 **2 May** Revival of MacMillan's *Anastasia*, with new designs by Bob Crowley.

1997 **14 July** Farewell Gala and final performance before the Royal Opera House closes for refurbishment. During the closure The Royal Ballet performs at the Hammersmith Apollo, the Royal Festival Hall and the Barbican.

1999 **23 November** The Company marks the reopening of the Royal Opera House with 'A Celebration of International Choreography'. **17 December** Opening night of *The Nutcracker*, the first full-length ballet in the new House.

2000 **8 February** Revival of De Valois's production of *Coppélia*, using Osbert Lancaster's original designs. **29 February** Revival of Ashton's *Marguerite and Armand*, with Sylvie Guillem and Nicolas Le Riche. **6 May** Millicent Hodson and Kenneth Archer revive Nijinsky's *Jeux* in a programme with his *L'Après-midi d'un faune*.

2001 **8 March** De Valois dies. **July** Ross Stretton succeeds Dowell as Director of The Royal Ballet. **30 July** *Swan Lake* is the first full-length ballet to be broadcast to Big Screens. **23 October** Premiere of Nureyev's staging of *Don Quixote*. **22 November** Company premiere of Cranko's *Onegin*.

2002 **September** Ross Stretton resigns as Director. **December** Monica Mason becomes Director of the Company.

2003 **13 January** Company premiere of Jiří Kylián's *Sinfonietta*. **8 March** Premiere of Makarova's new production of *The Sleeping Beauty*. **April** Jeanetta Laurence appointed Assistant Director. **22 December** Premiere of Wendy Ellis Somes's new production of Ashton's *Cinderella*.

Francesca
Hayward as
Perdita in
Christopher
Wheeldon's
*The Winter's
Tale*
©2016 ROH.
Photograph by
Bill Cooper

2004 April The Company marks the 75th anniversary of Sergey Diaghilev's death in a programme that includes *Le Spectre de la rose*. **4 November** Revival of Ashton's full-length *Sylvia*, reconstructed and staged by Christopher Newton for the 'Ashton 100' celebrations.

2005 7 May Premiere of Christopher Bruce's *Three Songs – Two Voices*, inspired by the life of Jimi Hendrix.

2006 15 May The Company celebrates its 75th anniversary with a new production of the 1946 *The Sleeping Beauty*, realized by Monica Mason and Christopher Newton with Messel's original designs, re-created by Peter Farmer. It is followed by revivals of Ashton's *Homage to The Queen*, with additional choreography by Christopher Wheeldon, Michael Corder and David Bintley, and De Valois's *The Rake's Progress*. **8 June** HM The Queen attends a gala performance of *Homage to The Queen* with *La Valse* and divertissements. **November** Premieres of Wayne McGregor's *Chroma* and Wheeldon's *DGV: Danse à grande vitesse*. **December** McGregor becomes Resident Choreographer of The Royal Ballet.

2007 March Premiere of Alastair Marriott's *Children of Adam*. **April** Premiere of Will Tuckett's *The Seven Deadly Sins*. **June** Barry Wordsworth is appointed Music Director. **23 November** Company premiere of Balanchine's *Jewels*.

2008 28 February Premiere of Wheeldon's *Electric Counterpoint*. **23 April** Premiere of Kim Brandstrup's *Rushes – Fragments of a Lost Story*. **October** The 50th anniversary of Ashton's *Ondine*. **13 November** Premiere of McGregor's *Infra*. **28 December** *The Nutcracker* is broadcast live to cinemas around the world, in the Company's first cinema broadcast.

2009 March Anthony Russell-Roberts retires as Artistic Administrator and is succeeded by Kevin O'Hare. **April** Jeanetta Laurence is appointed Associate Director of The Royal Ballet. **17 November** Memorial service dedicated to the founders of The Royal Ballet held at Westminster Abbey.

2010 January 50th anniversary of Ashton's *La Fille mal gardée*. **5 May** Premiere of Liam Scarlett's *Asphodel Meadows*.

2011 28 February Premiere of Wheeldon's *Alice's Adventures in Wonderland*, to a commissioned score by Joby Talbot. **17–19 June** The Company appears at The O₂ Arena for the first time, performing MacMillan's *Romeo and Juliet*.

2012 23 March 'Royal Ballet Live', a day behind the scenes with The Royal Ballet, is broadcast live on the internet. **5 April** Premiere of McGregor's *Carbon Life* and Scarlett's *Sweet Violets*. **2 June** Revival of MacMillan's *The Prince of the Pagodas* after a 16-year absence from the Company's repertory. **15–20 June** Premiere of *Metamorphosis: Titian 2012*, a triptych of new works by Brandstrup and McGregor, Marriott and Wheeldon and Scarlett, Tuckett and Watkins, in collaboration with the National Gallery. **20 June** Mason retires as Director, succeeded by O'Hare. **July** Wheeldon is appointed Artistic Associate. **30 October** The Company celebrates HM The Queen's Diamond Jubilee in a gala performance. **November** Scarlett is appointed the Company's first Artist in Residence.

2013 22 February Premieres of Ratmansky's *24 Preludes* and Wheeldon's *Aeternum*. **February–March** Members of the Company tour to Brazil. **8 May** Premiere of Scarlett's *Hansel and Gretel*. **24 May** Premiere of McGregor's *Raven Girl*. **20 June** Premiere of Brandstrup's *Ceremony of Innocence* at the Aldeburgh Festival. **5 October** Premiere of Carlos Acosta's production of *Don Quixote*. **9 November** Premiere of David Dawson's *The Human Seasons*.

2014 7 February Premiere of McGregor's *Tetractys*. **10 April** Premiere of Wheeldon's *The Winter's Tale*. **May** 50th anniversary of Ashton's *The Dream*. **31 May** Premiere of Marriott's *Connectome*. **June** The Company tours to the Bolshoi Theatre, Moscow, Taipei and Shanghai. **7 November** Premiere of Scarlett's *The Age of Anxiety*.

2015 27 March Premiere of Hofesh Shechter's *Untouchable*. **11 May** Premiere of McGregor's *Woolf Works*. **June** The Company tours to the USA for the first time in six years. **September** 50th anniversary of MacMillan's *Romeo and Juliet* **26 October** Premiere of Acosta's *Carmen* **18 November** Revival of Ashton's *The Two Pigeons* after a 30-year absence from the Company's repertory.

2016 12 March Premiere of Wheeldon's *Strapless* **4 May** Premiere of Scarlett's *Frankenstein* **28 June** Premiere of McGregor's *Obsidian Tear* and revival of MacMillan's *The Invitation* after a 20-year absence from the Company's repertory. **June** The Company tours to Japan.

Director
Kevin O'Hare

©Joe Plimmer

Opposite page:

(top, left to right) Royal Ballet Music Director Koen Kessels, Resident Choreographer Wayne McGregor, Artistic Associate Christopher Wheeldon and Artist in Residence Liam Scarlett

(bottom) The full Company on stage at the end of the 2015/16 Season. © ROH 2016. Photograph by Andrej Uspenski

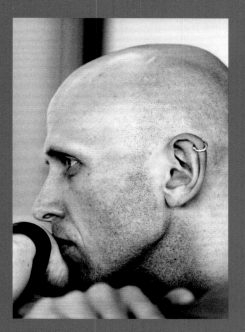

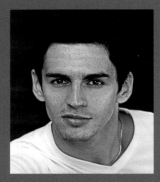

Federico Bonelli
Joined as Principal 2003
Born: Genoa, Italy
Trained: Turin Dance Academy
Previous Companies: Zürich
Ballet (1996), Dutch National
Ballet (1999)

Alexander Campbell
Joined 2011
Promoted to Principal 2016
Born: Sydney, Australia
Trained: Academy Ballet,
Sydney and The Royal Ballet
School
Previous Company:
Birmingham Royal Ballet

Lauren Cuthbertson
Joined 2002
Promoted to Principal 2008
Born: Devon, England
Trained:
The Royal Ballet School

Matthew Golding
Joined as Principal 2014
Born: Sasketchewan, Canada
Trained: Royal Winnipeg Ballet,
Universal Ballet Academy and
The Royal Ballet School
Previous Companies: American
Ballet Theatre (2003), Dutch
National Ballet (2009)

Francesca Hayward
Joined 2011
Promoted to Principal 2016
Born: Nairobi, Kenya
Trained: The Royal Ballet
School

Ryoichi Hirano
Joined 2002
Promoted to Principal 2016
Born: Osaka, Japan
Trained: Setsuko Hirano Ballet
School

Nehemiah Kish
Joined as Principal 2010
Born: Michigan, USA
Trained: National Ballet
School of Canada
Previous Companies: National
Ballet of Canada (2001),
Royal Danish Ballet (2008)

Sarah Lamb
Joined 2004
Promoted to Principal 2006
Born: Boston, USA
Trained: Boston Ballet School
Previous Company: Boston
Ballet (1998)

Steven McRae
Joined 2004
Promoted to Principal 2009
Born: Sydney, Australia
Trained:
The Royal Ballet School

Laura Morera
Joined 1995
Promoted to Principal 2007
Born: Madrid, Spain
Trained:
The Royal Ballet School

Vadim Muntagirov
Joined as Principal 2014
Born: Chelyabinsk, Russia
Trained: Perm Choreographic
Institute and The Royal
Ballet School
Previous Company: English
National Ballet (2009)

Marianela Nuñez
Joined 1998
Promoted to Principal 2002
Born: Buenos Aires
Trained:
Teatro Colón Ballet School,
The Royal Ballet School

Natalia Osipova
Joined as Principal 2013
Born: Moscow
Trained: Bolshoi Ballet
Academy
Previous Companies: Bolshoi
Ballet (2004), American Ballet
Theatre (2010), Mikhailovsky
Theatre (2011)

Thiago Soares
Joined 2002
Promoted to Principal 2006
Born: São Gonçalo, Brazil
Trained: Centre for Dance,
Rio de Janeiro
Previous Company:
Theatro Municipal, Rio de
Janeiro (1998)

Akane Takada
Prix de Lausanne scholarship
2008; Joined 2009
Promoted to Principal 2016
Born: Tokyo, Japan
Trained: Hiromi Takahashi
Ballet Studio and the Bolshoi
Ballet Academy

Edward Watson
Joined 1994
Promoted to Principal 2005
Born: Bromley, England
Trained:
The Royal Ballet School

Zenaida Yanowsky
Joined 1994
Promoted to Principal 2001
Born: Lyon, France
Trained: Las Palmas, Majorca
Previous Company: Paris
Opéra Ballet (1994)

PRINCIPAL CHARACTER ARTISTS, CHARACTER ARTISTS, FIRST SOLOISTS AND SOLOISTS

PRINCIPAL CHARACTER ARTISTS
Left to right:
Gary Avis
Alastair Marriott
Elizabeth McGorian
Christopher Saunders

CHARACTER ARTISTS
Left to right:
Jonathan Howells
Philip Mosley

FIRST SOLOISTS
Left to right:
Claire Calvert
Yuhui Choe
Helen Crawford
Bennet Gartside

Melissa Hamilton
James Hay
Valeri Hristov
Hikaru Kobayashi

Itziar Mendizabal

Yasmine Naghdi

Johannes
Stepanek

Beatriz Stix-Brunell

Valentino
Zucchetti

SOLOISTS
Left to right:

Luca Acri

Christina Arestis

Matthew Ball

Olivia Cowley

Tristan Dyer

Nicol Edmonds

Elizabeth Harrod

Tierney Heap

Meaghan Grace
Hinkis

Fumi Kaneko

Paul Kay

SOLOISTS, FIRST ARTISTS AND ARTISTS

Mayara Magri
Emma Maguire
Laura McCulloch
Kristen McNally

Fernando
Montaño
Marcelino Sambé
Eric Underwood
Thomas
Whitehead

FIRST ARTISTS
Left to right:
Tara-Brigitte
Bhavnani
Camille Bracher
Reece Clarke
David Donnelly

Benjamin Ella
Kevin Emerton
Hayley Forskitt
Isabella Gasparini

Nathalie Harrison

Tomas Mock

Erico Montes

Anna Rose O'Sullivan

Romany Pajdak

Demelza Parish

Gemma Pitchley-Gale

Leticia Stock

Lara Turk

ARTISTS
Left to right:

Lukas Bjørneboe Brændsrød

Grace Blundell

Mica Bradbury

Annette Buvoli

Harry Churches

Leticia Dias

Ashley Dean

Leo Dixon
Téo Dubreuil
Solomon Golding
Hannah Grennell

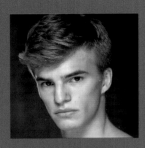   

Chisato Katsura
Isabel Lubach
Calvin Richardson
Julia Roscoe

Mariko Sasaki
Joseph Sissens
Gina Storm-Jensen
David Yudes

**AUD JEBSEN
YOUNG DANCERS**
Left to right:
Estelle Bovay
**Maria Castillo
Yoshida**
Arianna Maldini
Giacomo Rovero

Francisco Serrano

**Charlotte
Tonkinson**

**PRIX DE
LAUSANNE
DANCER**

**Vincenzo Di
Primo**

THE ROYAL BALLET 2016/17

In 1956 Queen Elizabeth II granted the then Sadler's Wells Ballet, Sadler's Wells Theatre Ballet and Sadler's Wells School a Royal Charter, and they became respectively The Royal Ballet and Royal Ballet School. Under the Charter a body of Governors was set up whose ultimate duty it is to safeguard the future of the Company (now The Royal Ballet and Birmingham Royal Ballet) and School and to be the custodians of the traditions established by Dame Ninette de Valois in the formation of the Company and School in 1931.